Precedent
&
Possibility

The (ab)use of law in South Africa

Dennis Davis

Michelle le Roux

DOUBLE
STOREY
a juta company

PRECEDENT & POSSIBILITY

First published 2009

by Double Storey Books,
a division of Juta & Co, Ltd
PO Box 14373, Lansdowne, 7779, Cape Town, South Africa

ISBN 978-1-77013-022-7

Typeset in 10/13 Galliard

Project Manager: Sharon Steyn
Editor: Rae Dalton
Proofreader: Caryl Verrier
Typesetter: AN dtp Services, Cape Town
Cover designer: Marius Roux
Print management by Print Communications
Front cover photograph: Dale Yudelman
Back cover photograph: Alix Carmichele

Contents

Acknowledgements

This book comes from an idea originally floated by Russell Martin and Bridget Impey, for which inspiration we are truly grateful. It set us on an intellectual and personal journey, which had the added benefit of affording us the opportunity to discover not only our past, but also some pointers to the future of constitutional democracy in South Africa. In this, it was an experience without precedent for either of us, and revealed the possibilities available to our nation.

Of course, a project such as this never succeeds without countless hours of assistance from many other people. First among this lengthy list are those who so generously gave us their time, and memories, insights and thoughts, in interviews about the cases that follow. Thanks are due to Chief Justice Arthur Chaskalson, Justice Richard Goldstone, Judge Edwin Cameron, Sir Sydney Kentridge QC, advocates George Bizos SC, Gilbert Marcus SC, Marumo Moerane SC, Wim Trengove SC, Anton Ackermann SC and Geoff Budlender, Zackie Achmat, Alix Carmichele, Professors Dennis Cowen, Halton Cheadle, Neville Rubin and Nicholas Haysom, Perino Pama, Justine White, Leon Levy and Ahmed Kathrada. In addition, we are grateful to Tom Rihkotso, and to Professor Steven Ellman for generously affording us access to an interview he conducted with Mr Rikhotso, and to Veli Komani, courtesy of video interview footage to which we had access facilitated by Zackie Achmat.

Our second source of information was the newspaper articles, op-ed pieces, journal articles and books written by so many, hopefully all credited in the end notes, many of the most inaccessible of which were gathered with such generous diligence by Herschel Miller of the National Library in Cape Town. Thanks must also go to Michele Pickover at the Cullen Library Wits University archive who provided access to the archives of the *Rivonia* trial, *Wendy Orr* inquest and *LRC* papers.

We both owe thanks to those who suffered through earlier drafts of the manuscript, and dreadful formatting (particularly from Dennis): Judge Edwin Cameron, Professors Halton Cheadle, John and Jean Comaroff, Advocate Rob Petersen SC and Gilad Stern. Their thoughtful comments and helpful criticisms only enriched the final work. So too did the responses from the audiences at the UCT Summer School and Grahamstown Festival. Special thanks to Rowena Bihl and Hester Opperman for all their assistance.

To the team at Juta, Sandy Shepherd, Sharon Steyn, Rae Dalton, Caryl Verrier and the marketing department: thanks for your efforts and patience as the project took far longer than initially promised.

Cyril Ramaphosa generously agreed to pen a foreword and we are grateful for this significant addition to our book.

And finally, to the huge team on three continents consisting of our respective partners, families, friends, and all the waiters, chefs, baristas and barmen who kept us buoyant, fed, caffeinated and hydrated in the endless hours of discussion, drafting and debate that produced this book: we really, and tritely, could not have done it without you.

Dennis Davis, Michelle le Roux — September 2008

Foreword

Apartheid made many South Africans ambivalent about the law. A legal system, we believed, should protect all citizens against the abuse of power from whatever quarter. The law, we felt, should serve the interests of the powerless and not of the ruling elite.

Yet we experienced the law under apartheid as a repressive instrument. It provided the foundation for a system that denied rights on the basis of race, and it was abused to crush legitimate political opposition. At the *Rivonia* trial it came perilously close to sending Nelson Mandela and Walter Sisulu to the gallows.

Even in those dark times, many of us retained our faith in the potential of the law. We recognised that it could be abused to entrench an evil political system. But we also saw that the rule of law could be turned against our enemies and used to constrain the arbitrary exercise of their power.

As general secretary of the National Union of Mineworkers in the 1980s, I discovered that laws intended to oppress us could also be used to curtail the violent and inhumane abuse of power by mine managers.

In those years we looked on, enthralled, as brilliant lawyers like Arthur Chaskalson used legal reasoning to fight back against the pass laws and detention without trial.

Apartheid's legal battles drew attention to issues at the heart of the country's political struggle and contributed to a new constitutional order with human rights at its centre.

Our Bill of Rights, however, has changed the character of the battle for justice rather than ending it. The courts remain sites of intense contestation in which the moral and political conflicts of our society continue to be fought out.

In the past, as is revealed in the cases described in this book, a number of lawyers and litigants displayed great courage during the tumultuous apartheid years by standing up for justice and equality. Fundamentally at odds with the dominant ideology of legalised oppression and dispossession, many of these South African patriots paid a heavy professional and personal price for their convictions.

It is a tribute to the tenacity and intellect of these people that, even within the constraints of a legal system moulded to sustain an unjust regime, they were able to challenge the abuse of power and the violation of .the rights of the individual.

An ambitious Constitution such as ours, however, should not and ultimately cannot be protected by lawyers and judges acting on their own. Citizens in general need to respect the obligation upon the courts to defend the values that our Constitution embodies, even when this defence results in judgments that are widely and profoundly unpopular.

Political leaders, likewise, need to respect the spirit of the Constitution and to abide by the culture of justification it seeks to promote. Leadership in a constitutional order must rest on persuasion and justified action and not upon the bald compulsion of state or party power.

This informative and instructive work is a welcome addition to the growing body of South African legal knowledge. It also stands as a tribute to the courageous men and women who have been prepared to fight to reclaim the law for the people of South Africa.

Cyril Ramaphosa — September 2008

one

Introduction

L aw is deeply embedded in popular culture. Daily headlines announce developments in the latest murder trials that grip the public imagination. Movies like *Michael Clayton* and television series like *Boston Legal* attract huge audiences. The arguments of counsel and decisions of judges in high-profile cases are dissected over cups of coffee and dinner tables across the country.

The law has also played an important role in the history of this country. But do we ever consider the precise manner in which that law shaped the politics and economics of our society?

During the long night of apartheid, courts were often sites of vigorous political struggle, being the places where different visions of the country were presented to the public by the competing litigants, usually the state against accused persons or applicants whose rights were at stake. Since 1994 and the advent of constitutional democracy, similarly significant contests have taken place in our courts. There is, however, a major difference: Litigation now takes place within the context of the Constitution which provides a vast range of rights for all who live in this country. This book seeks to examine some of the crucial cases in which battles for justice in its various forms have been fought.

But first, we venture into the terrain of the theoretical and the conceptual. Hopefully some readers will join us to consider the reasons for our selection of the cases and the links between the old and the constitutional order. Before taking this detour, may we offer this guidance to readers who are more interested in the cases themselves: They should feel free to skip ahead to Chapter 2 and avoid the conclusion as well, where we move beyond the stories to speculate about the future of our constitutional democracy.

The cases—a difficult choice

Our primary reason for choosing the cases that appear here is that all of them, as we shall show, contributed to a change in the South African political landscape. In other words, they were chosen on the basis of their legal and political importance to South Africa at the time of their contest in the courts, as well as because of their implications for the nature and development of South African society.

There are, of course, many cases which assumed critical legal and political importance to South Africa at the time that they were litigated. The choice therefore proved to be very difficult, particularly in a one-volume work of this nature. Ultimately, we chose cases for which it truly can be said that the country held its breath awaiting the courts' decision.

Legal cases are no more than stories. This may sound strange to some readers in that laws are framed in arcane texts and legalese, or professional jargon, which courts interpret and apply to the facts of the case. Of course, these stories are mediated through these legal texts and a process which uses a particular language. Cases take place within a particular political and moral context. But the unfolding of the case and its outcome is a narrative which directly affects the lives of individual litigants and, possibly indirectly, millions of citizens in this country.

The cases in this book are thus stories that tell of our past, present and future. We have attempted to tell these stories without the legalese that complicates them, and with due recognition to the individual role players, being the lawyers and judges who were responsible for the outcomes, and the litigants whose life experiences were the source of these cases.

When all of these and similar cases are considered together, they reveal a remarkable faith in the process of law, even during the decades of determined efforts by successive racist governments to destroy the very normative foundations of the legal system. Naturally, these cases also reveal the presence of many lawyers who sought during the apartheid era to maintain a racist *status quo*. But, at the same time, they highlight the role of others who strove to use the law in an effort to mitigate the worst effects of that government policy. Each of these cases held implications, at the time often unknown, for the possibility of a constitutional democracy for South Africa. When that time finally came, a tangible faith in law's possibility was rewarded.

By their nature, laws can both promote and constrain the exercise of power

Law and the government: the past fuses into the future

Within a decade of democracy, litigation was again launched based on the claim that government failed to listen to the people. Ironically, those who allegedly refused to listen to the claimants were often government leaders who had made similar demands of the apartheid state.

To many, this assertion of the link between the law of the past and future may seem decidedly incorrect, in that today's legal dispensation bears little resemblance to its apartheid predecessor. But consider the following: during apartheid, the law created the very foundations essential to the construction of the system that allocated and denied rights and privileges on the basis of race. The cruelty of apartheid was maintained by volumes of laws and regulations. But, by their nature, laws can both promote and constrain the exercise of power. In other words, litigation can be used to undermine the law itself. Let us first examine law as a form of struggle during apartheid.

Many of these legal struggles were based upon the following idea: A law may be introduced by government to achieve a pernicious purpose yet be employed by a resourceful litigant for an opposite end. Of course, the outcome may also depend on the approach to law of the particular judge before whom the case is heard. Take the case of Dullah Omar, later to become the first Minister of Justice in a democratic South Africa.[1] He was detained without the benefit of a trial under a draconian piece of legislation called the Public Safety Act. His legal representatives argued that, unless the Public Safety Act expressly authorised the State President to issue emergency regulations which included a denial of so important a right, the regulations could not deny a detainee the right to make representations to the authorities as to why he or she should not be detained.

The majority of the Court rejected this argument, holding that the State President was granted the implied power to promulgate regulations which excluded the rights of detainees to make these kinds of representations. In a significant minority judgment, Judge Gerald Friedman insisted that a right as fundamental as that of being heard when rights to liberty are affected by an adverse decision, could be removed expressly only by an Act of Parliament. The pro-executive judge was prepared to accept anything that the government called law, but a judge like Friedman insisted that the bedrock of law is the protection of the rights of citizens which can be taken away only by an express legal provision, not by reading an ambiguous text to negate the protection of rights.

In a country where the courts claimed adherence to the principle of the rule of law, certain judges took these claims seriously. But Judge Friedman was in a minority. From time to time, however, his approach did prevail. On occasion, the government was held accountable leading to unexpected outcomes. Judges would read apartheid statutes in ways that revealed their open texture or ambiguity in their meaning. This finding then allowed these judges to favour an interpretation that could produce an outcome which minimised the impact upon the existing rights of individual citizens. They read the law to mean something other than the interpretation claimed by the government. In the early 1950s, the courts often adhered to this model of adjudication. In 1950, for example, the Appellate Division held that a regulation authorising racially separate railway coaches in circumstances where only black passengers were subjected to criminal sanction for travelling in the 'wrong' coach was illegal because it promoted unequal and partial treatment.[2]

The bedrock of law is the protection of the rights of citizens

This approach, as we shall see, became rare as the apartheid state gained strength but the possibility of similar victories was never completely extinguished. Throughout apartheid a contest between legal results which either preserved or destroyed rights took place in the courts. In a work that heavily influenced a generation of progressive lawyers in this country to conceive of a legal theory that could justify human rights litigation, the English social historian Edward

Thompson in *Whigs and Hunters* clarified the difference between a system of power which claimed adherence to the rule of law and one based on pure arbitrary power, absent any recourse to law. The key passage of his text reads thus:

> The inhibitions upon power imposed by law seem to me a legacy as substantial as any handed down from the struggles of the seventeenth century to the eighteenth and a true and important cultural achievement . . . The notion of the regulation and reconciliation of conflicts through the rule of the law—and the elaboration of rules and procedures which on occasion made some approximate approach towards the ideal—seem to me a cultural achievement of universal significance . . . I am not starry eyed about this at all . . . I am insisting only upon the obvious point, that there is a difference between arbitrary power and the rule of the law. We ought to expose the shams and iniquities which may be concealed beneath this law. But the rule of the law itself, the imposing of effective inhibitions upon the power and the defence of the citizen from power's all-intrusive claims, seems to me to be an unqualified human good.[3]

Thompson understood well that power worked through law but that the power-holder was, on occasion, held accountable to a legal text which, given the nature of that text, was open to a litigant's interpretation. For this reason, governance under apartheid was sometimes vulnerable to challenges in the courts. Legal battles continued to rage throughout the period between 1948 and 1994. In most cases, the battle was fought without much success for the powerless. Sometimes, however, significant and surprising results were achieved. These victories were the product of many interrelated factors: the quality of lawyering, the ideology of the presiding judges, the political context in which the cases were fought, the intensity of political struggle at that time and the nature of the factual and legal materials relevant to the particular case.

Law and strategy

Lawyers who understood the nature of law in this way developed their litigation strategy to exploit the law's contradictions and to help create space for both political activity and the curbing of gross excesses of state power, all the while undermining the efficacy of government policy.

The then Chief Justice, Pierre Rabie, who, as we shall later see, was the leader of an excessively executive-minded judiciary during the 1980s and whose court was described as having declared a war on law during the states of emergency of the 1980s, commented on the way in which lawyers, who brought cases in many different courts challenging the state of emergency declared by P W Botha in 1985 and again in 1986 and 1987, appeared to have coordinated their legal strategies.[4] To an extent, he was correct—the human rights Bar certainly knew it was in a ferocious fight and each case litigated was followed carefully by other litigators anxious to explore any possibility for a rights-based defence which emerged from previous encounters.

The adverse context in which these legal fights took place is well illustrated by the approach adopted by the senior judiciary, particularly Rabie. Rabie presided over a court which was determined to reduce the space for any legal challenge against government repression. An interview conducted by Steve Mufson with Rabie, published in the *Sunday Star* of 3 May 1987, threw a bright light over this approach adopted by the overwhelming majority of the judiciary at that time: "[Rabie] seemed unperturbed by the Government's encroachment on the rights guaranteed by Roman-Dutch common law; that is, rules of law inherited from our Roman-Dutch and English heritage and fashioned by our courts over a century to meet the perceived needs of the country. As far as Rabie was concerned, there was no question of more than one outcome in a case because, once Parliament enacted a law, 'It is the law,' he said. He viewed a Bill of Rights with scepticism and said that, in the United States, 'It has produced a bit of a shambles.' To him, the United States represented 'freedom run mad'. He then went on to tell Mufson: 'We must be realistic. We have strangers coming in across the borders with bombs and mines. There is nothing in the common law to deal with a situation like that. The ordinary law of criminal procedure would require that a man be charged within 48 hours so that you can't question him any more after that. We must get information from people we arrest, especially when they are carrying weapons from the Soviet Bloc, otherwise we can't defend ourselves … The situation in the country is pretty near that of a civil war. It is naïve to think you can quell it by bringing people to court."

Contrary to the Rabies who dominated the bench, there was a small group of exceptional judges who were prepared to listen to arguments about abuses of rights and to read oppressive and racist legislation as narrowly as possible in order to give effect to the values of the common law.[5] According to this reading, the law, at its core, protected and promoted human rights such as the freedom of the individual and the civil rights of all citizens. Lawyers continued to use Thompson's theory of law in their litigation strategies, knowing that some judges might see law as a limitation on unaccountable state power.

'We have strangers coming in across the borders with bombs and mines'

Challenging the state of emergency

An unusual example of this judicial approach which demonstrates a belief in the possibility inherent in this form of litigation occurred at a conference held in 1986. It was organised by Professor John Dugard, the then Director of the Centre for Applied Legal Studies, an important human rights institution housed at the University of the Witwatersrand. Dugard is truly one of the heroic figures of the South African academy and a pioneer of human rights jurisprudence in this country. He had organised the conference so that lawyers, both in practice and in academic life, could meet to discuss the possibility of legal challenges that could be mounted against the declaration of the state of emergency. It was a time of great despair. The effect of the emergency had been to drastically circumscribe the space available for open political activity and dissent against government. Thousands of people had been rounded up and detained without trial. Chief Justice Rabie presided over the highest court in South Africa and had made his legal intentions clear. Vigilante organisations, whether directly or indirectly established by the government and buttressed by the police and army, had taken charge of many black townships, crushed political opponents, all under the cover of national legislation which empowered the declaration of a state of emergency and consequent suspension of many legal safeguards.

It was not surprising, therefore, that the conference began in muted terms. But, at this conference, a judge who, more than any other, represented the possibility of an independent, courageous and principled judiciary had been invited by Dugard to give the keynote speech. He was Judge John Didcott. Imagine the situation: a sitting judge comes to the University of the Witwatersrand to give an address in an open forum to a group of progressive lawyers, no doubt infiltrated by a number of security police spies. Didcott would have been aware of the risk he was taking in speaking so boldly in public. But he was not a person who was easily intimidated. He spoke of the need for lawyers, more than ever, to find innovative strategies for challenging government action in general and the emergency regulations in particular. He urged lawyers not to give up at this time because the very future of the legal system, which had the potential to underwrite a democratic country, was at stake.

John Didcott would have been aware of the risk he was taking in speaking so boldly in public

Any potentially progressive element of the existing legal tradition could disappear if the government had its way. He reminded the lawyers present that there were available potential legal challenges to the emergency regulations. Of course, he reiterated that it would be inappropriate for him to discuss the details of these avenues as he wished to be available to sit as a judge in some of those cases.

It was an extraordinary call to legal arms. A judge appointed by the apartheid regime was urging the best of South African human rights lawyers, with a brave, principled articulation of the innermost commitments of law, to be true to their calling. This speech was made at the very time when even the most progressive of South African lawyers were beginning to doubt the utility of their activities.

Didcott was almost unique on the South African bench. There were, however, other judges who were also prepared to adhere wherever possible to the underlying principles of the common law, including Gerald Friedman, Richard Goldstone, Ray Leon, Johan Kriegler, John Milne and Laurie Ackermann.[6] It is within this context of the contradictory qualities of law that the cases that were fought during the apartheid era and discussed in this book are perhaps best understood.

The bridge

The history of litigation before 1994 helps us understand the constitutional era that was born out of the legal rubble created by apartheid. The very form of constitutional democracy that took hold in South Africa after 1994 represented not so much a rupture of the old and a construction of the new but, as Etienne Mureinik wrote in a justly heralded article[7], the building of a bridge between a terrible past and the potentially liberating future. Mureinik wrote thus:

> If the new constitution is a bridge and this bridge is successfully to span the open sewer of violent and contentious transition, those who are entrusted with its upkeep will need to understand very clearly what it is a bridge from, and what a bridge to ... If the new constitution is a bridge away from a culture of authority, it is clear what it must be a bridge to. It must lead to a culture of justification—a culture in which every exercise of power is expected to be justified; in which the leadership given by government rests on the cogency of the case offered in defence of its decisions, not the fear inspired by the force at its command. The new order must be a community built on persuasion, not coercion.

Mureinik saw the new Constitution as a bridge designed to transport a country away from a culture of authority to what he termed a culture of justification, that is, a culture where every exercise of power has to be justified by the power holder. Under apartheid, decisions of the government were based on fear which was, in turn, inspired by the force at its command. Mureinik argued that leadership of government under the new Constitution had to rest on the cogency or persuasive quality of the case which it offered in justification of decisions it made. The bridge would assist in the journey which society undertook to travel away from arbitrary and brutal exercises of power to decisions which could be subjected to debate, deliberation, public examination and, above all, justification.

The rich metaphor of the bridge needs to be extended beyond its use as offered by Mureinik. The bridge also represents the model of transformation that was followed in South Africa. There was no revolution, no violent rupture from the past. The old was, in many instances, to remain although the substance of the old would be changed in incremental stages. This path of negotiated evolution rather than violent, sudden revolution can be illustrated by the manner in which the bridge was constructed.

The constitutional bridge was to be created mostly by bridge-builders who were fluent in the old legal traditions. Their construction was undertaken with the only tools in their possession, namely our inherited legal traditions, together with a constitutional mandate to engage in reconstruction of these traditions through the new text. Here we mean the inherited legal traditions, such as the structure of the Bar, the side Bar, the form of the judicial institution in this country that was inherited from Britain with black gowns and frilly bibs, and much reference to 'M'Lord' and 'M'Lady' and to 'my learned friend'.

The dominant conception of the common law is that of a timeless, universal body of truth inherited from the days of the Dutch occupation of the Cape. Through this, precedent retains its tenacious hold on progress as courts, in the main, follow decisions handed down in the distant past. A court is not free to decide a case without constraint. An earlier decision by the higher court which set out a rule of law or interpreted a provision of legislation which is applicable in the case before the later court is now binding and therefore must be followed. All these legal rules and conduct form the traditions of which we speak. But it now becomes mixed with the new constitutional text and the interpretive moves of the courts in giving meaning to the new text. In this way, fresh legal material is manufactured which, in turn, is employed in the construction of the legal bridge.

Models of adjudication for a constitution

In addition there is the not insignificant matter of models of judicial adjudication. As will be illustrated in this book, before 1994, the performance of the judiciary broadly can be explained by way of two models. Until the late 1950s, the courts, particularly the Appellate Division in Bloemfontein, were staffed by judges who were essentially libertarian: they distrusted state interference in the private lives of citizens. For them, the State was a night watchman which operated to guarantee the negative liberties of all citizens.

Old styles of adjudication proved unsuitable for the new challenge of legal transformation After 1960, the courts endorsed the law as a tool of social engineering by the state, no matter the effect upon individual freedom. Neither of these models was suitable to the adjudication of a constitutional text which endorsed social democracy, meaning guarantees of negative liberty together with positive obligations of the state to ensure a minimum floor of goods and services for all who lived in the country. Whatever the chosen model, change was clearly a necessity. Old styles of adjudication proved unsuitable for the new challenge of legal transformation.

The bridge is also constitutive of the new society that is to be constructed by and with laws. As apartheid had built a legal system powered by race, so too was the new democracy to be created by laws sourced in the Constitution.

Hence the bridge continues to be constructed whenever Parliament enacts legislation; each new transformative statute is like another span in the bridge.

This metaphor of the bridge has still further implications for our story: the crossing of the bridge never really ends. At best, the journey is a movement by society away from the past and in the direction of a community prefigured in a coherent reading of the constitutional text. That idea of community is never attained completely. The journey itself becomes an essential part of the transformative exercise. As the constitutional custodians, the judiciary therefore moves into critical focus.

The effectiveness of the judiciary

An important implication arising from the *Harris* cases, dealing with the constitutional crisis of the 1950s, is that when judges are isolated by governments and faced with negative public opinion, their role as potential instruments in the struggle to retain rights under attack, let alone transformation, are truly limited. A constitution is not merely the sum of the provisions contained in its text. This text must be given life by the decisions of the courts. If the text constitutes the design of the bridge, the courts begin to build the bridge in terms of their particular conception of the design.

Of course, the construction of a constitutional bridge can only happen successfully if the community continually accepts the efforts of the court in building the bridge. With this kind of acceptance, the bridge gains legitimacy when it is increasingly viewed by the population as a viable means to be used for the journey away from the apartheid past.

Legitimacy and efficacy are the very cement of the project. Efficacy means that the decisions of the courts are recognised and rendered effective by those in power. After all, it is now trite to parrot the American constitutional theorist, Alexander Bickel,[8] who observed that the courts are the weakest arm of government with no police or army to command in order to enforce their orders. The process of enforcement depends upon the cooperation of the other arms of government. It is mainly the police force which is used to enforce court orders, if necessary, and the police are under the control of the executive. Efficacy is reinforced by legitimacy; that is, the more the public respects and regards the importance of court decisions, recognising that their content broadly reflects the moral convictions of the community, the more legitimate the courts become as an institution. In turn, this level of public regard develops into a form of public practice which does not take lightly to manipulation of the constitutional system.

Legitimacy and efficacy are the very cement of the project

By this, Bickel means that the institution of rule by constitutional law is then defended by the public in the face of executive or legislative attempts to curb the power of the courts. If the public, mainly through institutions of civil society and the media, defends the legal institutions, government becomes more wary about interference. With a legitimate institution as the key agency of construction, it is possible for the bridge to transport society in a direction away from that which existed prior to its construction. However, if there is fundamental public disagreement about the construction, the project becomes stillborn, like the bridge on the Foreshore in Cape Town depicted on the cover of this book, waiting in a forlorn fashion to be connected to some other part of the city. With this background, we turn to our selection of cases.

The coloured vote cases

This book canvasses cases from both the apartheid past and democratic South Africa. In each of these cases, the stakes were enormous. The trilogy of coloured vote cases heralded the end of the liberal legalism that had flickered throughout the first part of the 1950s. With the decision in *Collins*, the last of this trilogy of cases, the South African legal system finally and definitively eschewed the idea that a common law, which placed the freedom of the individual at the centre of the legal enterprise, should trump legislation which took away these rights, save where the legislation in question made a denial absolutely clear. In the wake of the first two cases in the trilogy, the National Party responded to its legal defeats by altering the composition of the Appellate Division in order that its judgments would increasingly reflect the will of the (white) people of South Africa. Not only did this help give it eventual victory in *Collins* but it destroyed the last vestiges of a liberal court which may have challenged the executive.

In summary, these cases tolled the bell for the burial of liberal legalism, albeit of the weak kind that endured into the 1950s. Thereafter, it would be rare for government's race laws to be overturned by a court determined to preserve the rights of individuals, even those long existing in the common law of the country. By the time the final decision in the trilogy was made to approve the constitutional changes that disenfranchised the coloured voters of the country, the National Party had gained control of the Appeal Court. Its campaign to alter the composition of the Bench had borne fruit which it harvested for more than two decades. Thus the institution of an independent judiciary was seriously jeopardised.

Rivonia

Next up is the *Rivonia* case, a quintessential political trial as defined by the Frankfurt School political scientist, Otto Kircheimer,[9] in that it adopts the form of criminal law to vindicate the existing social and political order by imposing criminal sanctions for the political actions of legitimate political opponents. In these ways, political acts designed to criticise the government or to organise opposition to government policy are subjected to a criminal censure. By censure, we mean the attempt of government to categorise this political activity as nothing more than criminal conduct devoid of 'legitimate political purpose'. After all, the courts impose severe sanctions upon people convicted of criminal conduct. The possibility is then open for government to equate this 'criminalised' political conduct with, for example, common law murder or robbery.

Rivonia was a trial of the political ideas of those leaders who represented the majority of the country. The state sought to present the leadership of the African National Congress as no more than a group of violent criminals. Of course, as in any political trial, the 'accused' contested this attempt of the state to invoke a criminal censure with all the vigour that their testimony and legal team could muster. But the ultimate conviction of the accused held the possibility that South Africa's greatest leaders, including Mandela and Sisulu, could have been hanged. That alone was cause for the country to hold its breath. The trial also represents the story of a diminishing faith in the law. The defence lawyers well knew of these limitations as they confronted a more confident, oppressive state and increasingly pro-executive judges. The scope for legal resistance had narrowed. *Rivonia* was not only about Nelson Mandela and the other accused, but it was also about Bram Fischer, lead counsel for the accused, and his journey after *Rivonia* from a leading senior counsel at the Johannesburg Bar to a full-time revolutionary. In brief, it appears that, not long after the end of the trial, Fischer recognised that the existing legal system could hardly be employed meaningfully to effect significant social change.

Residence and relocation

The two other cases litigated during the apartheid era discussed in this book represented far more strategic and less defensive conceptions of litigation. In these cases, the law was used to curb the excesses of apartheid in key areas of state policy. Even before 1948, influx control had diminished the freedom of movement of most South Africans on the grounds of race alone. By the late 1970s, literally hundreds of thousands of black South Africans had been made criminals in their own country by attempting to live with their families or work in urban areas from where they were barred by a system of laws designed to prevent their permanent residence in the urban centres. Millions of people worked in exploitative conditions for the benefit of an economy controlled by the few. The system of influx control empowered government officials to treat millions of South Africans as pawns on a giant chessboard.

Along came two tenacious litigants, Messrs Komani and Rikhotso, and the Legal Resources Centre (LRC). In two separate cases, the director of the LRC and future Chief Justice of South Africa, Arthur Chaskalson, managed to persuade a National Party-appointed Appellate Division that the administration of these pass laws was illegal. By the end of this litigation, the pass laws could no longer be properly enforced and the way had been cleared for black South Africans to live and work in urban South Africa. Not only did Messrs Komani and Rikhotso succeed in their quest to live legally where they had resided for years but the outcome justified the choice of a legal strategy during the height of apartheid rule where the very laws attacked in a conservative court had been designed as a main strut in the apartheid edifice.

Atrocities in incarceration

From the 1960s, the government employed a system of detention without trial to incarcerate its political opponents. As is the case today in the United States and Britain, governments seek to bypass the law in their 'war against terror'. The South African government employed the justification of a 'communist onslaught' against its alleged 'civilised standard of life' to incarcerate people without any proof of an offence which could be tested by a legal system. The police were not prepared to be rendered accountable to even a generally sympathetic judiciary which government had carefully appointed.

During the early 1960s, the system of detention began with incarceration without the authority of a court for a maximum defined period of 90 days. Within a decade, this period had been extended to indefinite detention. The cloak of secrecy and lack of accountability that was thrown over the system did not prevent the regular publication of allegations of police torture of detainees. But it was only when a courageous district surgeon came forward to expose the atrocities committed by the police, invariably denied or covered up by government and rarely believed by the courts, even when they were confronted with detailed allegations of torture, that the sheer horror of the system was exposed to the nation through litigation. The *Wendy Orr* case was a piece of strategic litigation designed to expose the system of detention without trial. The use of existing law and legal procedure to achieve this aim within the context of a state of emergency, where the country was controlled by police and not the courts, is a remarkable illustration of strategic human rights lawyering.

*The **Wendy Orr** case was a piece of strategic litigation designed to expose the system of detention without trial*

These four cases were part of a legal tradition upon which constitutional democracy during the late 1980s and early 1990s could be based. These cases showed that there was value in a rights-based legal culture and that the promise of a transformed jurisprudence had never been destroyed in its entirety.

Cases based upon a Constitution

The cases that were litigated after the advent of constitutional democracy and which are discussed in this book all illustrate the manner in which the bridge has been constructed since the designs were approved by the Constitutional Assembly. Each of these cases represented a challenge for the nascent South African constitutional project. On each occasion, the Constitutional Court, an institution created by the same new Constitution, was tested by the challenge of taking the law into uncharted territory, thus extending the bridge a little further towards the society promised in the constitutional text.

The very first case heard by the Constitutional Court concerned the legality of the death penalty. The death penalty had been employed with increasing regularity in South Africa. Between 1978 and 1987, 1218 people were hanged; in 1987 alone, the figure was 164. By the 1980s, the issue had become the subject of great political controversy. The death penalty was a punishment of first choice. As a prominent political commentator, Herman Giliomee, noted in 1988: '[a]lmost unnoticed South Africa has got itself in a situation where it is hanging people at a rate which would cause even the most sordid banana republic to hang its head in shame.'[10]

In the late 1980s, South Africa experienced its own *intifada*. During this period of resistance, a number of apartheid bureaucrats who did the government's bidding in the townships were killed in the unrest. The State then employed the legal doctrine of common purpose to charge groups of people who were present at these killings with murder—the rationale being that as the 'mob' made common purpose with the unidentified killer(s), any member of the 'mob' was guilty of murder. In a case which became known as the *Sharpeville Six*, the six accused were convicted and sentenced to death. The application of the doctrine of common purpose enabled the state to obtain convictions without proving that any of the individual accused had been directly involved in the murder. The decision was upheld by the Appellate Division. Few decisions of this kind have prompted such discord. The lives of the six men were spared not only by way of a legal challenge heroically led by their counsel, Jack Unterhalter and Edwin Cameron, the latter now a leading member of the Supreme Court of Appeal where he had fought so hard to save the lives of the six, but primarily due to political campaigns which aroused local and international pressure.

In the late 1980s, South Africa experienced its own intifada

By 1990, the campaign against the death penalty had reached fever pitch as a result of cases like the *Sharpeville Six*. F W de Klerk, then President of the country, placed a moratorium on all executions. However, no agreement could be reached by the constitutional negotiators as to whether the death penalty should be declared unconstitutional. The decision was left to the Constitutional

Court which decided the matter in the very first case argued before the court. The case of *Makwanyane* is not about the way brutal murderers succeeded in their argument that the death penalty was unconstitutional. The accused hardly featured in the arguments before the court. Rather, in their judgments, the newly appointed justices of the court not only reflected on the history of the death penalty as a metaphor for a brutal history of government in which life and dignity, particularly of black South Africans, was not respected, but asserted the importance of constitutional democracy and the vision the constitutional text held for the future of the country. The case was not about an individual criminal; it concerned the articulation of the core commitments of the new Constitution.

HIV/AIDS, together with crime, is arguably the single most pressing social problem confronting democratic South Africa. Faced with a government that has steadfastly adopted policies which have failed fully to acknowledge or address the problem, civil society, mainly through the Treatment Action Campaign (TAC), contested government's inaction with great vigour, courage, innovation and some significant success. As part of this campaign, the TAC took the government to court to compel it to provide pregnant mothers with anti-retroviral drugs to prevent the transmission of HIV to their children. The case finally reached the Constitutional Court. The successful litigation by the TAC represented a victory in a new form of political trial. The Constitutional Court asserted that residents of this country could approach the court for basic goods and services as promised in the Constitution. This case is a story of a new form of human rights litigation in a democracy accompanied by great official hostility where government initially indicated that it was not prepared even to abide by the decision of the court.

The TAC took the government to court to compel it to provide pregnant mothers with anti-retroviral drugs

The Constitution and its centrepiece, the Bill of Rights, mandated constitutional scrutiny not only of the relationships between the state and the individual but also, where applicable, relationships between private actors exclusively. It also empowered the courts to extend the principle of accountability by the state to its citizens.

Alix Carmichele was subjected to a brutal attack by a man who should have been behind bars awaiting trial. Prosecution and police negligence allowed him to roam free so that he could brutally confront Carmichele in the idyllic setting of Knoetzie beach in the Western Cape. Like Messrs Komani and Rikhotso, she pursued her rights with great courage and tenacity. Five courts later, she established an important legal principle in that our law of delict[11] required adaptation through the guiding spirit of the Bill of Rights to entitle Carmichele and similar victims to sue the state for damages as a consequence of its failure to protect her.

The transition to democracy is never easy. The law and hence the judiciary can also be used by those who wish to subvert the new enterprise. The crossing of the bridge was challenged by both left and right. Hence two further cases merit examination. When Louis Luyt, the president of the South African Rugby Union, challenged a government-appointed commission of inquiry into rugby, Nelson Mandela found himself summonsed by one of the most conservative judges in the country to explain why, as President of the country, he had appointed this commission. When the case went on appeal to the Constitutional Court, many judges of that court were impugned by Luyt who called for their recusal claiming that they would be biased against him. The *SARFU* case represented an attack by the old order on key instruments of the new democratic system of government. It is a story of political contest with a very different result from the previous time Mr Mandela appeared in court, at the *Rivonia* trial.

The left also resisted a key design of the bridge. Critical to the process of change was the Truth and Reconciliation Commission (TRC). The legislation that brought the TRC into existence guaranteed a process of amnesty for those who had committed and fully disclosed political crimes.[12] If they were granted amnesty, the Act granted applicants criminal and civil immunity. A number of families, including those of great South African leaders, Steve Biko and Griffiths and Victoria Mxenge, challenged the constitutionality of this provision. In what is now known as the *AZAPO* case, the Constitutional Court, palpably torn by the moral dilemma of the case, found that the postamble to the interim Constitution had provided expressly for such immunity. Without this provision, the court opined that the construction of the bridge could have been blown up at its very inception; hence the families had to lose their application.

All these cases raised critical social and political questions. Each affected many who lived in the country. Each shows the contested nature of the law, as well as the different claims and visions of those who litigated these cases. For many readers, the recitation of these cases may serve to tell some of our history and the inherent drama of the law. And that is a purpose of this book. But the deliberate linkage between the old and the new tells another, equally important story: of a constitutional democracy like South Africa built on the old, whether because the text of the Constitution responds to the old or because the old continues to haunt our attempts to move beyond it. More than that, it reveals that constitutional democracy cannot be imposed—its values must be continually asserted and justified. The bridge must be diligently and continually built. Indeed the bridge may prove to be too limited a metaphor, for constitutional democracy is rather a journey which never ends.

Endnotes

1   *Omar and Others v Minister of Law and Order and Others* 1986 (3) SA 306 (C). By contrast, see the judgment of Judge Goldstone in *Momoniat and Naidoo v Minister of Law and Order* 1986 (2) SA 264 (W). Mr Omar at the time was one of the most tenacious and courageous human rights practitioners in the country.

2   *R v Abdurrahman* 1950 (3) SA 136 (A).

3   E P Thompson *Whigs and Hunters, The Origin of the Black Act* (1975) 265-266. There was also a liberal approach to law that proved equally influential. See, for example, E Mureinik 'Dworkin and Apartheid' in H Corder (ed) *Essays in Law & Social Practice* (1988).

4   Nicholas Haysom and Clive Plasket 'The War against Law: Judicial Activism and the Appellate Division' (1988) 4 *SAJHR* 303.

5   When we refer to the common law, we mean that body of law which is not sourced in legislation and which, rather, is drawn primarily from Roman-Dutch and English law, itself a reflection of our colonial past. This body of law was then adopted by the courts to meet the judicially perceived needs of the country. Thus the rules developed by the courts, together with the legal materials of both the Roman-Dutch and English legal systems to which courts may have recourse, constitutes the structure of the legal system upon which is built a superstructure of legislation which amends, corrects, repeals and adds to the existing body of common law. Today, the common law ultimately derives its authority from the Constitution which is also the source for judges to effect changes to the common law. For a detailed discussion, see Francois du Bois (ed) Wille's *Principles of South African Law* (9ed) ch 4.

6   Laurie Ackermann later left the bench to promote human rights as a law professor, heading up the first human rights centre at Stellenbosch University.

7   Etienne Mureinik 'A Bridge to Where? Introducing the Interim Bill of Rights' (1994) *SAJHR* 31, 31-32.

8   Alexander Bickel *The Least Dangerous Branch* (1962).

9   Otto Kirchheimer *Political Justice: The use of legal procedures for political ends* (1961).

10 *Sunday Times* (27 August 1988).

11 Briefly, the law of delict is that body of law which seeks to afford a right of compensation to a person who, as a result of an act of another person performed in a wrongful and culpable way, has suffered harm.

12 Section 20(7) of the Promotion of National Unity and Reconciliation Act 34 of 1995.

two

Who can rid me of this troublesome court? The first instalment

H istory has a curious way of repeating itself. A legal crisis occurred more than half a century ago and there is a current concern that a similar chain of events could happen again. Once more, the judiciary is in the eye of a political storm and the implications of the present controversy compel us to look back to the political turbulence of the early 1950s.

On the hot summer's day on 20 February 1952, the finest legal minds of the Cape Bar congregated in the majestic courtroom of the Appellate Division of the Supreme Court in Bloemfontein.

They had travelled from Cape Town to appear in a case that held massive implications for the last vestige of constitutional protection in apartheid South Africa—the right of 'coloured' South Africans to vote together with whites for members of Parliament. Although the case had been brought nominally by individual voters, the challenge to the National Party's new scheme had been launched on behalf of a significant section of the population.

The seven samurai

The legal team assembled on behalf of the voters was led by Graeme Duncan KC and included Harry Snitcher KC and Donald Molteno.[1] Duncan was later to be described by one of his opponents in this case as 'one of the greats of the legal world over the past few decades'. At the time a truly dominant intellectual figure at the Cape Bar, Duncan was probably best classified politically as a Cape liberal. In contrast, Harry Snitcher had been a prominent member of the South African Communist Party until 1948 and one of its leading intellectual figures. Whereas Duncan looked every bit the patrician lawyer, Snitcher was small and elf-like. Duncan was the team leader but Snitcher, too, was an advocate of great legal skill and forensic shrewdness. He was truly one of the most eloquent lawyers, arguably the best of the last group of jury advocates.

The third member of the team was Donald Molteno. He had served as the 'Native Representative' in Parliament from 1937 to 1948. At one time, he had been the vice-chairman of the Liberal Party. Later, he was to leave practice and become professor of public law at the University of Cape Town. In 1959, the newly formed Progressive Party employed his services to formulate its policy on qualified franchise whereby black voters were required to meet certain requirements before they could be eligible to vote. For an erstwhile member of the Liberal Party, this policy was an exercise in expediency in that it clearly was designed to soften the non-racial commitment of liberals in order to attract white votes. But it was a policy that, in part, was faithful to the case that Molteno was about to fight in Bloemfontein.

The government team was led by Andrew Beyers KC. A large and seemingly avuncular individual, he had a most intimidating presence. Beyers first shot to prominence as the losing United Party (UP) candidate in the Oudtshoorn constituency during the 1938 parliamentary general elections. Unsuccessful in politics, he enjoyed a successful practice at the Bar which led to an appointment on the Cape Bench in 1956 and a speedy promotion to the Appellate Division at the beginning of 1959. Shortly thereafter, he was appointed as the Judge President of the Cape High Court, a position he occupied until his retirement.

Whereas Beyers was a man of pronounced personality and sometimes humanity, Theo van Wyk KC possessed none of the latter. He did have a formidable intellect which was evenly matched by a parsimonious and mean-spirited view of the world, a true apartheid ideologue. Van Wyk was later appointed to the position of *Ad Hoc* Judge at the International Court of Justice at the Hague. He, too, would become the Judge President of the Cape High Court. Unlike Beyers, he never showed an inch of compassion when confronted by the inhumane consequences of apartheid.

The third member of the team was Dawid de Villiers, who was *It was well known* to take silk in 1954 and serve as an acting judge in 1959 and again *that the National* from later that year to 1961. An outstanding legal mind, he declined *Party was* a permanent appointment to the Bench to concentrate, first, on *desperately keen to* legal and, later, commercial interests. In the 1960s, he was the leader *appoint De Villiers* of the South African legal team that argued the South West African *as a judge* case at the Hague. It was well known that the National Party was desperately keen to appoint De Villiers as a judge, from which position it would have been likely that he would have achieved the status of Chief Justice. He refused these offers and, instead, became the Managing Director of Nasionale Pers.

De Villiers was the exact opposite of Van Wyk. He was a sophisticated intellectual. In his later life, he embraced a non-racial South Africa with great enthusiasm. He returned to the Bar to argue a number of significant cases on behalf of people who had suffered the most under the grinding rule of the National Party he had so enthusiastically embraced in his earlier career. The final member of the team was George Wynne. Like Beyers, he had had an unsuccessful political career, in his case on behalf of the National Party. Later, he was to be appointed to the Senate and ended his career as a judge in the Eastern Cape. Apparently, he had been added to the team because some of his government clients thought he had a contribution to make, a view not shared by Beyers.

All these men had been to the Appeal Court many times before 1952. But it is fair to say that, on 20 February 1952, they argued a case which was more important than any other they had undertaken during their distinguished legal careers. When the Court convened on that day, it was to hear argument in a dispute which, in various forms, lasted five years and was to lead to a constitutional crisis of considerable proportion. The effect thereof would be felt for the next four decades.

The nature of the dispute

To understand the case, we need to take a short historical tour. Before 1910, the voting laws for the Cape Colony permitted all males over the age of 21 to vote providing each person 'is able to sign his name and address and occupation'. There were two further qualifications, namely ownership of property to the value of £75 or earnings of £50 per annum as a salary or wages. After 1910, changes to the electoral law permitted women to vote subject to the same property qualifications that were applied to white males. There was thus a common roll but not a common franchise. In 1936, africans were taken off the common roll in the Cape Province and given separate representation in Parliament. They were represented by whites. For a time, Molteno was one of these representatives. The coloured community remained on the common voters' roll when the National Party won its electoral victory.

The principle of the common roll had been protected by section 152 of the South Africa Act, being the Constitution of the Union. That section provided that any law which sought to change the common voters' roll had to be passed by a joint sitting of the two Houses of Parliament and by a two-thirds majority of the total number of members of both Houses. The provision did not appear to be under any threat to South Africa when the country celebrated the end of World War II. But on 26 May 1948, the National Party pulled off a stunning electoral victory aided by the electoral system which, at that time, weighted votes heavily in favour of rural constituencies. The National Party and its allies won 79 out of the 150 seats in the House of Assembly. The fact that General Jan Smuts's United Party and its allies won 50,9 per cent of the vote compared to 41,2 per cent for the National Party was irrelevant. The minority party came into power and, with its victory, it was determined to engage in the implementation of its racist project.

One of its first steps was to consolidate its tenuous hold on power. In 1950, the National Party successfully introduced the Suppression of Communism Act which outlawed the Communist Party and ensured the removal from Parliament of Communist Members of Parliament who had been elected to represent 'Cape Natives'. This Act gave considerable power to the police to curb political opposition to the government. Over the next 40 years, the police would increasingly employ this and similar legislation to take control over civil society.

The National Party then turned its attention to the common voters' roll in the Cape, a province of the country which significantly was still under the control of the United Party. In 1951, after a furious debate in Parliament, the National Party succeeded in passing the Separate Representation of Voters Act. As the law stood before the passing into law of this Act, all voters voted in the same constituency, whether white or coloured. With the introduction of the Act, coloured voters would be able to vote only in separate constituencies in which they were registered. That the National Party considered this Act to be important was crisply illustrated by a statement made by the then Prime Minister, D F Malan, when he responded to the possibility that the United Party would challenge the validity of the Act in court. Malan told Parliament: 'If the court should declare this Act of Parliament invalid . . . it stands to reason that it would be a serious matter for Parliament and for the country. It would mean the undermining of Parliament's sovereignty; it would mean that the judicial authorities would assume powers belonging exclusively to a Legislature . . .'[2]

The United Party ignored these threats and found four voters who acted as the plaintiffs in the case. They were Ganief Harris, a Malay bricklayer who lived in Woodstock, Cape Town; Edgar Franklin, a van driver who also lived in Woodstock; William David Collins, a merchant of Cape Town; and Edgar Arthur Deane, a trade unionist and secretary of the Furniture Workers' Union. Collins and Deane were members of the Coloured Peoples' National Union and they later became Cape Town city councillors. The United Party could not itself bring the application against the constitutional change. So it needed to find individuals who would be affected by the new law and were willing to be used to initiate the case. Ganief Harris gave his name to this famous case but in truth he played little, if any, role in the proceedings.

Coloured voters would be able to vote only in separate constituencies in which they were registered

The litigation was not launched without apprehension. Once relegated to the position of leader of the opposition after the electoral defeat of the United Party in 1948, Smuts began to concern himself with the possibility that the new government would change the Constitution in order to remove the coloured citizens from the common voters' roll. But, a few days after the election defeat, Smuts summoned prominent lawyer, successful entrepreneur and UP spokesperson on Coloured Affairs, Abe Bloomberg, to Pretoria to discuss a possible fight against such a move. Bloomberg was instructed to procure a legal opinion on the legality of such a move by the NP government. Bloomberg briefed Duncan, Snitcher and Molteno who opined that the Constitution could be changed only by a super majority of both Houses of Parliament.

At roughly the same time, the NP obtained their own legal advice. Prof Ignatius Coertze of the University of Pretoria, who was in his own words 'a passionate supporter of the NP', cautioned against trying to change the Constitution by way of a simple majority of both Houses sitting together.[3]

Smuts remained uncertain, the opinion of senior counsel notwithstanding. He approached Denis Cowen, then a young law professor at the University of Cape Town, who had written an article about the National Party's proposed legislation which was published in the *Cape Times* in 1949 and later amplified in a far longer, academic article which was published in 1951 as *Parliamentary Sovereignty and the Entrenched Sections of the South Africa Act*. Smuts had read *'Do we have a good case ... can we win?'* Cowen's article and invited the author to his private suite at the Mount Nelson Hotel for a chat. Over sherry, Smuts probed Cowen over the possible success of a case based on his article. Over and over, Smuts asked Cowen, 'Do we have a good case ... can we win?' But more ominously, Smuts told Cowen that if the case were won the NP would not rest until it achieved its objective, even if it meant instituting a constitutional revolution bypassing the authority of the courts. Cowen left the meeting with the clear impression of Smuts's conviction that a winning case may herald the end of the rule of law as Smuts understood that concept.[4]

By the time the litigation was launched, Smuts was dead. The new leader of the United Party, J G N Strauss, proceeded to ensure that Duncan and his team were briefed to challenge the manner in which the Constitution had been altered.

Harris I

Ostensibly on behalf of the four voters, but in substance on behalf of a larger constituency of voters, Duncan rose to address the five members of the Appeal Court and argue that the Act was unconstitutional. He argued for some six hours and fifteen minutes. Briefly, his argument was that section 152 of the South Africa Act remained in force notwithstanding that in 1936, by way of the Statute of Westminster, the Union of South Africa had been granted a sovereign parliament which was no longer under the control of Britain. Although South Africa was a sovereign state, nothing in the 1936 legislation indicated that the protection of the common voters' roll had to be altered by the abolition of a special majority. In essence, the voters' case was that if the constitutional protection of the coloured vote had to be removed, it could be done only by a two-thirds majority vote of both Houses of Parliament.

Beyers and Van Wyk's arguments took even more time. Early on in his address, Beyers had introduced a political note which underlined the government's entire argument. This was that, in his view, no country which emerged from a colony into a dominion[5], and thus into a sovereign state, could claim to be sovereign unless it had a Parliament functioning in a bicameral manner as did the British Parliament, which was free to pass a statute of any kind, in any manner it so chose. In short, unless the legislature elected by the voters was completely sovereign, South Africa could not be considered to be a sovereign state. Over many hours, Beyers and Van Wyk sought to persuade the court to this proposition. But it became clear to the government team that, whatever precedent it had in its favour, Duncan's argument clearly held sway with the five judges.

A brouhaha before judgment

Before judgment could be handed down on 20 March 1952, politicians had already intervened. The moderator of the Dutch Reformed Church in the Cape, Dr A J van der Merwe, was the chair of the Central Committee of the Van Riebeeck Festival due to take place in April 1952 and designed to commemorate the 300th year of the arrival of Jan van Riebeeck at the Cape. In January 1952, on behalf of the Central Committee, he requested an interview with Chief Justice Centlivres. At this stage, the hearing had not yet taken place and perhaps Dr van der Merwe had some religious insight into the outcome of the case. He was concerned that the controversy that would inevitably surround the judgment would interfere with the celebratory mood the festival was designed to promote among white South Africans.

By the end of February, Van der Merwe had received no response from Chief Justice Albert Centlivres. He grew impatient and approached the Prime Minister to support a move which would encourage the Court to postpone the handing down of judgment until after the Van Riebeeck celebrations. Dr Malan wrote to Centlivres requesting a postponement of the judgment until after the conclusion of the festival. The Chief Justice informed Malan that courts could not deliver delayed judgments without the consent of the attorneys concerned. Pressure was now put on the attorneys for Harris and the other plaintiffs. On 18 March 1952, it was announced that judgment would be handed down on 20 March. Van der Merwe had believed that a postponement would be obtained. He was disappointed. A few days after the judgment was handed down, he issued a statement to the press concerning the need for a postponed judgment. He also released correspondence between the Chief Justice and Malan. This prompted the Chief Justice to issue a statement setting the record straight and, in particular, emphasising that the court could not delay judgment without the consent of the attorneys concerned.

In his comprehensive examination of this case, David Scher describes a less important but illuminating event leading up to the delivery of the judgment. Abe Bloomberg had acted as the United Party's attorney in the litigation. Shortly before the appeal he had drinks in the private bar of Parliament with the Minister of Interior, Dr Dönges, who was responsible for the legislation, and the government's senior counsel, Andrew Beyers. Beyers, in his typically flamboyant fashion, was very confident of winning the case. He asked Bloomberg if he was prepared to bet on the outcome of the appeal. A £200 bet was concluded between the two men. When the appeal was lost by government, Bloomberg received a cheque for £200 together with a note which read 'My dear Bloomberg, herewith my cheque and best of luck. This is the easiest money you have ever won. I'm afraid I never even had a run for my money.'

Beyers asked Bloomberg if he was prepared to bet on the outcome of the appeal. A £200 bet was concluded between the two men

In this assessment, Beyers was completely correct. The major difficulty that confronted Chief Justice Centlivres and his colleagues was an earlier decision of the Court in *Ndlwana v Hofmeyer NO* where the Court had decided that, as the South African Parliament had become sovereign after the passing of the Statute of Westminister, the appeal court had no power to pronounce upon the validity of any Act of Parliament. It was upon this decision that government lawyers had relied almost exclusively to contend that a South African court had no power to test the validity of legislation in South Africa after 1931. It was hardly a cavalier argument. After all, it had a 1937 precedent as support.

Chief Justice Centlivres refused to follow the *Ndlwana* precedent. After a careful examination of that case, he found that the earlier court had not dealt properly with the question of whether the Statute of Westminster impliedly repealed the entrenched provisions, including section 152 which provided that a two-thirds majority of both Houses of Parliament was required before the voting arrangements concerning coloured voters could be changed.

Reading the judgment of Chief Justice Centlivres in the yellowing pages of a law report which is now more than half a century old, it is fascinating to find the detail to which the Chief Justice went to show that the 1937 decision had pronounced on a question of vital constitutional importance without the benefit of proper argument. Centlivres noted, by way of reference to the record of the *Ndlwana* court, that the appellant had argued for 55 minutes. Counsel for the respondent had argued for a quarter of an hour and the reply had taken but 10 minutes. As the Chief Justice correctly noted: 'This short argument contrasts strangely with the argument in this case which lasted six days.' In short, the decision had not been properly considered.

Once the Appellate Division had found that the *Ndlwana* decision was wrong, the government's case was fatally torpedoed. The entrenched clauses remained part of the Constitution. The Separate Representation of Voters Act had been passed by simple majority with the two Houses of Parliament sitting separately. The constitutional guarantee of a mandated special vote by two-thirds of the members of both Houses of Parliament had not been followed. For this reason, the legislation had to be set aside.

The reaction

The government's reaction was swift and predictable. Dr Malan told Parliament in a special statement on 20 March 1952 that:

> The judgment of the Appeal Court . . . has created a constitutional position which cannot be accepted. Neither Parliament nor the people of South Africa will be prepared to acquiesce in a position where the legislative sovereignty of the lawfully and democratically elected representatives of the people is denied and where an appointed judicial authority assumes the testing right . . . it is imperative that the legislative sovereignty of Parliament should be placed beyond any doubt in order to ensure order and certainty.[6]

It did not take long for the government to come up with yet another legislative initiative to implement its voting programme. On 22 April 1952, Dr Dönges introduced the High Court of Parliament Bill. According to the Bill, the power to review any order of the Appeal Court which invalidated a piece of national legislation would be vested in a special committee of Parliament composed of all members of the Senate and the House of Assembly of whom 50 would constitute a quorum. It would be called 'The High Court of Parliament'. The 'Court' would be served by a judicial committee consisting of 10 members of Parliament. The Bill provided that the High Court was to be a court of law, the decisions of which were final and binding. The orders would be executed in the identical manner to those of the Appeal Court. Dr Dönges told Parliament that this Act merely says that 'when a judgment has declared an Act of Parliament invalid, such judgment is subject to review by the elected representatives of the people. This court merely creates the opportunity whereby the elected representatives of the people express themselves clearly and unambiguously with regard to certain questions of the utmost importance. Those who oppose the Bill are begrudging the "Volkswil" (the will of the people).'[7]

The National Party representatives again trumpeted the question of the will of the people, being the will of the small white minority. Thus, H J van den Berg, an NP member of Parliament, asked the House: 'Can you expect me to have any respect for a Constitution and for entrenched clauses in that Constitution which were entrenched against the wishes of the majority of the people of South Africa?'[8]

Harris II

The High Court of Parliament Act was passed on 3 June 1952. A judicial committee was then appointed. Four United Party members resigned from the committee. It had a quorum of six National Party members. Andrew Beyers QC, assisted by Dawid de Villiers, appeared for the applicants on an application to review the *Harris* judgment. No-one represented the coloured voters, but no matter said Andrew Beyers, he would not confine himself solely to his own case but place all possible points of view before the judicial committee. In what must have been one of the most unsurprising decisions ever to emanate from Parliament, or any tribunal for that matter, the Judicial Committee recommended the reversal of the decision of the Appellate Division to declare the Separation of Voters Act invalid.

The High Court of Parliament then convened on 25 August 1952 to study the report of the Judicial Committee. The United Party boycotted the proceedings. As expected, the High Court of Parliament unanimously accepted the legal grounds set out by the judicial committee and declared the judgment and orders of the Appellate Division in the case of *Harris* to have been set aside.

'They really are monkeys in dinner jackets and the sartorial elegance of that garb does not in the least conceal the barbarian beneath'

Back went Harris, Franklin, Collins and Deane to court to set aside the High Court of Parliament Act. They contended that it was invalid. The matter finally reached the Appellate Division on 27 October 1952. The same teams convened to argue before the same court. The high stakes were felt clearly by all the parties, including the two senior counsel acting for government, Beyers and Van Wyk. The voters' attorney, Pilkington-Jordan, wrote to United Party leader J G N Strauss as follows: 'Beyers again treated the Court with scant courtesy and both he and Van Wyk were thought thoroughly rude to Duncan. They really are monkeys in dinner jackets and the sartorial elegance of that garb does not in the least conceal the barbarian beneath . . .'.[9]

The tension between the parties notwithstanding, this time the dispute was far simpler. As Chief Justice Centlivres said: 'The approach to the problem before the court is to ascertain by looking at the substance and not merely the form of the Act whether the High Court of Parliament was in fact a Court of Law.' It was clear, said the Chief Justice, that the entrenched provision of the Constitution, namely section 152, conferred on individuals the right to call on the courts to help them resist any legislative or executive action which offended against the entrenched sections of the Constitution. The Chief Justice then said: 'These sections contain constitutional guarantees creating rights in individuals, the duty of the Courts, where the question arises in litigation, being to ensure that the protection of the guarantee is made effective, unless and until it is modified by legislation in such a form as under the Constitution can validly effect such modification.'[10]

Viewed in this way, the Constitution provided individuals the right to approach the court for relief when their constitutional rights were infringed. There may not have been many rights under the Constitution but some remained, including the right of coloured voters to be included on the common voters' roll. The question was whether the High Court of Parliament was really a court to which citizens could proceed in the event that they were dissatisfied with the decision of the Appellate Division. Chief Justice Centlivres said that, whatever the High Court of Parliament might have been called by Parliament, it was still Parliament and not a court. It may have been described as a court of law but this description could not alter the fact that it was not a court of law but Parliament and it was courts which had to adjudicate upon the Constitution.

The Court was unanimous. The High Court of Parliament Act breached the Constitution and had to be set aside.

'It is undemocratic that six old men in Bloemfontein have the final say'

Certain members of the National Party knew that the advice given to Dönges by Beyers, Van Wyk and the chief legal adviser to the government, D H Botha, had been poorly conceived. Dönges had been under great pressure to deal with the Appellate Division and, in desperation, had latched onto the opinions offered by his lawyers. That did not prevent the Court from being blamed for the outcome. As former rugby captain, Dr P K Albertyn, said, if one read the earlier judgment of the Appellate Division of 20 March 1952, it felt 'as if his team had played the entire match with the referee determined to cheat'.

Whatever the reason, the National Party stopped short of using its High Court of Parliament to set aside the second *Harris* decision, which would unquestionably have created constitutional chaos. It had most certainly considered radical measures to restrict the independence of the judiciary. According to documents found in the papers of Eben Dönges, the National Party contemplated initiatives which ranged from compelling judges to sign a contract recognising the sovereignty of Parliament to only appointing 'Nasionale' candidates to the Bench.[11] Paul Sauer, a senior member of the National Party, captured the sentiments of the ruling party when he said in a well-published speech 'It is undemocratic that six old men in Bloemfontein have the final say. Who is the boss—the six in Bloemfontein or you (the voters)?'[12]

Eric Louw, then Minister of Economic Affairs, later to be a long-serving Foreign Minister modelled along the style of Hitler's Von Ribbentrop, in that he similarly sought to cultivate an aloof and urbane approach while defending brutal racism, was even more strident: 'Whenever these judges deal with cases involving "non-whites" they are inclined to view these cases within the context of their liberal outlook and convictions.'

Revealing the racism that characterised apartheid South Africa, Louw went on to bemoan the fact that the judges in Bloemfontein were not prepared to accept that 'natives, due to a far lower level of civilisation and other inherent factors, could not enjoy the same civic opportunities as whites'.[13]

Dönges echoed the same racist bile, albeit indirectly, when he threatened that 'unless Parliament is convinced that its laws will not be invalidated, it will be obliged to employ American precedent and appoint only judges who have the same set of values.' He called upon the 'volk' to tell the judges in Bloemfontein that it was tired of the kind of 'legal cunning' the court had employed to subvert the will of the people.[14]

The government, however, did not implement these strident strategies immediately. Rather, it considered its position carefully and with surprising caution. A few years later, it came up with a definitive legislative strategy to remove coloured voters from the common voters' roll. At the same time, it ensured that the overwhelming number of judicial appointments were 'Nasionale appointments'.[15] It is to these developments that we must turn to understand the final collapse of the legal challenge.

The *Collins* case

Three years passed before the government first introduced the Appellate Division Quorum Act which provided that on the hearing of an appeal dealing with the validity of an Act of Parliament, a quorum of 11 judges of the Appellate Division was required. In the earlier *Harris* cases, a quorum of five had been sufficient, five who had been appointed under different political conditions. Now the gloves were taken off by government. A bench of 11 was constituted, allowing for reliable hands to be appointed. The government packed the Court in preparation for a third challenge to its constitutional plans.

The extension of the composition of the Court was not the only reason for government optimism. The Court had already begun to change, owing to retirements of key judicial figures and their replacement by reliable supporters of apartheid. By March 1955, Leopold Greenberg, one of the five judges who had sat on the *Harris* cases, had retired upon reaching the age of 70. In his place came Lucas Steyn. Steyn had been a judge for less than four years. Before his appointment, he had held the post of Chief Law Adviser to the government. In this capacity, he had participated in the South African delegation to the United Nations. In 1950, he presented the government's case in the first advisory proceeding about Namibia before the International Court of Justice. He has been described by Edwin Cameron in a celebrated article which analyses his devastating contribution to South African law as someone who had 'a towering but

He called upon the 'volk' to tell the judges in Bloemfontein that it was tired of the kind of 'legal cunning' the court had employed to subvert the will of the people

parsimonious intellect; he was a scrupulous but ungenerous judge; his attempt to rid South African law of its unique and fundamental connection with English law was not only jurisprudentially and historically unjustified but ultimately quixotic; he was an unfettered but—of his own volition—executive minded judge and that during his term of office a legal temperature, already chill for the survival of human rights and the preservation of fundamental freedoms turned several degrees colder.'[16]

The government now had Steyn on its side. Of that it was sure. It may well have also had Henry Fagan. According to a letter that Dawid De Villiers sent to Prime Minister Strydom on 19 November 1956, the government counsel were confident that, had he sat in the House's Court, Fagan would have decided in their favour.[17] But the other four judges, Centlivres, Van den Heever, Hoexter and Schreiner, were clearly a problem for the government which did not want to fail a third time; hence the new strategy of expansion of the court.

Its previous reluctance to implement the crude proposals to strip the judiciary of its earlier independence notwithstanding, the government now moved decisively to pack the Court with judges made in its political image. In 1955 it introduced the Quorum Act. The Minister of Justice, Mr C R Swart, told Parliament:

> The government intends to take steps ... to reinstate the sovereignty of parliament. By the sovereignty of parliament we mean the state of affairs which obtained immediately after the 1937 decision ... viz that Parliament can pass legislation without any limitation. ... We say that where there is another case in future in regard to measures adopted by the government we desire to have a quorum of eleven judges. The government desires to have a larger court than the ones which in the past decided on these matters and contradicted each other to decide future cases.[18]

Five further judges of appeal were appointed, being De Beer, the Judge President of the Orange Free State; Reynolds, Judge President of the Eastern Districts; together with his colleague Judge de Villiers, Judge Brink of the Free State and Judge Hall of the Cape—reliable hands all.

The government now felt it had put in place a court which would cause it no further trouble. Thereafter, the government passed the Senate Act. The Act enlarged the Senate through the granting of a greater representation to the larger provinces together with an increase in the number of nominated senators, the election of senators by a simple majority in an electoral college instead of by proportional representation and a dissolution of the existing Senate by the end of 1955. The enlarged Senate guaranteed the presence of many more National Party Senators. When the two Houses of Parliament sat together, the National Party was now assured of its two-thirds majority which was necessary to change the Constitution.

The government did not disguise its intentions to Parliament. In his second reading speech on the Bill, the Minister of Interior, Dr Dönges, said:

> 'The government cannot run away from its mandate . . . it has to take the necessary steps to carry out the mandate given to it. In the first place, it tries to do so by using its ordinary powers in the ordinary methods. However, if these do not succeed it has no alternative, if it is continuously thwarted and condemned to ineffectiveness, then to use the reserve powers and the special methods given to it by the South Africa Act in order to carry out the will of the voters . . .. In fact it is the essence of a democratic government that it should use all constitutional means at its disposal to give effect to a mandate it received at an election.'

The Prime Minister, J G Strydom, was even more blunt: 'In the first place the object of this Bill and the legislation which will follow later is to put the coloureds on a separate roll . . . The second aim of this Bill [is] to put the sovereignty of Parliament beyond all doubt in accordance with our interpretation of the Statute of Westminster and in terms of the 1937 decision of the Appeal Court.'[19]

The new court

Before we turn to the third challenge before the appeal court, mention must be made of the new court which was to hear the final case in this saga.

The existing members of the Appellate Division had not been consulted about the new appointments. Oliver Schreiner was the only judge who remained faithful to the common law principles that the Court had steadfastly upheld in the earlier *Harris* cases. When he wrote to his wife on the new appointments, he did not disguise his disdain: 'I have little doubt that most of the cases will be decided fairly rightly—the job is not so difficult that every case calls for high quality, thank heaven. But it isn't going to be a court to be proud of being one's country's highest court. But we'll live through these interesting unattractive bounds—any rate in the long run the country is fairly certain to come right.'

The senior judges' lack of regard for their new colleagues took on an odd spin through the ancient game of bowls. There was a custom that judges of appeal played bowls on Wednesday afternoons when the court did not sit. What could have been a clearer condemnation of these new political appointments than refusing to invite them to play bowls! That is indeed what happened, as is apparent from another letter which Oliver Schreiner sent to his wife: 'I was glad to get your support for the view that we should be reasonably firm about extra-judicial associations with the newcomers. Whether there will be modifications over the years remains to be seen; but for the present, and especially with the most thick-skinned of them, it is clearly necessary to maintain a reasonable distance.' Schreiner also made it clear what he thought of the intellectual capacity of the newcomers when he wrote to his wife: 'There is the problem of dealing with the judgments of the new men—they take a good deal more working than do those of the old hands ... most of the burden falls on Albert (Centlivres) ... When one thinks of the number of people who believe that the additional judicial appointments must at least lighten the work for the seniors it makes one laugh a bit sourly.'[20]

This divided Court heard argument on the Senate Act on 15 October 1956. There was only one appellant this time, William Collins. He had been one of the individual voters who had appealed against the judgment of the Cape Supreme Court which had given the government a taste of success when it upheld the validity of the Act. The debate between Graeme Duncan and the judges on the first day was far less interesting than was a remark by one of the new judges, Eddy de Beer. Dawid de Villiers, on behalf of the government, had sought to attack the first *Harris* decision and invited the Court to reconsider its validity. What he wanted was a fresh finding that the Court had acted incorrectly in its first *Harris* judgment when it set aside legislation duly passed by Parliament.

There was only one appellant this time, William Collins

At some point in the hearing, De Beer said that he and the new judges had accepted their appointments only on the understanding that the *Harris* decision was not to be challenged. Suddenly, De Villiers withdrew his threat to attack the first *Harris* judgment. As Oliver Schreiner remarked to his wife: 'You can imagine, can't you, what a bombshell Eddy's announcement was. But can you picture people accepting the position on this court on condition that certain issues will not be raised before them? The inference is natural, that they were prepared to consider any other issues of a related kind and were consulted as to whether they felt prepared to deal with such issues. One assumes they were not invited to express their views in advance, but fancy any sort of talk of that kind, it just shows what we have come down to.'[21] Brink was the only other judge who told his colleagues that he had given a similar undertaking to the Minister of Justice, Swart.

Minister Swart sought to explain De Beer's bizarre but honest outburst when he addressed Parliament in January 1957.[22] He said that, when De Beer was approached to take an appointment on the Appeal Court, he had raised his difficulty with the court's decision in the first *Harris* case. Minister Swart said: 'There had never been any intention of the conditional appointment, for the government does not impose conditions when appointing a judge, nor does the judge accept appointment on certain conditions.' He had simply tried to help Judge de Beer with his personal problem. This was one of the few occasions during the apartheid period when the public, had they paid attention, would have realised the extent to which direct political considerations played a part in the appointment of judges.

The Judgment

Whatever the motivation of the government, its strategy finally bore fruit on 9 November 1956 when the Appeal Court handed down its judgment in the *Collins* case.

The majority judgment was delivered by Chief Justice Centlivres. He held that the House of Assembly and the Senate, sitting separately, could, by ordinary majority, reconstitute the Senate. Indeed, if the ordinary majorities altered the Senate so that it should consist entirely of government supporters, that too would be valid. It may have been that the Senate could not be abolished without using a special voting procedure but that it could be reconstructed in the way the National Party had done did not make the legislation unconstitutional. Lucas Steyn, the government's 'pre-eminent legal gauleiter', delivered a concurring judgment, the essence of which was that, whatever the purpose of the government in passing the legislation, this consideration was utterly irrelevant. The law had been passed legally and there was nothing that a court could do about such legislation. In keeping with the view articulated so often by the government during the entire crisis, Steyn found that the only sanction for passing such legislation was that the electorate 'would provide an adequate and more appropriate curb on the activities of Parliament'. Decoded: so long as only white people voted, majority rule was clearly acceptable. The National Party would jealously guard the interests of the 'volk'!

So long as only white people voted, majority rule was clearly acceptable. The National Party would jealously guard the interests of the 'volk'!

Steyn had laid down the legal philosophy that was to remain dominant in the Appellate Division until 1994. So long as the law expressly empowered the executive, a court would not examine the substance of the law. Form, not substance, was the overwhelming test. Issues of justice, as protected in the common law, were of little concern.

In the second *Harris* case, the Court held that the High Court of Parliament was not a court but was merely a group of parliamentarians constituting themselves as a court for one purpose, namely to subvert a court structure of which they did not approve. Here the substance, that is, the purpose of the legislation, was critical to the court's decision. But now it was significant only to Oliver Schreiner. Schreiner began by asking the question whether the body constituted by the Senate Act was a Senate in substance and therefore a House of Parliament within the meaning of that word. If answered in the affirmative, this would be sufficient to pass the legislation. Theoretically, Schreiner maintained, Parliament could, by acting bicamerally, appoint or create any body whatsoever and call it a Senate. A court would be bound, if invited to do so, to enquire whether such body was really a House of Parliament. But that was to be myopic. It was impermissible to look only at the form of the Act. By looking at its purpose, he held that the revamped Senate was nothing more than a body devised by government lawyers to produce a sufficient majority to ensure that coloured voters would be taken off the common voters' roll. The Senate Act was but a mechanism to obtain a vote in a joint session to take coloured voters off the common voters' roll. Thus the new Senate could not be considered to be a Senate for the purposes of being a House of Parliament. The Senate Act was a legal fraud.

Schreiner cut a lonely figure. The two other judges who had formed part of the two *Harris* judgments, Centlivres and Hoexter, were now part of the majority that upheld the government. Schreiner remained in splendid philosophical isolation. Writing to his wife he said: '[s]trictly between ourselves, I've written a dissenting judgment but no one else agrees with me, so I must be wrong. It happens that way and one mustn't think the sky is going to fall because of the result of the appeal.'[23]

Edna Schreiner's response was insightful: 'It was amusing to think that the Government need not have gone to the expense of packing the AD with their minions.'[24] It is interesting to consider why Judges Centlivres and Hoexter were not prepared to sign on to the Schreiner dissent and why, by contrast, Centlivres felt compelled to author the majority judgment. It seems possible that these judges knew the game was up. The Court had changed, a majority of the Court in favour of 'coloured' voters was no longer possible, and, arguably of greater significance, the Court was running heavily against (white) public opinion which could be employed against the Court in even more virulent measures than had to date been the case—better to withdraw and live to fight another battle in the future.

Extra-parliamentary politics

There is another important part of the explanation. During the period in which the two *Harris* cases were decided, there was significant white, extra-parliamentary opposition, particularly in the form of the Torch Commando. This is not to underestimate the effect of the opposition of most of the population. On the contrary: those politics changed the country. However, to the extent that the approach of the Court was shaped by white opinion, opposition from these ranks proved influential. Formed by ex-servicemen who had returned from World War II, the Torch Commando was 'the channel of expression of tens of thousands of disillusioned and frustrated men and women who were uneasy at the trend of events in South Africa. It particularly appealed to the returned soldiers and their families throughout the country.'[25] It managed to obtain a paid-up membership of over 125 000 and initially drew vast crowds to its protests against the impending legislation. But it was a movement riddled with contradiction. David Scher observed:

The movement was fundamentally in harmony with South African social patterns and its members nurtured no incentive to revolutionary action. It certainly did not seek a frame of reference beyond that of protecting the Constitution against the attack of the Government. Their deep constitutional regard convinced many Torchers that their extra-party movement was incongruous in a democratic society. It was almost apologetically that Sailor Malan told his audience in July 1952 that the Commando was not a permanent feature in the political life of South African and would, as soon as the need for it fell away with the return to power of the United Party, 'be dissolved like, morning mist'.[26]

By 1955, the movement was no more and, with it disappeared the last vestige of serious white opposition to the disenfranchisement of coloured voters.

Does history repeat itself?

The constitutional crisis of the 1950s set a judiciary which had an established tradition of independence sourced in English colonial origins against a government determined to implement its own political programme without restrictions placed upon it and unfettered by judicial interpretation of existing law. This meant, as we have seen, that the National Party government grew increasingly intolerant of the judiciary which it saw as subverting 'the will of the people'. The fact that the National Party's racist vision of the world equated the will of the people with the will of white people is irrelevant to this argument.

Fifty years later, and almost one decade into constitutional democracy, the ANC produced a statement which, save for the significant distinction that its conception of the will of the people embraced all South Africans, was stunningly similar to the National Party's approach to the judiciary during the 1950s. In its annual statement of 8 January 2005, the ANC stated as follows:

We need to ensure that all enjoy protection under the law, and that all have access to the institution the State designed to protect and uphold their rights. We face the continuing and important challenge to work for the transformation of the judiciary. Much work has already been done to address the race and gender imbalances within this institution. Nevertheless, more progress has to be achieved in this regard. However, we are also confronted by the similarly important challenge to transform the collective mindset of the judiciary to bring it into congruence with the vision and aspirations of the millions who engaged in the struggle to liberate our country from white minority domination. The reality can no longer be avoided that many within our judiciary cannot see themselves as being part of these masses, accountable to them, and inspired by their hopes, dreams and valued systems. If this persists for too long, it will inevitably result in popular antagonism towards the judiciary and our courts, with serious and negative consequences for the democratic system as a whole.

This statement understandably promoted a public controversy, which died down briefly only to be resurrected when government introduced proposals to amend the Constitution. These proposals would place the administration of courts firmly under the control of the Department of Justice and introduce a Superior Courts Bill which made further changes to the manner in which courts are organised and further increased the power of the Minister of Justice. If these proposals are passed by Parliament, the most powerful judges in the provincial courts, the Judges President, will no longer be appointed by way of the Judicial Service Commission but, rather, directly by the President of the country.

At the time of writing, it is perhaps too early to speculate with any precision as to whether these proposals represent the beginning of the implementation of the promise contained in the statement of 8 January 2005 to ensure the transformation of 'the collective mindset of the judiciary'. But there is a parallel between what occurred during the 1950s and what may bring an independent judiciary of the first decade of the 21st century into significant conflict with an executive, albeit this time democratically elected. The possibility cannot be discounted, however remote.

The events of 50 years ago provide a salutary warning of a possible threat to the judicial institution. When senior judges are called 'counter-revolutionaries' by influential members of the ruling party, the threat recalls the conduct of the ruling party of that period, however distant the present threat may yet be on the political horizon. Constitutional democracy is not asserted; it is continuously defended by political action. Absent the latter, it may be that another chapter will yet be written about the removal of a troublesome South African court.

Endnotes

1   'KC' refers to King's Counsel, the most senior rank of advocate. Today, senior counsel are designated by 'SC' after their names.
2   *House of Assembly Debates* col 4584 (17 April 1951).
3   David Scher *The Disenfranchisement of the Coloured Voters* (unpublished DLitt and Phil thesis Unisa 1983) 96-97. This chapter owes Dr Scher a great debt in that his superb research provided a goldmine of material.
4   Author's interview with Cowen (November 2006).
5   Canada and Australia were the other countries now recognised by Britain as dominions.
6   *HOD* col 3124-3126 (20 March 1952).
7   *HOD* col 4922-4925 (5 May 1952).
8   *HOD* col 5181 (7 May 1952).
9   J G N Strauss Papers as cited by D M Scher 'The Court of Errors: A Study of the High Court of Parliament Crisis of 1952' *Kronos* 23:33 (1988) *Kronos* 23:33.
10 *Minister of the Interior and Another v Harris* 1952 (4) SA 769 (A) 779.
11 These suggestions are gleaned from the Dönges papers as accessed by Scher *ibid* 521.

12 *Die Burger* (18 March 1953).
13 *Die Vaderland* (25 March 1953) (translation).
14 *Die Vaderland* (23 March 1953) (translation).
15 In the Liberal Party's magazine, *Contact* (February 1955), there appears a discussion of appointments to the bench and the likelihood that these would produce a servile and weak bench.
16 1982 *SALJ* 38 at 40.
17 Scher *ibid* 632.
18 *HOD* col 4430 (25 May 1955).
19 Both speeches can be found in *HOD* cols 6003ff (23 May 1955).
20 Ellison Kahn (ed) *Fiat Justitia: Essays in Honour of Oliver Denys Schreiner* (1983) 40.
21 Kahn *ibid* 40.
22 *HOD* cols 189-191 (19 January 1957).
23 Letter cited by Kahn *ibid* 44.
24 Letter cited by Kahn *ibid* 44.
25 G Heaton Nicholls *South Africa in my Time* 243.
26 Scher *ibid* 332.

three

The *Rivonia* trial: Competing visions for South Africa

'The white state has thrown overboard every pretence of rule by democratic process. Armed to the teeth it has presented the people with only one choice, and that is its overthrow by force and violence.'

Operation Mayibuye[1]

Today, Pretoria is a city that feels and looks like a part of the African continent. Take a walk down the anachronistically named Andries or Vermeulen streets at lunch hour and the transformation of the city from the apartheid military fortress of a few decades earlier is palpable. Forty years ago, however, Pretoria was the white capital of the Afrikaner kingdom. Huge white men, many with epaulettes weighed down with small crowns distributed by the police and army, strode the streets of the city. Pretoria was the centre of apartheid power; its white inhabitants were supremely confident of the future of their city, their country and the fortunes of their rugby team, the Blou Bulle, the 'blue bulls'.

It was into this citadel of repression, at the height of the power of the National Party, that the key leaders of the African National Congress were transported. They were being taken to a trial which sought to criminalise their political activity aimed at producing a non-racial democracy.

The case became known as the *Rivonia* trial. As the government moved to destroy the ANC as a political organisation, the central command of the ANC met regularly at a farm in Rivonia. The farm had been made available to the ANC by the Communist Party.[2] This secret venue was itself reflective of another part of privileged white South Africa. Liliesleaf farm covered some 11.5 hectares in the suburb of Rivonia on the northern outskirts of Johannesburg. In the early 1960s, suburbs such as Rivonia were no more than farmland, a far cry from the blocks of gated townhouses and marbled shopping malls that now characterise the northern suburbs of Johannesburg.

The farm was bought through a company which had been incorporated by the South African Communist Party. Legal records showed that the occupants were a well-known architect, Arthur Goldreich and his family, while farming activities were conducted under the supervision of Thomas Mashitane, who was a member of the South African Communist Party. These arrangements were designed to create a veneer of a normal family, with the Goldreichs purported to be the residents and Mashitane 'the foreman'. The arrangement worked well for a while. As Mashitane later testified before court, among the most regular customers for fresh produce from the farm were members of the Rivonia police station.

Initially, security around the farm was very strict and few members of the ANC, other than the Central Committee of the SACP, knew of its existence or the purpose to which it had been put. Ahmed Kathrada later wrote '[h]owever a number of us had started feeling uneasy about the continued use of the Rivonia farm. We were aware that the "need-to-know" principle had not applied to Liliesleaf for some time, and that far too many people—one of whom was Bruno Mtolo, a saboteur from Durban and leader of the Natal branch of the ANC's armed wing Umkhonto we Sizwe (MK)—had visited the farm.'[3] Mtolo's visit to the farm was to prove critical to the fate of its occupants, but more of that later.

On 6 July 1963, members of the High Command of MK met at the farm to discuss a draft document which had been prepared by Joe Slovo. Lionel 'Rusty' Bernstein, like Joe Slovo a key member of the Communist Party, had raised strong objections to this document which sought to alter MK strategy from that of a sabotage campaign to guerrilla warfare. For Bernstein, the document was predicated on a completely inadequate analysis of the real balance of power in the country and had not taken sufficient consideration of government strength and MK weakness.[4]

Mtolo's visit to the farm was to prove critical to the fate of its occupants

Absent from these central discussions was Nelson Mandela. He had already been in prison for some time. In 1962, Mandela had left the country as 'David Motsamayi' and travelled abroad for several months. During this trip, Mandela met up with the first group of 21 MK recruits on their way to Addis Ababa for guerrilla training. Not long after his return to South Africa on 5 August 1962, Mandela was arrested and charged with illegal exit from the country and incitement to strike. He was in Natal at the time, passing through Howick on his way back to Johannesburg, posing again as David Motsamayi, now the driver of a white theatre director and MK member, Cecil Williams.

On 7 November 1962, Mandela was convicted and sentenced to three years' imprisonment for incitement, together with an additional two years for leaving the country without a passport.

The document setting out Operation Mayibuye envisaged a process of determining a date whereby, in pre-selected areas, trained and armed guerrillas would seek to join the MK. These groups would catch the state forces by surprise, creating as much chaos and confusion for the enemy as possible. Before these operations could take place, 'political authority would have been set up in a friendly territory with a view to supervising the struggle ... It is visualised that this authority would in due course of time develop into the "Provisional Revolutionary Government".[5]

The ultimate aim of the plan was to ensure that an external guerrilla force would join some 7 000 armed men in four key areas to wage war on the South African government.

It was, as Anthony Sampson noted in his biography of Mandela[6], a 'reckless and unrealistic scheme'. Among the leadership, there was a clear divide. Govan Mbeki, Joe Slovo and Arthur Goldreich were enthusiastic proponents of the plan. Walter Sisulu, Ahmed Kathrada and other members of the High Command had strong reservations and it was to debate these reservations that the High Command leadership had gathered at the farm in July 1963. In Kathrada's opinion, the plan was almost naïve in its scope and promise. Its architects had been advantaged by the dispersion of ANC leadership at the time as a result of government repression.[7] There were many influential leaders of the ANC who, therefore, did not have the opportunity of debating the plans and who would, in Kathrada's view, have resisted its adoption.

An external guerrilla force would join some 7 000 armed men in four key areas to wage war on the South African government

The security police, with the benefit of legislation which empowered them to detain political opponents without recourse to a court, had launched a ferocious campaign to destroy the ANC and the Pan African Congress by incarcerating its leadership after the Sharpeville uprising of 1960. By 1963, the police net was closing in on the High Command of the ANC. Three months earlier, in April 1963, a mass arrest of key members of the PAC and its military wing, *Poqo*, had taken place. The Minister of Justice, John Vorster, told Parliament in June 1963: 'We dare not lose sight of the fact that we are still faced with the problem of the ANC and it is a very real problem because it is *par excellence* the organisation which has many more white brains at its disposal, not only overseas, but here as well ... the immediate danger is the ANC with its militant wing, the Spear of the Nation, and we are busy taking just as effective action against this organisation as we did with the PAC'.[8]

On 11 July 1963, the police hit the jackpot. They raided Liliesleaf with the express aim of capturing Walter Sisulu, then the senior member of the High Command. But they found far more than they had expected. When they arrived, a large group of key members of the ANC had congregated with Sisulu at the farm.

Kathrada maintains that neither the ANC nor the SACP ever found out who or what had led the police to Rivonia on that fateful day. Ironically, it had been decided that this was to be the last meeting at the farm as it was considered too risky to continue meeting there. Whatever the source of police information, white South Africa rejoiced at the arrests. Even that most liberal newspaper in South Africa at the time, the *Rand Daily Mail*, captured a feeling of white relief when it carried the following headlines on 13 July 1963: 'Security swoop on Rand sparks huge investigation. Subversion: End Near. Arrests give new clues—police chief'.

The head of the Security Branch, the notorious Colonel Hendrick van den Bergh, proclaimed triumphantly: 'With these arrests the security branch has virtually smashed the various secret organisations which have threatened the safety of the states.'[9] Of those detained, Goldreich and Harold Wolpe, who were arrested after the Rivonia raid, managed to escape the country after bribing a prison warder. Theirs is an extraordinary story but it is not for now. Nelson Mandela, already imprisoned, was joined in the dock by Walter Sisulu, Dennis Goldberg, Govan Mbeki, Ahmed Kathrada, Lionel 'Rusty' Bernstein, Raymond Mhlaba, James Kantor, Elias Motsoaledi and Andrew Mlangeni. The case was technically known as the *State v Nelson Mandela and Others* but it has gone down in history as the *Rivonia* Trial.

The legal case against them was immense and they faced the probability of the death sentence

All the accused had been detained for 90 days without trial under the government's newly established security laws, of which more later in this book. Kathrada tells of police pressure on him to cooperate with the investigation. With their usual combination of racism and antisemitism, the interrogators asked him if he wanted to go to prison 'for a bunch of kaffirs and Jews'.[10]

At this meeting, they met their legal team. Bram Fischer, the team leader, and George Bizos were well known to them. Fischer was a leading member of the underground Communist Party who had been at many a meeting at Liliesleaf farm. As Kathrada recalled wryly, 'George was also well known to us because we were so often in trouble'. The other lawyers, Arthur Chaskalson and Joel Joffe, were less known at this stage. At the outset, the lawyers set out the legal options but, for the accused, this was to be a political trial in which they would present a political justification for their actions.[11] The accused were under no illusions: the legal case against them was immense and they faced the probability of the death sentence.

The trial's opening

Even before it began, the attendant press coverage had ensured that the political temperature surrounding the trial would be raised. When the trial finally began on 9 October 1963, the *Rand Daily Mail* headline proclaimed: 'State alleges conspiracy planned on a military basis. Revolt, invasion, charges—eleven arraigned in more than 200 sabotage attacks.'[12]

The proceedings opened amidst a massive police presence. Hilda Bernstein, wife of accused 'Rusty' Bernstein, wrote of the way in which 'the convoy sweeps through Pretoria's peak hour traffic, drives into the court building through the massive iron grill gates at the back of the building, and policemen with sten guns jump out and surround the prison yard while the prisoners, handcuffed are taken into cells below the court.'[13]

The trial took place at the Palace of Justice in Pretoria. The building was constructed in 1897, a relic of the old Transvaal Republic. It is a splendid brown brick building with an imposing set of stairs leading to the entrance, a magisterial landmark in the capital city. The external appearance of the building is marked by a symmetry of classical proportions. Its architecture has been described as that of 'centralised power and legal authority'.[14] Of the internal appearance of the court Hilda Bernstein said:

> The judge's bench is an elaborate pulpit of wood, carved and posted like an old-fashioned bed, at one end of the 60 foot court. He is enthroned there, dwarfed in his scarlet robes. On either side of this structure are beige curtains, draped and pleated from floor to ceiling, into which the voices of prosecutor, defending counsel and judge alike disappear and are lost. A huge-bladed fan, suspended on a long rod and ceiling directly above the prosecutor's head, wobbles slowly through the summer months, imperceptively stirring the thick air.[15]

The courtroom was segregated with separate benches for white and black spectators. The white benches were filled with members of the Security Branch and a few supporters of the accused. The black benches were packed with family and other relatives of the accused. Winnie Mandela, who was already banned and thus could not communicate with the public, was present and had to remain uncharacteristically silent. Albertina Sisulu, recently released from jail, was also present.

On the opening day of the trial, the presiding judge, Quartus de Wet, was immediately faced with an application for a postponement. Bram Fischer, the lead counsel for the defence team, rose to request three weeks to thoroughly consider the indictment, being the description of the charges. This line of defence had an important precedent. Lawyers who previously defended a larger group of ANC leaders in the Treason Trial of 1956 had material success in attacking the indictment. In that case, the government pressed charges against 156 of its political opponents, including many of the same men. The trial ended unsuccessfully for the government but only after five hard-fought years of litigation.

The point of this attack was that, even during this bleak legal period, the law of procedure guaranteed a measure of fairness for the accused and the State was obligated to let the accused know in clear terms what case they were required to meet in court. The accused were thus entitled to object to the charge sheet on the basis that the charges set out were vague in describing all of the necessary particulars or that it failed to specify elements of the crimes for which they stood charged. Where a court sustains such an attack, the State must be given a chance to remedy the charge sheet by amendment and failing which the charge will be quashed and the accused freed.

At *Rivonia*, the accused had not been charged with treason but with two counts of sabotage, the charge sheet alleging some 193 separate acts under the Sabotage Act, a third charge in terms of the Suppression of Communism Act and a fourth which concerned the financing of MK activities. But there were very few specific, detailed allegations to substantiate these charges. The indictment was a shoddy piece of work. Judge de Wet had no choice but to grant the three-week postponement.

Three weeks later, Bram Fischer rose again to attack the indictment. The atmosphere was now even more emotionally charged. The austerity of the legal process had given way to a political contest to be fought out in a courtroom. As the accused came up from the cells below the Court by way of the dark stairwell, they gave the ANC raised-fist salute, and shouted out '*Amandla*' (power) to which the gallery roared back '*Ngwethu*' (it is ours).

Judge de Wet, who had been appointed to the Bench in 1950, had risen speedily by judicial standards to become the Judge President of the Transvaal Supreme Court. Chaskalson thought that he was no National Party supporter. Although his father had been prominent in the white opposition party, the United Party, he was 'apolitical', although clearly possessed of the racist outlook of most whites at the time.[16]

The indictment was a shoddy piece of work. Judge de Wet had no choice but to grant the three-week postponement

De Wet looked down from his judicial throne. He was confronted with two lawyers of markedly different backgrounds, character and political vision. Lead defence counsel, Bram Fischer, had been born in 1908 into the very core of the political and legal establishment that ruled South Africa throughout his life. His father, Percy Fischer, had been the Judge President of the Orange Free State and his grandfather, Abraham Fischer, the Prime Minister of the Orange River Colony and later a member of the cabinet of the Union of South Africa. Fischer had been schooled at the prestigious Grey College in Bloemfontein and later at Oxford University. In 1940, he joined the South African Communist Party and shot to prominence in the party to become one of its leaders. By the time of the trial, he was 55 years old and a barrister of considerable standing. A short stocky man with striking grey hair and stern, black glasses, Fischer was a quietly spoken, polite but very skilled barrister. His politics aside, Fischer comported himself in the best traditions of the English Bar—to this day, the exemplar for South African advocates.

Of course, he was so much more than a talented counsel. As Chief Justice Ismail Mahomed said in the House of Assembly on 3 February 1998:

> Just occasionally in the life of a people history produces a citizen, the impact of whose life continues long beyond his physical demise to stimulate profound reflections on the complexity and the potential grandeur of our species and its unique need and capacity to formulate and to develop for itself a moral basis to regulate the interaction of its members *inter se*

between those members and the evolving environment in which it inherits and generates. Such a rare man was Bram Fischer.[17]

One can only imagine the stress experienced by Fischer throughout the trial. Of this, Steven Clingman, in his masterful biography of Fischer, wrote:[18]

> MK had effectively been destroyed at *Rivonia*. Fischer realised that it was necessary to reconstitute the organisation even in a minimal form. As the *Rivonia* trial proceeded, he worked with David Kidson to reactivate Umkhonto structures, this while the *Rivonia* trial was proceeding! Bram's involvement at *Rivonia* meant that he had been observed by a number of people, including the black workers at the farmhouse who were now to be called as prosecution witnesses. Any one of them, asked to identify any individual in the courtroom they had seen at Liliesleaf, could have turned to Bram and pointed him out. For Bram to enter into the trial was in that regard an enormous, even life-threatening risk—and it was for this reason that when Rusty Bernstein first heard that he would be leading the defence, he turned to his co-accused and said, 'He deserves the Victoria Cross.' That was also the reason why, during the opening stages of the trial, when most of the farm workers were called to give evidence, Bram managed to be out of court, engaged in an arbitration which he freely admitted was 'hopeless', but which had the advantage of keeping him busy elsewhere.

The prosecutor was a small bald-headed man with only a stub for a left hand, a legacy of an injury sustained while working in his father's butchery. Percy Yutar was born in Cape Town of parents who had come to South Africa from the Jewish ghetto in Lithuania, in similar fashion to most of the country's Jewish community. He was fiercely ambitious. He became the first student in South Africa to be awarded a doctorate in law, in his case by the University of Cape Town. The religious prejudice of the time meant that this qualification did not assist him to move rapidly in the legal profession. But his ambition was all-consuming. He finally obtained an appointment as a junior State prosecutor. His willingness to work long and hard and his indifference to the immorality of the apartheid system finally brought him the promotion he had craved for so long.

At the time of the *Rivonia* trial, he was the deputy Attorney-General for the Transvaal, the second most senior prosecutor in the province. His experience of the virulent antisemitism that had confronted him earlier in his career prompted him to show to extravagant excess that he was a loyal Jewish South African. He proudly wore a signet ring in the shape of the Star of David. He was president of one of South Africa's largest orthodox synogogues. *Rivonia* now afforded the ambitious Yutar an opportunity to show how useful he could be to the government, and how loyal 'this Jew' could be to the country. The outcome of the trial was terribly important to his campaign to gain the ultimate prize, Attorney-General of the Transvaal. Yutar knew about Fischer's political involvement. At one adjournment, he said to Fischer that he 'had enough in his bag to put him away'.[19]

In his quiet and determined way, Fischer's attack on the indictment began to have an increasingly positive effect on Judge de Wet. Fischer pointed out that there was a great deal of generality in the manner in which the charges had been set out. In particular, this was problematic because properly formulated charges would have clearly set out allegations tying each accused individually to each charge. For example, Nelson Mandela had been charged with 156 acts of sabotage, all of which were alleged to have been committed while he was in prison.

Fischer argued for two full court days. After he had completed his detailed argument, Dr George Lowen, who appeared for one of the accused, James Kantor, rose to address the court. He was the very opposite of Fischer. He presented his address in a dramatic and emotional style, and was not afraid to use sarcasm. He spoke passionately on behalf of Kantor. Lowen was a German-trained lawyer who had participated in a number of trials of opponents of the Nazi regime before leaving as a refugee from Hitler's Germany. Understandably, he viewed this trial in similar fashion to his previous experience. He concentrated his arguments on the manner in which the State had treated his request for further particulars to the charges levelled against his client, Kantor. At one point, he told the judge: 'Take for example question 5. The answer given by the State was dot, dot, dot!' Judge de Wet replied: 'In my copy there are 4 dashes, Mr Lowen.'[20] De Wet had now given a clear indication of his attitude to the indictment.

Fischer's attack on the indictment began to have an increasing positive effect on Judge de Wet

Yutar was in serious trouble with his indictment and he knew it. The case was not running well for the State. When he rose to answer the defence's submissions, his voice rose a number of decibels, almost to the point of a squeak, such was his great agitation. He implored the judge not to quash the indictment. In his anxiety, he continued to employ the word 'squash' rather than the legal term 'quash'!

But the judge was having nothing of Yutar's plea. The indictment was clearly vague and full of generalisations. It contained insufficient particulars of the charges against each accused.

The judge thus found for the accused, stating that:

> When details are required of the dates when and place and manner in which each of the accused was alleged to have commenced acting in concert with the alleged co-conspirators, the reply is this is peculiarly within the knowledge of the accused. The accused are assumed to be innocent until they are proved to be guilty. And it is most improper, in my opinion, when the accused ask for particulars in regard to an offence which is alleged to have been committed to say to them; this is a matter which you know all about. That presupposes that he is guilty and he will not be told anything about the offence.[21]

The accused had won round one and were technically free, but the decision in their favour did not help them for long. They were immediately rearrested.

Joel Joffe, an attorney who postponed his emigration plans to assist in the defence at *Rivonia*, recalls that, upon hearing the decision, Denis Goldberg bent down to kiss his wife. Warrant Officer Dirker 'grabbed him and hauled him off to underground cells'.[22] New indictments were prepared which alleged that the accused and 22 co-conspirators together with the South African Communist Party, the ANC and MK had committed sabotage by the employment of people for training and the preparation in the use of explosives for warfare, including guerrilla warfare together with 192 listed acts of violence and destruction. It was further alleged that the accused had conspired to acts of guerrilla warfare, given assistance to military units of foreign countries who would invade South Africa and a general participation in a violent revolution in South Africa. An additional count alleged that these acts were calculated to further the achievement of the aims of communism and that the ANC was controlled and dominated by the South African Communist Party.[23]

Dr Yutar rose to present his opening address to the Court. The press had been well primed. *Die Burger*, the leading Afrikaans daily newspaper in the Cape, included a double-page spread describing the state case in detail. Significantly, its header screamed: '*Rivonia*—case: Goldreich and the others planned to build an armaments factory'.[24] The racist discourse of the newspaper could only see the *Rivonia* trial as that of the state versus a group of white miscreants leading a larger group of black followers. The readers of *Die Burger* were informed that the plan the accused had allegedly hatched was to manufacture sufficient explosives to blast Johannesburg skyhigh. *The Star*, the widely read Johannesburg afternoon paper, also carried a similar feature entitled 'Reds backed revolt plan'. The report confirmed 'Behind the accused was a vast communistic machine and organisation with all its manifold avenues of co-operation and assistance'.[25]

Yutar summarised the state's case against the accused as follows:

> The accused deliberately and maliciously plotted and engineered the commission of acts of violence and destruction ... The planned purpose thereof was to bring about in South Africa chaos and disorder and turmoil, which would be aggravated according to their plan by the operation of thousands of trained guerrilla warfare units deployed throughout the country at various vantage points. These would be joined in the various areas by local inhabitants, as well as specially selected men posted to such areas. Their combined operations were planned to lead to confusion, violent insurrection and rebellion followed at the appropriate juncture by an armed invasion of the country by military units of foreign powers.[26]

Throughout his address, Yutar continued to employ this form of emotive language designed to excite white fear. For example, he claimed that 'The State will show that the accused gloated over the first explosion . . . and brought out a special poster of Umkhonto we Sizwe to mark the occasion.'[27]

In this way, Yutar tailored his opening address, not only to the judge, but to the white electorate. When the legal teams arrived on 3 December 1963, the defence was surprised to see that microphones had been installed in the court for the purpose of broadcasting Yutar's opening address live on SABC radio. Yutar immediately enquired of the judge whether it was in order for his opening address to be so broadcast. Judge de Wet looked particularly uncomfortable, saying that he had initially given instructions that the recording of the opening address could proceed 'in order to inform the public'. He went on to say that the position had changed, despite the fact that he never clarified what or how it had changed but he refused permission to broadcast Yutar's speech on the state-controlled radio.

This was a small but not insignificant victory. The ability of the State to present its case without an immediate counter from the defence is a powerful mechanism by which to frame the case in the public mind. The public often assumes that the State case is the truth. By the time the accused have presented their case, which can occur only at the close of the State's case, public curiosity has waned and the damage against the accused has been done. In a political trial of this magnitude, Yutar would have used the state-controlled radio to inflict as much damage upon public perceptions of the accused as he possibly could within the confines of an opening address. De Wet was at least intent on running a fair criminal trial and this afforded another small victory to the defence.

The State's case

The State introduced 173 witnesses. Twenty-nine of these witnesses had been detained without trial. Some of these witnesses had agreed to testify after great pressure had been exerted upon them to give evidence against their former comrades. The key witness for the State was Bruno Mtolo, who had been a member of the ANC and the South African Communist Party, as well as a key figure of MK in KwaZulu-Natal. As was always the case with Yutar, he began leading the witness dramatically:

Yutar: Bruno, are you a saboteur? Mtolo: Yes I was. Yutar: Did you blow up pylons and other government property in Durban?[28] Mtolo: Yes I did.'[29] Mtolo provided the court with considerable detail of the sabotage campaign of which he had been a part. For three days, Mtolo described his activities for MK in detail.

Hilda Bernstein correctly observed:

He, who spent three years as the most active saboteur in the country, one of the most energetic members of Umkhonto, incriminates everyone who has ever worked with him, everyone he has ever known in the ANC and

> Umkhonto, including his younger brother whom he identifies in court as
> the young man recruited by Umkhonto to be sent abroad for military
> training. He now accuses the men on trial for their lives of having lived in
> luxury.

Mtolo described at length how Walter Sisulu had furnished his home with
expensive items. Although these were false statements, this evidence was an
important component of Mtolo's testimony. He sought to confirm the State's
interpretation of the accused as violent, self-serving and greedy. In his own
book, he spoke of the self-serving and selfish nature of the accused: 'The people
who would be in court . . . would not even know that these leaders did not care
but kept on asking for more recruits without trying to take steps to avoid
arrests.'

Mtolo also raised the spectre of the ANC being dominated by the
Communist Party:

> I thought of the women who would be wearing green and black uniforms,
> instead of red and black because these people were not what they pretended
> to be. These were the leaders who, when I was sent to find out what steps
> were being taken to avoid the arrest of the youngsters for military training,
> told me, 'When soldiers are fighting these things should be expected.' They
> were the same people who made us and our families starve while they and
> their families were living in luxury.[30]

Yutar pressed this theme of greed and opportunism throughout the trial. In
his closing address, he contended: 'It was tragic to think that the accused,
who, between them, did not have the courage to commit in person one single
act of sabotage, should nevertheless have incited their followers to acts of
sabotage, guerrilla warfare, armed insurrection and open rebellion and
ultimately civil war.'[31]

The defence's case

The approach adopted by the defence was made very clear at the outset when
Nelson Mandela responded to the full charges: 'My Lord, the government, not
I, should be in the dock. I plead not guilty to all charges.'[32]

The strategy of the defence was not to deny responsibility for actions that
they had indeed taken but rather to utilise every opportunity during the trial to
explain their position and to put forward reasons for the political activity in
which they had engaged. The trial was a political forum. Yutar had presented
the government's political programme. Now the accused were intent on
exploiting the platform afforded by the trial in order to define and explain the
nature of their political struggle.

Early on in the strategic discussions between the legal team and the
accused, it was decided that Nelson Mandela would not give evidence as a

witness but, rather, would address the Court from the dock. In legal terms, this meant that any testimony he would provide by way of his address could not be challenged by the prosecution but it would have far less evidential weight in persuading the judge to bring in an acquittal.

Part of the defence strategy was to keep Yutar guessing as to the nature of the defence plan. That itself was not easy. All consultations took place in a hastily constructed room at the Pretoria prison in which the accused were held. Hilda Bernstein described the room thus:

> The room is long and narrow, with a wooden counter partitioned down the centre. The partition is hardboard perforated with holes; a few Perspex windows are set into the hardboard, with speaking holes beneath them. If requested the warders can, with great difficulty and sweating and swearing, remove the Perspex windows leaving a heavy metal grating in their place. A row of bar stools are fixed on either side of the counter.[33]

When the defence legal team first came into the room and found their clients seated on stools on the one side of the counter, they were compelled to sit on stools on the other side of the counter. It was if they had entered an icecream parlour. Nelson Mandela captured this moment when, smiling politely, he said to his lawyers: 'What will it be today, gentlemen—chocolate or icecream soda?'[34]

Part of the defence strategy was to keep Yutar guessing as to the nature of the defence plan

It was extremely difficult to consult in confidence because the room was bugged so that the recorded consultations could later be analysed by Yutar and his legal team. This, of course, did have certain advantages. When the preparation for Mandela's evidence commenced, defence lawyers produced the voluminous record of the 1956 Treason Trial, which ran to tens of thousands of pages. As a result, Percy Yutar began to pore over these vast volumes as he worked on an anticipated cross-examination of Mandela. Of course, none of this record was ever used by the defence but Yutar was not to know that until Mandela took the witness stand!

The defence team's turn to present their clients' case came on 23 April 1964. In his quiet style, Fischer outlined the case for the defence. In particular, he told the judge that the defence challenged the state's argument that the ANC was a tool of the Communist Party and that the objects of the ANC were the same as those of the Communist Party. Fischer said that the defence would show that the leaders of MK and the ANC had decided to keep these two organisations entirely distinct and that MK had never adopted the military plan known as Operation Mayibuye which had been so central a plank of the state's case against all the accused.

Judge de Wet was visibly astonished by this opening statement and said almost disbelievingly: 'That will be denied?', to which Fischer replied:

Yes that will be denied. The evidence will show why it was hoped throughout that such a step could be avoided. The court will be asked to have regard to the motive, the character and the political background of the men in charge of Umkhonto we Sizwe and its operations; to have regard to the tradition of non-violence of the ANC; to the reasons which led these men to resort to sabotage in an attempt to achieve their political objectives, and why, in the light of these facts, they are to be believed when they say that Operation Mayibuye had not been adopted.[35]

When Fischer concluded his address, he informed the Court that the defence case would begin with a statement from the dock by Nelson Mandela. Yutar, who had been preparing for weeks for the cross-examination of Mandela, was visibly shocked. In his best falsetto voice, he said: 'My Lord, my Lord, I think you should warn the accused that what he says in the dock has far less weight than if he submitted himself to cross-examination!' By now, Judge de Wet, who possessed a notoriously short temper, had endured more than enough from Percy Yutar. Icily, he admonished the now almost hysterical lead counsel for the state: 'I think, Mr Yutar, that counsel for the defence has sufficient experience to be able to advise their clients without your assistance.'[36]

'The government which uses force to maintain its rule teaches the oppressed to use force to oppose it'

Yutar's rather pathetic attempt at cajoling Mandela to be subjected to cross-examination having ended, Mandela rose slowly, a sheaf of papers in hand. He adjusted his spectacles, which he wore for reading. For hours, Mandela explained to the Court the political and intellectual background and development of his political ideas, his early commitment to nationalism and his conversion to non-racialism. He told the judge that it was wrong to suggest that the ANC had responded to the influence of foreigners and, particularly, communists: 'I have done whatever I did as an individual and as a leader of my people because of my experience in South Africa and my own proudly-felt African background, not because of what any outsider might have said.'[37]

The speech involved a direct challenge to the political authority of the government. He told the Court: 'The government which uses force to maintain its rule teaches the oppressed to use force to oppose it ... [violence was adopted] not because we desire such a course, solely because the government left us with no other choice.'

It is easy today, with the benefit of more than 40 years of hindsight, to gloss over the extraordinarily clear and direct challenge Nelson Mandela laid down to the very heart of the South African political system, which had been fashioned over more than 300 years of racist rule. The press, the Security Branch agents who sat in court, Percy Yutar and his prosecution team, together with Judge de Wet, appointed as a Judge President by the National Party, all had to listen without interruption while Mandela contended: 'Our fight is against real and not imaginary hardships, or to use the language of the state, "so-called hardships". Basically, my Lord, we fight against two features which are hallmarks of African life in South Africa, and which were entrenched by legislation which we seek to have repealed. These features are poverty and lack of human dignity and we would not need communists or so-called "agitators" to teach us about these things.'

Mandela then spoke of the long history of non-violent struggle that had been led by the ANC. He told the Court: 'For a long time, the people had been speaking of violence and we, the leaders, had nevertheless always prevailed upon them to avoid violence and to preserve peaceful methods and achieved nothing, and our followers were beginning to lose confidence in this policy.' He spoke of the violence perpetrated on innocent women in Zeerust in 1957, who were ordered to carry passes, and the violence of the state agent protests in Pondoland in 1960 when the government had attempted to introduce 'Bantu authorities' into those areas. He concluded that, 'In 1961, the leaders, I and some of my colleagues came to the conclusion ... that it would be unrealistic and wrong to continue preaching peace and non-violence at a time when the government met our peaceful demands with force.'

Mandela was coming to the end of his speech and thus to the part that had caused his lawyers grave concern. He wanted to end his exposition of his political ideology by saying: 'This was an ideal for which I am prepared to die.' His lawyers were concerned that this might provoke the judge to hang Mandela. He refused to leave these words out, but eventually agreed to insert the words 'if need be' into the speech. He ended what Anthony Sampson[38] correctly described as the most effective speech of Mandela's career with words that carried the central theme of the political struggle for a further 30 years, until the democratic Constitution of 1996 enshrined these commitments into law:

> During my lifetime, I have dedicated myself to the struggle of the African people. I have fought against white domination and I have fought against black domination. I have cherished the idea of a democratic and free society in which all persons live together in harmony with equal opportunities. It is an ideal which I hope to live for and achieve. But if needs be, it is an ideal for which I am prepared to die.

These words were uttered in a still voice. When Mandela ended, silence descended upon the entire court. Even Judge de Wet appeared moved and, after what seemed an eternity, with an equally quiet voice, he turned to Bram Fischer and said 'You may call your next witness.'

The Nobel Laureate, Nadine Gordimer, has a different recollection of the speech:

> The address, after going through many changes, returned (I thought) to the simple verity of the second version, and read much better than it was spoken: Mandela's delivery was very disappointing indeed, hesitant, parsonical (if there is such a word), boring. Only at the end did the man

come through and when he had spoken that last sentence the strangest and most moving sound I have ever heard from human throats, came from the 'black' side of the court audience. It was short, sharp and terrible, something between a sigh and a groan. Afterwards, silence. Sisulu was splendid; what a paradox—he is almost uneducated, while M has a law degree! He was lucid and to the point—and never missed a point in his replies to [the apartheid prosecutor Percy] Yutar.[39]

If Mandela's speech was claimed to be the high public point of the defence case, Gordimer was at least correct in her assessment of Walter Sisulu. The performance of Sisulu, who was vigorously cross-examined by Percy Yutar, was nothing short of remarkable. The contest was between a man of rudimentary formal education and a lawyer who had more tertiary qualifications than any practising lawyer in the country. Quietly but firmly, the short, bespectacled Sisulu asserted the very core of the morality of ANC political action: 'The African people, like all oppressed people, have got a moral right to revolt against oppression.'[40] As Kathrada said in his recollection of the trial: 'At the end of it all, Walter emerged from the witness box as cool, as calm and unruffled as when he entered it. Our lawyers and even the accused were amazed at his composure, his phenomenal memory and the masterly way in which he had acquitted himself.'[41]

One of the many mistakes Yutar made during the trial was to engage directly in the political issues underlying the trial. Normally, prosecutors would eschew such an approach and concentrate upon the legal hurdles that required to be negotiated if the state was to be successful. But Yutar was determined to show the accused that their politics led only to violent crime. As with so many whites, Yutar had conflated academic qualifications with intelligence. This led him into engagements with Walter Sisulu from which he emerged a distant second.

It was during the evidence of Sisulu that De Wet revealed the dominant judicial mindset of that time. When Sisulu insisted that the 'masses' wanted the vote, the judge interrupted Yutar's cross-examination to ask Sisulu: 'Is that correct? You think they should have the vote, but how do you know that the ordinary Bantu about town wants the vote? . . . You only know that you think he ought to have it, but how do you know he wants it?' Sisulu exposed the judge's thinking with the reply: 'Well, I have not come across meetings where I have heard people saying "No, we don't want the vote!" People always support the idea of the vote.'[42]

The judgment

The evidence was at an end. Both sides then presented their arguments. At the end of arguments, the judge adjourned the case for three weeks to consider his verdict. The only truly hopeful point for the defence was the apparent acceptance by the judge during Fischer's argument that Operation Mayibuye had been only a proposed plan which had not been accepted by the accused or the ANC. Had that not been the case, a conviction would surely have led to death sentences for the architects of the plan that called for mass production of explosives and an ambitiously widespread armed struggle.

On 11 June 1964, Judge de Wet returned to court to deliver his judgment. It took but a few minutes for him to say the following:

> I have very good reasons for the conclusions to which I have come. I don't propose to read these reasons. The verdict will be 'Nelson Mandela is found guilty on all four counts; Walter Sisulu is found guilty on all four counts; Dennis Goldberg is found guilty on all four counts; Govan Mbeki is found guilty on all four counts; Achmed Kathrada is found guilty on count 2 and not guilty on counts 1, 3 and 4. Lionel Bernstein is found not guilty. He will be discharged; Raymond Mhlaba is found guilty on all four counts; Andrew Mlangeni is found guilty on all four counts; Elias Motsoaledi is found guilty on all four counts.' I do not propose to deal with the question of sentence today. My reasons will be made available in a statement.[43]

Mandela told his legal team that he, Walter Sisulu and Govan Mbeki had discussed with their colleagues the question of appealing against a possible death sentence. They had decided that it was politically inadvisable to appeal against the death sentence. Their trial would end after Judge de Wet had sentenced them.

Harold Hanson, a very senior member of the Johannesburg Bar, was then brought into the defence team to deal with the argument relating to sentence. Hanson was a large, ebullient man possessed of a booming voice and with a great talent for legal oratory. Arthur Chaskalson recalls Hanson as being a superb advocate, perhaps not as a fine a 'black letter lawyer' as Oscar Rathouse, then a dominant legal figure at the Johannesburg Bar, but about as good as anyone when it came to articulating legal argument in court.[44] It was considered prudent *Their trial would end after Judge de Wet had sentenced them* to employ so distinguished a counsel who was not known to be politically active. In addition, Fischer was under great stress at the end of this long trial of his comrades and friends. He regarded Hanson as a fine advocate and with whom he was comfortable to leave the plea in mitigation. What was less known was that Hanson had once been a member of the Communist Party.[45]

Hanson called one witness, Alan Paton, best known for his novel *Cry the Beloved Country*. Paton was also the leader of the South African Liberal Party. Hanson asked Paton why he testified in this case, a deeply brave move in the light of white hostility towards the accused and the vicious reaction that could be expected from government as a result of his testimony. Paton replied: 'Because I was asked to come. But primarily because, having been asked to come, I felt it was my duty to come here—a duty which I am glad to perform, because I love my country. And it seems to me, my Lord with respect, that the exercise of clemency in this case is a thing which is very important for our future.'[46]

Paton explained to the Court how the failure of the peaceful political campaigns that had been pursued by the accused for decades had compelled them to the conclusion that there were only two alternatives left, to bow their heads and accept continued racist rule or to resist by force. Ominously, Judge de Wet interjected:

> There were many cases where people resisted and were convicted of high treason and executed. I have in mind the famous gunpowder plot in England. In the light of subsequent history, these people have legitimate grievances but they are not entitled to break the law by force. And what happens to people like that, historically, is that they get convicted of high treason and are condemned to death.[47]

It might have been expected of Percy Yutar to behave as prosecutors generally do in these cases, that is, to refrain from questioning Alan Paton who had appeared solely for the purpose of giving evidence in mitigation of sentence. The purpose of this evidence is solely to provide the Court with information and insight into the accused. It assists the Court in balancing the interests of the accused and society, when deciding on an appropriate sentence. Prosecutors generally allow this evidence to be presented without contest.

However, Yutar was no ordinary prosecutor. He was running his own political trial. He rose aggressively to cross-examine Paton. The introduction to his cross-examination set the scene:

> Yutar: Mr Paton are you a communist?
> Paton: No.
> Yutar: Are you a fellow traveller?
> Paton: I don't understand what a fellow traveller is, but I understand your implication. No, I am not a fellow traveller.
> Yutar: You are understanding my implications?
> Paton: Correct.
> Yutar: Do you share the aims and objects of the Communist Party?
> Paton: Some of the aims I would share, such as the more equitable distribution of land and wealth, better economic opportunities.
> Yutar: What don't you approve of in the Communist Party?
> Paton: I disapprove entirely of their totalitarian methods which they adopted to bring about such changes.
> Yutar: Do you disapprove of that?
> Paton: Entirely.

Yutar continued to cross-examine Paton in great detail for reasons he had set out at the beginning: 'I propose to cross-examine this witness with your

Lordship's leave. And I don't do so in order to aggravate the sentence, but in order to unmask this gentleman and make perfectly clear that his only reason for going into the witness box, in my submission, is to make political propaganda from the witness box.'[48] Attorney for the defence, Joel Joffe, correctly described Yutar's cross-examination as 'a degrading exhibition ... But the police at least enjoyed it, they tittered gleefully as this honest man, of undeniable courage, was smeared and demeaned by Yutar. Mr Justice de Wet, probably by reason of his own political prejudice, rather than of law, also appeared to be enjoying Paton's discomforture.'[49]

The tension in the courtroom was almost tangible. The accused faced the prospect of the death penalty. One man other than the judge knew for certain that this would not occur. He was Harold Hanson. Before he argued in mitigation of sentence, Hanson went to see De Wet. When he returned, he told Arthur Chaskalson, a member of the defence team: 'He is not going to impose the death sentence.' Chaskalson asked how he knew. Hanson replied: 'I asked the judge, who said: "Do not tell your clients but I am not going to impose the death penalty on them".'[50]

The tension in the courtroom was almost tangible

Of course, neither the public gallery nor the accused knew of De Wet's attitude. As Chaskalson explained, there was no guarantee that De Wet would not change his mind and it thus was impossible for their clients to be told that there was to be no death sentence when the possibility could not be definitely discounted.

Hanson made an impassioned address about the need to recognise the political nature of the case. He reminded the judge of the struggles of Afrikaners earlier in the century. 'We in the country ... understood well the struggle for national liberation. We understand well the struggle for national liberation. We understand its motivation. We understand it better than the people of any other land.'[51]

Unfortunately, but not unexpectedly, the plea fell on deaf judicial ears. In a soft voice barely heard by the gallery, the judge began his decision and reasons for the sentence:

> I have heard a great deal during the course of this case about the grievances of the non-European population. The accused have told me and their counsel have told me that the accused who were all leaders of the non-European population were motivated entirely by a desire to ameliorate these grievances. I am by no means convinced that the motives of the accused were as altruistic as they wish the court to believe. People who organise a revolution usually take over the government, and personal ambition cannot be excluded as a motive. The function of this court, as is the function of the court in any other country, is to enforce law and order and to enforce the laws of the State within which it functions. The crime of which the accused have been convicted, that is the main crime, the crime of conspiracy, is in

essence one of high treason. The State has decided not to charge the crime in its form. Bearing this in mind and giving the matter very serious consideration, I have decided not to impose the supreme penalty which in a case like this would usually be the proper penalty for the crime but consistent with my duty that is the only leniency I can show. The sentence in the case of all the accused will be one of life imprisonment.

Ahmed Kathrada captured the reaction of the accused thus:

He (De Wet) spoke the crucial words 'life imprisonment' almost in a whisper, then hurried from court. A deep hush enveloped the courtroom, followed by an audible sigh of relief—not shock as one would normally expect at the prospect of a life sentence but relief, because it was not a death sentence. We turned and smiled at the packed public gallery and Dennis, [Goldberg] I think, shouted: 'Life sentence!' The enormity and full implication of the sentence would sink in soon enough, but for that moment there was only jubilation that we were not going to be hanged.[52]

Conclusion

It is difficult to imagine how South Africa could have developed into a non-racial democracy 30 years later, had Judge de Wet imposed the death sentence. He is long dead and there is no direct evidence as to what motivated him instead to impose sentences of life imprisonment. In a rather distasteful attempt to reconstruct his image in the new South Africa, Percy Yutar claimed he had saved the accused's life by charging them with sabotage rather than high treason because 'his instinct was that the judge would not hang the accused for sabotage but only for treason'.[53] That reconstructed version is not supported by any available evidence. Kathrada, in an interview, correctly poured scorn on Yutar's claim. In an interview in 1987 with Professor C H Albertyn which fully justifies Kathrada's reaction, Yutar claimed that the difficulties encountered by the state in the treason trial that ran between 1956 and 1961 was a significant factor in charging the accused with sabotage, which was easier to prove, than treason.

In an introduction to a rightwing, journalistic account of the *Rivonia* trial,[54] Percy Yutar wrote that he had consistently contended before the Court that the accused had been guilty in 'a classic case of high treason'. He informed retired Judge H H de Villiers[55] that he indicted the accused under the Sabotage Act, and not for high treason under the common law, because of the treason trial of 1956 in which all the accused were acquitted.

According to De Villiers: 'Yutar was concerned that because of the nature of the proof required by the common law, it was wiser to charge the accused under the Sabotage Act and not in terms of the common law of high treason.'

George Bizos, then a junior counsel who was a member of the defence team, has suggested that part of the reason for Judge de Wet's decision to eschew the death penalty was due to his own antipathy to capital punishment.

Bizos remembers that De Wet had been deeply affected by a previous case in which he had sentenced an accused to death, only for the latter's sentence to be commuted by the Governor-General on advice from a state law advisor who had discovered that events subsequent to the trial had shown that a key witness had lied to the Court.[56]

That some judges were fiercely racist but not in favour of the death penalty was known in South Africa. Thus this explanation is very powerful. But there are other possible explanations. Nelson Mandela writes in his autobiography that the judge was not entirely immune from outside pressures, with foreign governments and institutions campaigning in favour of the accused.[57] Of course, the judge would have been aware of the dominant white position. The National Party and its supporters were equally determined to see these key leaders of an organisation, which they saw as the greatest threat to continued white domination of the country, removed permanently from society. Kathrada, however, was certain that intense international pressure coupled with an internal political consideration that execution of these leaders would make martyrs of them all had exerted a significant influence on the judge. Bizos remembers a remark of Judge de Wet in which he told Fischer that the accused were receiving a good press, a sure sign that the judge was not unaware of the overwhelming sympathy and support for the accused from the international community.

Some judges were fiercely racist but not in favour of the death penalty

For Judge de Wet, life imprisonment was the manner in which he responded to these contradictory pressures. This explanation finds some support in a book published shortly after the conclusion of the trial written by the same retired Appellate Division Judge, H H de Villiers, one of the National Party appointees to the Appellate Division, to deal specially with the constitutional crisis documented in the previous chapter of this book. Loyal to white rule, De Villiers attempted in his brief book to justify both the need for the trial and the judicial conduct thereof. Significantly, in the preface to his book, retired Judge President of the Natal Provincial Division, Francis Broome wrote:

> Two recent overseas comments on the *Rivonia* trial indicate the need for a book like this. Both related to the sentence of imprisonment imposed by the presiding Judge instead of a sentence of death. One comment ascribed the Judge's leniency to government policy, the other to the pressure of public agitation. It is high time that the world realised the South African judiciary is independent and that its judges are not amenable to pressure from government, public or any other source.[58]

The manifest inaccuracy of the last sentence is indicative of the competing pressures which must have been felt by a judge whose default position was the maintenance of the then political system.

The verdict of even some of the conservative press was one of relief that the accused had not been hanged. *The Star* commented after the trial that: 'They were foolhardy in the extreme, and might have had disastrous results for many besides themselves if it had not been nipped in the bud. They have reason to be thankful that it ended as it did and so have we all.'[59] Even the 'liberal' press supported the verdict. An editorial of the *Rand Daily Mail* opined: 'The sentences pronounced by Mr Justice de Wet in Pretoria yesterday at the conclusion of the Rivonia trial were both wise and just ... Would they have not been summarily shot ... [after a conviction for a similar crime] if this had been an Iron Curtain country.'[60]

This was reflective of the dominant white discourse that Dr Verwoerd exploited to the full in a statement to Parliament which won the enthusiastic endorsement of the opposition United Party. In his statement he said:

> I want to state clearly and unequivocally that in this case we have not got to do with an opposition against the South African government's policy or the championship of the freedom and rights of people. We have to do with a Communist uprising which would have been brought about in South Africa ... should these Rivonia accused have succeeded, then a Communist-orientated government—whether white, black or mixed—would have been established.[61]

The South African government's few foreign friends appeared to adopt a similar view of pragmatic support for the sentence. Anthony Sampson relates that the British Ambassador to South Africa, Mr Hugh Stephenson, informed the British Foreign Secretary, Rab Butler: 'We could be thankful that the judge did not give a death sentence because it means that a leader of the calibre of Nelson Mandela with his credentials enhanced by a term of imprisonment, should be available for the dialogue between black and white which must eventually take place in South Africa.'[62]

The evidence given by Paton and the comments of Stephenson indicated that there were many outside the ANC camp who recognised presciently how important Mandela, Sisulu and the other *Rivonia* leaders convicted at the trial would be to a future South Africa. But, at the time, it was not how white South Africa saw the picture. The prevailing white attitude was well illustrated in an editorial in the *Sunday Times*[63]:

> For the people of South Africa the pervading lesson of Rivonia is that violence as a political weapon must be discarded once and for all. Moral considerations apart, violence never stood a chance of success. Any reasonable assessment of the forces available leads to this conclusion. Meanwhile the damage done in the hardening of white attitudes is incalculable. The delicate mechanisms of human adjustment to change has been shaken loose, there are gears no longer in mesh.

The judgment in the *Rivonia* trial was utilised by politicians to bolster attitudes against the ANC for more than two decades. This was best exemplified when

P W Botha made his so-called 'Rubicon speech' on 17 August 1985. He said that there could be no negotiations with Nelson Mandela, for the latter 'had planned violent insurrection, rebellion and the manufacture of a large number of bombs and grenades ... (and that) the crime of which Mandela had been convicted was in essence high treason punishable by death'.[64]

In her thesis on South African political trials, Professor Albertyn wrote:

> In the long term, the Rivonia trial initiated a process of social amnesia, the beginning of the white memory of the ANC where the censures of violence and communism were merged into the public image of the ANC. It also marked the beginning of a process whereby whites failed to distinguish between violent and non-violent political action and all extra-parliamentary opposition was increasingly incorporated under the censure of violence. Together with this was a growing acceptance of the authoritarian methods against such opposition, as whites gave up liberal values of the rule of law and rights in favour of their own perceived interests and survival.[65]

As white attitudes hardened, so black political leaders in South Africa began to challenge, with growing intensity, the censure of their political struggle as violent, communist and criminal activity. Albert Luthuli, then leader of the ANC, said of the accused on the day of their sentence:

> They represent the highest morality and ethics in the South African legal struggle ... Their policies are in accordance with the deepest international principles of brotherhood and humanity: Without their leadership, brotherhood and humanity may be blasted out of existence in South Africa for long decades to come. They believe profoundly in justice and reason; when they are locked away justice and reasons are departed from the South African scene.[66]

The immediate legal strategy employed by the defence at *Rivonia* was to save the lives of their clients. That significant achievement was crucial to the future of the country. But *Rivonia* may also be viewed as a classic political trial, a contest about the censure of political activity which the state sought, with increasing desperation, to impose upon its legitimate political opponents. It took more than 30 years to remove this censure. After the *Rivonia* trial, South Africa experienced an increasingly speedy descent into a state of official lawlessness. The rule of law became honoured more in the breach than in the compliance. But 30 years after the completion of this key trial, constitutional democracy dawned in this country. A part of the explanation as to how legal values persisted over this period emerges from the chapters that now follow.

Endnotes

1   Extract from document found by police at Liliesleaf farm (11 July 1963).
2   Kathrada interview (28 December 2007).
3   Ahmed Kathrada *Memoirs* (2004) 156.

4   Kathrada *ibid* 157.
5   Kathrada *ibid* 158.
6   Nelson Mandela *A Long Walk to Freedom* (1994) 184.
7   Kathrada interview.
8   *Hansard* col 7772 (1963).
9   *Rand Daily Mail* (15 July 1963).
10 Kathrada interview.
11 *Ibid.*
12 *Rand Daily Mail* (9 October 1963).
13 Hilda Bernstein *The World that was Ours: The Story of the Rivonia Trial* (1984) 120.
14 Wessel Le Roux 'Studying Legal History through Courtroom Architecture' (2003) *Codicillus* 55, 62.
15 Bernstein *ibid* 120.
16 Chaskalson interview (July 2007).
17 1998 *SAJHR* 209.
18 Steven Clingman *Bram Fischer: Afrikaner Revolutionary* (1998). Chaskalson (author's interview July 2007) recalls examining documents during the trial which had been seized earlier by the police and which should have been made available to the defence. He discovered documents that involved Fischer. When he was later asked by Fischer what he had found, he mentioned these documents. Fischer offered no comment.
19 Kathrada interview with authors.
20 Bernstein *ibid* 125.
21 Joffe *ibid* 43.
22 Joffe *ibid* 43.
23 *The Star* (4 December 1963).
24 Translation from the Afrikaans text.
25 *The Star* 5 December 1963.
26 *Rivonia* trial record vol 4 p 1.
27 *Rivonia* trial record vol 4 p 12.
28 Bruno Mtolo *Umkonto we Sizwe: The Road to the Left* (1996) 148.
29 Bernstein *ibid* 158.
30 Mtolo *ibid* 142.
31 *The Star* (20 May 1964).
32 Bernstein *ibid* 140.
33 Bernstein *ibid*.
34 Bernstein *ibid* 188.
35 Bernstein *ibid* 192.
36 The speech is to be found in the *Rivonia* trial record at the Cullen library, vol 19.
37 *Rivonia* trial record vol 14.
38 Mandela *The Authorised Biography* (1999) 193.
39 R S Roberts *No Cold Kitchen* (2006) 155-156.
40 *Rivonia* trial record vol 20 p 12.
41 Kathrada *ibid* 178.
42 George Bizos *Odyssey to Freedom* (2007) 249-250.

43 Joel Joffe *The Rivonia Story* (1999) 203.

44 Arthur Chaskalson interview (July 2007).

45 Kathrada interview with authors.

46 Joffe *ibid* 208.

47 Joffe *ibid* 208.

48 Joffe *ibid* 208.

49 Joffe *ibid* 211.

50 Joffe *ibid* 212.

51 *Rivonia* trial record vol 32.

52 Kathrada *ibid* 191.

53 Obituary of Percy Yutar by Fred Bridgland *Scotsman* (23 July 2002).

54 Louritz Strydom *Rivonia Unmasked* (1965) 8.

55 De Villiers *Rivonia: Operation Mayibuye* (1964) 28-29.

56 Interview with George Bizos (16 June 2007). The system by which the Governor-General (later the President when South Africa became a Republic in 1961) commuted a sentence of death has been documented and carefully analysed by Rob Turrell in *White Mercy: A Study of the Death Penalty in South Africa* (2004).

57 See also Mandela *A Long Walk to Freedom ibid*.

58 Foreword to *Rivonia: Operation Mayibuye*.

59 February 1964.

60 June 1964.

61 *Rand Daily Mail* (17 June 1964).

62 Anthony Sampson *Mandela: The Authorised Biography* (1999) at 198.

63 7 June 1964.

64 *Cape Argus* (18 August 1985).

65 C H Albertyn *A Critical Analysis of Political Trade in South Africa 1948 to 1988* (unpublished Phd, Cambridge University) 248.

66 Cited by Albertyn *ibid* 250.

four

The challenge to the pass laws:
The beginning of the end; or
they did not even know his name

SELLERS
  Can I see your ticket?
SEAGOON:
  I haven't got one.
SELLERS:
  You can't come up Blackpool tower wi'ot a ticket
SEAGOON:
  Well, where can I buy one?
SELLERS:
  At the bottom
SEAGOON:
  I'll go down and get one.
SELLERS:
  You can't go down wi'out a ticket
SEAGOON
  What am I supposed to do, jump off?
SELLERS:
  You can't jump off wi'out a ticket.
SEAGOON:
  (Megaphone) Oh ho ho ho Hello folks. Trapped at the top of Blackpool tower.
SELLERS:
  Wi'out a ticket
SEAGOON:
  . . . without a ticket.

from *The Goon Show: The Thing
on the Mountain*, courtesy of the BBC

T he border between tragedy and comedy is often porous. Spike Milligan
    mined the comedy of the 'Catch-22' logic of a bureaucrat confronting the
individual citizen with ever-increasing obstacles when he wrote the script of the
BBC radio comedy, *The Goon Show*. The system of pass laws was based upon a
similar form of Catch-22 logic but its purpose was egregious, arbitrary and
cruel. Dr Verwoerd and his predecessors, Hertzog, Smuts, Malan and Strydom,
ran the 'goon show' for the predominant benefit of an enthusiastic audience—a
few million white South Africans—and to the incalculable human cost of a

country. Theirs was a system of absurd 'logic' which imposed unspeakable hardship on millions of South Africans.

For almost a century, the lives of most of the South African population were stringently and brutally controlled by a complex web of legislation which constituted the core of the apartheid structure. That web was constructed by four primary pieces of legislation. They governed influx control; the denationalisation of millions of citizens who had 'Bantustan citizenship' conferred on them; an archipelago of labour bureaus, designed to control the employment of black labour; and job reservation provisions which had the effect of excluding black people from being hired for a specified range of occupations.[1] This system treated human beings as mere numbers. Their identity and hence their dignity were systemically stripped.

The irony of it all is that the major legal triumph over this web of inhumane laws is still known by the purported name of the plaintiff in the case, (Tom) 'Rikhoto', whose real name is Rikhotso.[2] The treatment of the identities of black South Africans as irrelevant seems to have lived on beyond apartheid.

But before we look at his case, we must refer to the pass laws and their legal intricacy and record of implementation.

Pass laws: the origins

The pass laws had a truly devastating effect on the rights of South African citizens. Between 1916 and 1984, more than 1 774 500 black South Africans were arrested and most prosecuted under a battery of pass laws and influx control regulations.[3] The daily average of prosecutions during this period fluctuated from 89 to 1 482. This intense level of criminalisation of a population took place in pursuit of an objective articulated by the Stallard Commission on Transvaal local government as follows:

> It should be a recognised principle of government that Natives—men, women and children—should only be permitted within municipal areas insofar and for so long as their presence is demanded by the wants of the white population and should depart therefrom when they cease to minister to the needs of the white man.[4]

The National Party succeeded in developing an even more heartless form of influx control. A general circular generated by the Secretary of Bantu Administration in 1967 captures the banality of this evil:[5]

> It is accepted government policy that the Bantu are only temporarily resident in the European areas of the Republic, for so long as they offer their labour there. As soon as, for some reason, they become no longer fit for work or superfluous in the labour market, they are expected to return to their country of origin or the territory of the national unit where they fit in ethnically if they were not born or bred in the Homeland.[6]

Critical to the attainment of this objective was legislation that restricted permanent urban residence to those who had been born in a particular urban area and who had resided there since birth and to those who entered the urban area legally and resided there continuously for at least 15 years or who had worked for one employer for at least 10 years. The spouse or child of a 'qualified person' was permitted to live permanently with the man.

Enter Mr Komani

In 1975, Veli Komani, a resident of Guguletu township in Cape Town, launched an action for his wife, Nonceba Kumani, to live with him in Guguletu. With the benefit of the constitutional order that now prevails in South Africa, it seems almost unbelievable that, only 30 years ago, a husband had to go to court to live with his wife and, as we shall see, be advised that the case was by no stretch a 'winner'. What Mr Komani certainly would not have known was that his action would herald the beginning of the end of a central part of the apartheid system. Together with later legal action by Tom Rikhotso, who demanded permanent legal status as an urban resident, the lives of millions were about to change after decades of hopeless struggle against this brutal form of oppression.

Komani: the first challenge

Veli Komani had been employed by the same employer since 1960. By 1975, he was therefore entitled to reside permanently in the Cape Town area. He now claimed rights on behalf of his wife, Nonceba Komani. When she entered Cape Town in 1974, she was given permission to stay with her husband for some 11 months. In April 1975, the authorities refused a further extension, contending that Mr Komani lacked suitable accommodation for her in terms of the applicable regulations. Simply, the authorities accepted that the law allowed a wife to stay with a husband who was qualified to reside permanently in an urban area, but only if the wife had permission, by way of a grant of a lodger's permit from the relevant housing authority. The grant of this permit would prove impossible for Mrs Komani. After all, the applicable regulation was a masterpiece of legal mendacity: to obtain a permit, the applicant had to be lawfully employed. Without permission to be in the area, Mrs Komani was hardly likely to obtain such employment, besides which she was required to read the applicable section of the law as giving her no such right, absent of course, the housing regulation.[7]

Mrs Komani was in the grip of the State's Catch 22—she could not gain employment without rights of residence so she could not obtain a lodger's permit. Without a lodger's permit, she could not gain the right to live with her husband in the urban area of the Cape Peninsula.

Mr Komani proceeded to the Cape Supreme Court to break the deadlock. Curiously, he was represented by Advocate Charles Louw, a tenacious but conservative lawyer who, ironically, did much work for the police during this period. Komani's opponents were represented by a legal team that included the brilliant and highly eloquent Jeremy Gauntlett, later to become one of the leading human rights advocates at the South African Bar.[8]

It took almost three and a half years for Komani to obtain a judgment which upheld the refusal of the authorities. Judge Phillip Shock, a fine and hugely respected commercial lawyer, as eccentric as he was conservative, handed down the kind of judgment that characterised most apartheid jurisprudence—a rigid application of the text without consideration for the human implications of this interpretation, save when it adversely affected government interests. Hence he held that, although the housing regulation effectively destroyed any right granted to Mrs Komani to live with her husband, it was nevertheless permissible for the government to insist that black women must comply with the relevant housing regulations.[9]

Komani was not prepared to give up the legal fight. But after his attorney filed an application for leave to appeal, the Legal Aid Board decided that Komani would receive no further funding for legal representation. At this point, the Athlone Advice Office, run by the Black Sash and the South African Institute of Race Relations[10] and which throughout this bleak and repressive period assisted thousands of people whose lives were ruined by influx control, became involved in the *Komani* case. One of the stalwarts of the office, Noel Robb, sought to ensure the proper prosecution of Komani's appeal. Realising that the lack of funds may compromise the law firm who had acted so professionally and bravely for Komani in his application before the Cape Supreme Court, she wrote to Geoffrey Budlender, an attorney at the Legal Resources Centre (LRC) which had been established in 1979 by Arthur Chaskalson, Felicia Kentridge and Budlender as the first public interest law centre in South Africa.

Budlender ... held a deserved national reputation as a human rights activist

It proved to be a stroke of genius. By 1979, Budlender, then a fairly junior attorney, held a deserved national reputation as a human rights activist. As a student, he had been an accomplished leader of the Students' Representative Council at the University of Cape Town and then of the National Union of South African Students, in which capacity he had been singled out by the then Prime Minister, John Vorster, for the latter's unique form of public abuse. Vorster had incorrectly informed the nation that Budlender was a failed medical student and this allowed him to smear Budlender as being at university masquerading as a student but in 'reality' a political instigator. Only a Vorster-style leader could have shown such interest in the academic record of a student leader.

Budlender's quiet and thoughtful manner disguises a remarkable firmness of principle and brave dedication to the cause of human rights lawyering. Noel Robb's letter had thus given Veli Komani access to the very best South African legal advice.

Both Budlender and the director of the LRC, the future Chief Justice of the country and one of the greatest advocates ever produced in South Africa, Arthur Chaskalson, were concerned that earlier precedent may prove an insurmountable obstacle for the Komanis. In 1963, the Appellate Division, then on its way to a reactionary jurisprudential destination under Chief Justice L C Steyn, had decided that, to be ordinarily resident for the purposes of the section, litigants like Mrs Komani had to be lawfully resident which, owing to her inability to obtain a lodger's permit, was not the case. Both men had understandable doubts as to the prospects of the appeal court changing its mind.

There was a legal option available to them. It was possible to argue that, since this 1963 case, the law had been changed and no longer required a dependant to obtain permission from the superintendent of the location before acquiring a right under the section. This change, it was hoped, may have supported the argument that ordinary residence did not mean lawful residence.

But consummate lawyers like Chaskalson and Budlender knew well that this line of attack was unlikely to succeed, a conclusion which proved accurate, for the Court had no compunction but to dismiss this argument. Nonetheless, Chaskalson felt that the case may, at the very least, afford a long-term benefit in that it would test the boundaries the Court wished to maintain in policing this area of law.[11]

The Goon Show script was cruelly applied throughout the country

There was, however, a second argument that was to prove more decisive. Chaskalson contended, in his heads of argument prepared in advance of oral argument to be presented before the judges and thus filed with the Court long before the oral hearing, that the housing regulation was unreasonable. It meant that women like Mrs Komani could never obtain residence rights as spouses, the express wording of the section notwithstanding because, as a wife even of a 'man who was qualified to reside in the urban areas', she could never obtain a lodger's permit. Without a lodger's permit, she could not be lawfully resident and hence she would have no right to live permanently with her husband. The Goon Show script was cruelly applied throughout the country.

A section of an Act appeared to give Mrs Komani a right, but a regulation, being a lower form of law, destroyed any possibility of the enjoyment of this right. Consequently, a husband and wife in the circumstances of the Komanis could never live as a family. Family life was thereby destroyed. The legal attack was directed towards a result which was expressly authorised by the Act but was subverted by a regulation which, therefore, had to be contrary to public policy as represented by the Act of Parliament.

The case before the Appeal Court

The lawyers for Komani knew the formidable hurdles that awaited them in Bloemfontein. But they had some cause for optimism. The Bench chosen to hear the case was favourable: two of the judges were as liberal jurists as could be hoped for in a court in those days. Michael Corbett and Solly Miller were fair men, leaning towards the view that the common law still remained the basis of the legal system, rather than the racism of the apartheid legislation. Both were outstanding technical lawyers, respected by their more conservative colleagues. In addition, Chief Justice Frans Rumpff, a most conservative lawyer, was reasonably fair. He had been one of the three judges in the Treason Trial of the late 1950s who had acquitted Nelson Mandela and the (initial) group of 155 co-accused in the main political trial of the ANC prior to *Rivonia*.

When the argument was heard by the Court, the Chief Justice, a formidable, domineering man, leapt upon Chaskalson's argument to the effect that the housing regulation subverted the basic human rights of the Komanis. Chaskalson had contended that the Komanis were entitled to the basic human right of family life unless the law expressly negated such right. 'What human rights are you talking about?' was the Chief Justice's response. For him, the growing body of international human rights law was of no consequence to a South African court.

The hostility to this line of argument was palpable. But, as Budlender later reflected, he had never seen a counsel so dramatically persuade a court during the course of oral argument. Chaskalson argued that, while South Africa did not include, at that stage, any of the international human rights instruments in its legal system, the common law did recognise at root certain individual liberties and freedoms of the citizenry. And slowly but definitely, Chaskalson began to turn the Court towards his basic assumption: unless the law expressly removed a right, the citizen continued in his or her enjoyment thereof.[12]

All five of the judges were listening intently to Chaskalson's distinctive, clipped delivery

Once that argument had been accepted, Chaskalson was able to press on. Now all five of the judges were listening intently to Chaskalson's distinctive, clipped delivery. The initial hostility from the Bench was clearly on the wane. The key question for decision was: did a South African resident, even a black resident, enjoy residual rights to stay with his or her family, which could be taken away only by means of an express legal provision, or did such a person enjoy only the rights expressly conferred by law? This was a truly brilliant move by Chaskalson. He had shifted the debate away from a direct confrontation about human rights to the role of legislation in constituting the source of rights. A basic premise of the common law supported the idea of circumscribed government, that is, a citizen was permitted to act as he or she wished save where an express law prevented or limited this freedom.

For the judges of the appeal court to dismiss this argument, they would have needed to reject it for the legal system as a whole. It had always proved conceptually problematic to use the common law to divide people on the basis of race, hence the need for a battery of racist legislation to subvert the idea of an individual legal subject as enshrined in the common law, which did not expressly recognise race. The Chief Justice must have known that he could not write a judgment of so dramatically a racist nature that the residue of common law applied only to whites. How would this be done and what would its effect have been upon the limited but remaining legitimacy of the Court?

Once the premise was accepted that rights needed legislative removal rather than the converse, the lawyers for the government were in trouble. Gerrit van Schalkwyk, a bald, cherubic man of few but measured words who

The Court probed this argument with ever-increasing irritation

led Jeremy Gauntlett for the government, and who himself would later do sterling work as an advocate on behalf of the Legal Resources Centre, tried to argue that section 10 of the Act conferred no right upon the Komanis to remain in a prescribed urban area, but rather gave those who qualified in terms of the Act immunity from prosecution. Further, the so-called 'right to remain' did not confer any right to reside in a particular place in a prescribed area. In short, the housing regulation could limit the already limited right, which meant no more than that anyone who qualified under section 10 could not be prosecuted for being in the area.

The Court probed this argument with ever-increasing irritation because Van Schalkwyk had no answer to the basic premise developed by Chaskalson, being the absence of the provision of a law which prevented people like Mr Komani from remaining in the urban area of Cape Town. Had the law not recognised some rights based upon birth and continuous residence? Van Schalkwyk provided no response and an exasperated Rumpff proceeded to round on him with the terrifying force that he could and did bring to the Bench. Budlender recalls, thinking that the tide had truly changed, that one of the judges, C P Joubert, a crusty, self-appointed Roman Law purist who delivered a number of judgments which contained more Latin than English, and who had appeared to be asleep for much of the argument, suddenly asked Van Schalkwyk a question and, when no proper answer was forthcoming, rolled his eyes and returned to his position of repose.[13]

Chaskalson recalls that he was not truly confident when he completed his initial argument and that his opponents certainly considered that they were on the winning side at the first tea adjournment. They were almost laughing aloud at the difficulties Chaskalson had confronted from the Bench. But Chaskalson remembers the irritation of Rumpff when Van Schalkwyk could not satisfactorily answer the Bench's question and, by the end, 'Rumpff had destroyed him'. At one point, Rumpff suggested to Van Schalkwyk that he felt the Court was being 'led up the garden path'. When Chaskalson replied, he expressed the hope that he (Chaskalson) was not leading the Court up the garden path. Rumpff was at pains to assure him that that was not the case! At one point, Rumpff allowed himself a moment of humour. Chaskalson had contended that Komani and others in his position could not be regarded as temporary sojourners, to which Rumpff drily replied: 'We are all temporary sojourners, Mr Chaskalson.'

But the lawyers for Komani could not be too confident. At almost the very end of oral argument, Judge Miller asked whether the argument on behalf of Komani did not ultimately turn on those legal rights negated by the regulations. When Chaskalson replied in the affirmative but said it was unnecessary for the Court to go so far to find for Komani, the Court requested further written argument on the point of whether the housing regulation was invalid because it appeared to negate the rights to reside in the urban areas granted in terms of the Act. This gave the team more time to refine this argument.

'We are all temporary sojourners, Mr Chaskalson.'

When the judgment was finally delivered, the Chief Justice reviewed the history of residence in the urban areas by black South Africans from before the commencement of Union in 1910, concluding that there had been no absolute right to reside conferred by any legislation. But, focusing on a section of the Act which was not directly relevant to the case, he destroyed the argument the government lawyers had employed to justify the validity of the housing regulation.

The Chief Justice's reasoning went thus: section $10(1)(a)$ of the Act provided a black person who was born and lived continuously in the urban area the right to remain there on a permanent basis. Nothing in the Act nor in the history leading up to the Act indicated that this category of person had not acquired a right to so remain, yet if such a person did not possess the correct housing permit, he would have no such right. The right recognised by the Act could not be removed by a ministerial regulation which, of course, is a lower form of law. Thus, if the regulation sought to destroy a right, it was unlawful, not only in respect of section $10(1)(a)$ of the Act but generally. Consequently, the housing regulation had to be set aside and with this decision the regulation would no longer apply to Mrs Komani. She could now use the right she enjoyed in terms of section $10(1)(c)$, being the wife of a man who was qualified to reside in the urban area.

Aftermath

It was a dramatic victory, a triumph for the lawyering of Chaskalson, Kentridge and Budlender and the tenacity of Komani. It was also a remarkable and rather isolated example of the Appeal Court holding in favour of the liberty of the individual against the government. For almost two decades, the Court had shown little enthusiasm for curbing the excess of the government by asserting the importance of the common law in the process of interpreting ambiguous legislation. But, in this case, prodded by superb advocacy, the Court revealed a surprising willingness to explore the contours of ambiguous legal language to the benefit of a lonely, individual citizen whose case, however, affected the status of millions of black South Africans.

Small wonder that the doyenne of the Black Sash, Sheena Duncan, proclaimed: 'This is the most exciting news we've ever had . . . The judgment actually makes nonsense of the whole house permit system. It means that no permits will be required except by persons who are not entitled to residence under the law.'[14]

Mr Komani also had reason to feel optimistic. When he returned to the Langa pass office to ensure implementation of his court victory on behalf of his wife, he overheard a pass law official exclaiming, 'Now that kaffir has won, it's all over—no one will need a pass.' [15]

'Now that kaffir has won, it's all over—no one will need a pass.'

But Dr Piet Koornhof, the Minister responsible for these pass laws and a man who, early in his career, had written a doctorate at Oxford University which showed the futility of much of the very apartheid enterprise that he spent the balance of his political career enforcing, had other ideas. He said that the Court had ruled on only one case in but a single province and 'it would be completely wrong to infer that a large scale influx of wives and children . . . will now be possible as each case will have to be judged on the facts concerned'.[16]

This time, as was usually the case when repression was to be increased, Koornhof was as good as his word. Within two weeks, the relevant government department, inappropriately named the Department of Co-operation and Development in the light of the government's lack of commitment to integrity and honesty, issued a circular stating that, while a lodger's permit was not required for legal residence, nevertheless the Black Urban Areas Act was not affected by the Court's ruling and hence people who did not qualify to be in an urban area had to obtain permission to remain in the area.

So began a long and difficult process of forcing the government department to enforce the judgment. As Rick Abel documents in his superb study of this and other cases which characterised the apartheid period: 'Each case was different but only in the arbitrariness of official action. Applicants were asked to provide irrelevant documentation . . . told to obtain employment or rejected because they were too old or had inadequate housing.'[17]

For almost five years after the *Komani* judgment had been handed down, government bureaucrats sought to subvert its effect. But, as they fought their slow retreat against the demands for humanity, another blow was to be struck against the pass laws.

The *Rikhoto* decision

One of the main obstacles facing black South Africans who wished to obtain permanent residential rights in the urban areas was section 10(1)(b) of the same Act. The right was obtained if an applicant could show that he had worked for one employer for 10 years on a continuous basis or had lawfully resided in the urban area for a period of at least 15 continuous years. The problem was that permission was granted to work on a basis of 11 months each year thereby forcing the person to vacate the area during 'his leave'. In this way, the authorities hoped that a person could not prove continuous residence for 10 or 15 years.

But could the word 'continuous' mean 'without any break'—not even for a period of annual leave? If this question could be answered in favour of the applicant, the very structure of the pass laws would be significantly damaged. After all, it would then mean that a growing class of urban workers would gain permanent residence rights and, with the application of the *Komani* judgment, could then live with their wives and dependants. Some form of right to family life might then be restored.

The LRC, in general, and attorney Charles Nupen, in particular, were desperate to litigate in this area. Nupen was an ex-president of NUSAS, deeply committed to social and political change and later to become the leading mediator of industrial and other disputes in the country. A victory would seriously torpedo the very structure of influx control. Chaskalson recalls urging caution and patience until the 'right case could be found'.[18]

Finally, Nupen obtained his litigation wish. Mehlolo Tom Rikhotso had worked for one employer from 1970 to 1981 when he came into contact with the Black Sash advice office. Like millions of black workers, Rikhotso had to take leave each year when he returned to his village in the homeland of Gazankulu. He was refused rights of permanent residence under section 10(1)(b) and could not understand the reason therefor. The government's response was, of course, predictable: Rikhotso was not entitled to permanent rights of residence because his yearly visits to Gazankulu broke the requirement of continuity. Each time he returned to Gazankulu, he was obliged, in terms of the relevant regulations, to enter into a fresh 11-month contract with his employer; hence he had not worked continuously for a 10-year period.

The matter was again taken up by the Legal Resources Centre. The responsible lawyer was Charles Nupen. The case reached Nupen from the Hoek Street Law Clinic by way of a referral from Paul Kennedy, then a law student and now a silk at the Johannesburg Bar, who was approached by Rikhotso on 5 March 1983. According to Kennedy's note to Nupen, Rikhotso told him the following:

Like millions of black workers, Rikhotso had to take leave each year when he returned to his village in the homeland of Gazankulu

> Mr P Khumalo, a spokesman for the Community Council . . . told us that the authorities were preparing a new residential area in Katlehong—were still putting in services such as sewerage. When this was completed in about August or September, people in our area who presently have lodgers' permits and are on the housing waiting list would be moved to the new area where they could build their own homes . . . if they were not citizens of independent homelands (such as myself—I am a Shangaan, from Gazankulu) they would have to live in hostels. . . . I have a lodger's permit at present (at home) but my name is not on the housing waiting list. I am concerned that I will be removed from the house where I presently stay . . . my lodger's permit will be cancelled and I shall be forced to live in a hostel.[19]

The LRC brought an application for an order declaring that Rikhotso was entitled to remain in the urban area of Germiston. This time the case was heard by a judge of the Supreme Court, Brian O'Donavan, who was sympathetic to the problems faced by Rikhotso. Judge O'Donavan followed an earlier ruling by the great liberal judge of the 1950s whom we met in Chapter Two, Oliver Schreiner, namely that it was absurd to conclude that a person could never occasionally depart from the prescribed urban area in order to gain rights under the section. Rikhotso had worked for only one employer for the 10-year period. The system of annual contracts was but a government requirement which did not detract from the conclusion that the intention of Rikhotso and his employer was that he be continuously employed. Arrangements for the renewal of his contract were concluded before he went on paid leave, the annual break was granted as leave and his absences from work for 'other causes' had occurred on isolated occasions only . . . The question is one of substance not form.[20] Judge O'Donavan thus concluded that Rikhotso had acquired rights to reside permanently in the prescribed urban area.

This was a major victory against a key part of the system of influx control. Dr Koornhoff's reaction was that the record and judgment would now require careful study. This announcement subdued the enthusiasm. As the *Sowetan* noted, 'People will continue being bulldozed out of their jobs, out of the towns and sometimes out of their minds. As usual, this will be done by petty officials who simply disregard or even worse are ignorant of such breakthroughs or changes to the law.'[21]

Rikhotso was more confident than most observers that he would win before the Appellate Division once the government decided to appeal. He said that the highest court would uphold Judge O'Donavan because 'Johannesburg is just a town but there . . . there was not the law. And the Transvaal it was a territory. But all the laws it was from Bloemfontein.' As Stephen Ellman who conducted an interview with Rikhotso noted, for him Bloemfontein was the site of the Appeal Court and it was the 'head office' for the whole country. Its distance from the daily reality of ordinary South Africans made it appear a fairer tribunal than was their experience with the daily racism exhibited so expressly in the lower courts.[22]

Almost two years after his initial victory, Rikhotso's case was argued on appeal before the Appeal Court. In the period before the appeal, as had been the case with Komani, the authorities had done everything their obstructive minds could imagine to subvert the hard-won right. In particular, the authorities were determined to place as many obstacles in the way of Rikhotso, whose simple intention was to ensure that his family could live with him. After all, if the victories in *Komani* and *Rikhoto* were taken together, that was the indicated result. The wife and dependent children of a person who had rights like Rikhotso could live with him in the prescribed urban area.

Within this uncertain context, Arthur Chaskalson and Karel Tipp, another of the supremely talented and principled lawyers off the NUSAS leadership production line, proceeded to Bloemfontein to defend the judgment of Judge O'Donavan. This time, their opponent was a more typical government lawyer, Renier Kruger, who had much experience in taking cases for government in order to ward off any gains occasionally made by the human rights bar.

The authorities had done everything their obstructive minds could imagine to subvert the hard-won right

Kruger was a truly unimaginative lawyer and it showed in his argument. In essence, he repeated the arguments that had been rejected by Judge O'Donavan. Kruger pressed the point that Rikhotso had entered into a new contract each year and that no contract with a black employee could be concluded for longer than 11 months without official approval. Absent this approval, as was the case here, there was no continuous employment as required by the Act. The judges had clearly been persuaded by the Chaskalson argument that the substance of the arrangement between employer and Komani was the key to the case. Kruger had no response to the question: 'Yes, we know the form of the arrangement as required by the regulations but what did the two contracting parties intend?'

This time, the Court did not require further argument. The judgment was delivered by Judge Hennie van Heerden, austere but much respected for his intellect and who, unlike some appeal court judges at that time, was never accused of being influenced by the 'party's line'. He decided the case purely on the point to which Kruger had no answer. Rikhotso may have not been able to show that he had entered into one unbroken contract for 10 years but he had been employed continuously for that period by one employer. The breaks between each contract were treated by both sides as Rikhotso's legitimate right to leave. He enjoyed, at the very least, a legitimate expectation that, at the end of the leave period, he would continue to be employed even if he was required, for regulatory purposes, to complete another formal contract. For this reason, he had met the requirements of the section and hence had acquired a right to reside in the urban area.

An interesting aspect of the judgment was the comment by Judge van Heerden that the sets of regulations, together with the battery of legislation that governed the system of influx control, were complex even for lawyers, and thus posed a huge obstacle to those enjoined to administer the system and, even more so, to the millions whose lives were directly controlled by the system.

Yet, reading the judgment all these years later, one cannot but be struck by the irresistible simplicity of the reasoning employed by Judge van Heerden on behalf of the unanimous Court. The question immediately arises: Why did it take so long for this argument to be raised and the result to be achieved? We shall return to some tentative explanation shortly.

The consequences

It was a major victory, not only for Rikhotso[23] but potentially for millions of black South Africans. As Arthur Chaskalson wrote after the judgment:

> The *Rikhoto* judgment enables migrants to take advantage of the provisions of s 10(1)*(b)* of the Urban Areas Act and by so doing to upgrade their employment opportunities and to create for themselves opportunities for a family life in the towns—a right which the administration boards and labour officers sought to deny them.[24]

Chaskalson had expressed the consequences in his typically studied and measured fashion. The *Sowetan* captured the implication more bluntly: 'The judgment was a blow at the cornerstone of Government influx control policies,'[25] although it cautioned that legislation will doubtless be introduced to reverse the court decision. The government appeared to understand the implications perfectly. Abel cites an unnamed government source as saying, 'Those rulings defeat the purpose of government policy. Contract workers were not meant to get section 10 rights.'[26]

That implication was clearly considered by government. Apart from its own supporters, others were also apprehensive about the consequences of the decision. The *Natal Mercury* typified the position of the 'moderate white':

> From the human aspect, the ruling should be a matter for rejoicing, since it opens the way for tens of thousands of black migrant workers to live permanently in the cities with their families. But it would be foolish not to temper one's gratification over the human benefits with some sober reflection on the practical consequences.[27]

Similarly, the Afrikaans press warned of a black flood of new migrants into the urban areas.

Koornhof was under pressure from the breakaway Conservative Party, which advocated a 'pure' application of apartheid policy, as well as his own supporters and part of the press. In Parliament, the Conservative Party's Frank le Roux attacked Koornhof for delaying government's response to the Court's judgment as follows: '[T]he Appeal Court in Bloemfontein passed the same judgment, almost word for word, as the Witwatersrand judgment. The question is what the Hon. the Minister has done since September 1981 to counter the possibility of an unfavourable Appeal Court judgment.'[28] The racist discourse that so overwhelmed white South Africans at the time[29] contributed to the fear of a massive migration of black citizens into the hitherto almost exclusively white urban areas. Koornhof was alive to this 'problem' and hence assured members of the Conservative Party that the government had no intention of 'throwing in the towel' as regards influx control.[30]

But outside pressure and increasing concern from industrialised capital created a measure of ambivalence, or at least caution, on the part of the government. Illustrative of industrial capitalism's approach was a statement by Fred Ferreira of Ford (SA):

> [C]ampaigns to pull tens of millions of rand out of companies doing business with South Africa could gather steam if the Government took this step [overrode the *Rikhoto* judgment] ... The Americans are certain to view an attempt to circumvent the judgment as an attempt to muzzle the courts ... For this and many other reasons, I believe the Government would do well to implement the judgment.[31]

Not only was Koornhof aware of these pressures but he appeared to recognise the importance of the courts. Thus he told Parliament in rather different tones from his predecessors, Louw, Sauer and Dönges: 'Whatever the judgment of the Appeal Court may be, a responsible Government will surely consider, in the first place what it can learn from that judgment and, in the second place be filled with pride that the courts in this country have built up a very good name world-wide ... All we have to do is ensure that this finding is strictly adhered to.'[32]

This strategy of trying to use the legitimacy of the courts to best advantage in those relatively few defeats that the government suffered in the courts, without allowing the latter to circumscribe its racist vision, is reflective in a further announcement from Koornhof:

> The government is obviously bound by the judgment. ... it is my duty to avoid at all costs that unrealistic expectations of instant accommodation in urban areas are not created in the minds of migrant workers and their families ... They have not created legal rights to demand a house in black urban residential areas ... squatting will not be permitted under any circumstances.[33]

Shortly thereafter, Koornhof showed his hand. He introduced an amendment to the law, not to set aside the *Rikhoto* judgment but designed rather to make it more difficult for black citizens to employ the judgments of *Rikhoto* and *Komani* together so as to broaden radically the scope of the applicants' rights to reside in an urban area. The amendment revealed the plan: it applied solely to the wives and children of people qualified in terms of section 10(1)(b), the scope of which had been significantly extended by the court in *Rikhoto*. The amendment stated that those wives and children who did not ordinarily reside with the qualified male before 26 August 1983, the date of the commencement of the amendment, could reside with their husbands or fathers only in a house for which he had leasehold rights, a site or residential permit. A simple lodger's permit was no longer of any use. With the chronic shortage of suitable housing, such housing rights as leasehold or a residential permit were as rare as the proverbial hens' teeth.

The government's idea was clear. It could now claim that influx control by way of pass laws was no more and that it had abided by the two adverse court decisions. All it had done was to ensure that urbanisation took place in an 'orderly way' by ensuring that all who came to reside in the cities possessed 'proper' accommodation. In truth, government knew well that the scarcity of accommodation could work the same injustice as the pass laws.

The government had one final throw of the litigation dice. The issue around the meaning of continuous residence for the purpose of qualifying to live permanently in an urban area had not been decisively determined in *Rikhoto's* case. Thus a Mr Mthiya was compelled to go to court because, in his case, he had taken more than a month's leave on three separate occasions. Like Rikhotso, he had worked for the same employer for more than 15 years and had taken leave at the end of each 'separate contract'. But, on three occasions, the absence from work had been for periods of four, six and eight months repectively. 'Ah!' said the Black Affairs Administration Board, unlike Rikhotso, whose break from employment was always for one month, the length of these three breaks was clear proof that there had not been an uninterrupted period of employment for 15 years.

The government had one final throw of the litigation dice

Again, Arthur Chaskalson went off to Bloemfontein, this time with Jeremy Gauntlett as his junior counsel. The Bench was hardly a liberal one, although the judgment was delivered by one of the finest private lawyers to grace the Court during this period, Judge Ernest Jansen. He appeared to have no problem with the argument that the lengthy absences were not decisive in that there was an agreement that Mthiya would return to work on completion of personal business.[34] The Court eschewed the formalism that had dominated its work for more than two decades to decide the case on the substance of an undefined agreement. Small wonder that one commentator observed that this decision 'put an end to the make-believe Alice in Wonderland attitude of regarding blacks who in fact live in urban areas on a permanent basis as, not in law, being there at all.'[35]

Assessment

Two key questions need to be answered. Can it not be said, in the light of the bureaucratic insurrection against the *Komani* order, in particular, and the subsequent amendment to the law after the delivery of the *Rikhoto* judgment, that the enthusiasm for these legal victories needs to be tempered? Secondly, why did a Court, which since the coloured vote cases had been on a steady retreat from any liberal highwater mark of the early 1950s, hand down these two judgments?

The two answers may well be interrelated. The entire saga of litigation from *Komani* to *Rikhoto* needs to be located in the very endemic contradictions of apartheid policy as racist rule entered its last decade. It has been correctly noted that the context of the *Komani* or *Rikhoto* cases did not resemble the form of popular resistance against the pass laws that had characterised the Defiance Campaign of the 1950s. There were no strikes, no burning of passes and the Soweto uprisings notwithstanding, the government might have thought, with some justification, that repression had paid off, as it had in the 1960s and the consequent *Rivonia* trial.[36]

Komani and Rikhotso were single litigants, unsupported by anyone other than the Black Sash and the Legal Resources Centre. In short, there was no big, or indeed small, political campaign which powered the litigation.[37]

Perhaps that makes the outcome even more surprising. The two judgments were not automatically enforced by the apartheid bureaucrats. It took many years for the *Komani* judgment, in particular, to be recognised and, even then, the government amended the law. But, eventually, the litigants and many others did obtain relief.[38] Later, the government resisted sweeping these judgments into irrelevance by passing laws to set them aside in their entirety, as had been often been the case when the government suffered a rare defeat in court.

There was no big, or indeed small, political campaign which powered the litigation

It is easy, with the benefit of a decade of democratic hindsight, to question the importance of this litigation. But when these cases were launched, apartheid, its contradictions and the political effects of Soweto notwithstanding, was very much alive. Few would have predicted then that, within little more than a decade, the game would have been up for the racist men (and women) who had ruled with such confidence and for so long. These legal successes were therefore no small victories. They exposed the contradictions in the regulatory system of influx control and forced change, which in turn was to create conditions, at least in part, that gave rise to the growth in political resistance leading to the commencement of the political process of capitulation in 1990.

That leads to the second question and the linkage already mentioned. When Dr Koornhof, with his irritatingly mendacious enthusiasm, announced in 1980 that 'We can be and are, well on the way to achieving in my country equality for all people before the law and equal chances and opportunities',[39] he was reflecting the realisation that the present policy pertaining to measures such as influx control had run its course.

In August 1978, the government-appointed commission of Dr Riekert reported on its investigation into the problem of pass laws and labour needs of the country.[40] The core of the commission's proposals was that influx control should be shifted from control of mere presence in the area to far tighter control (if that were possible) of accommodation in urban areas, as well as employment. This would eventually lead to a division between a core of permanent urban workers housed with their families and a reservoir of peripheral workers in the rural areas to which the redundant, retired and sick urban workers would be sent when incapable of providing work or superfluous to the needs of capital.[41]

The arguments raised went to the heart of the apartheid system

This cruel and cynical move came with its own contradictions. Once the group of families who were permanent residents grew significantly, many of whom were unionised workers, the potential for political activity became easier. Indeed, within a few years, political resistance led by the United Democratic Front had begun to change the very foundations of apartheid rule.[42]

Perhaps it stretches the story too far to argue that the victories in the appeal court led to the breakdown of the pass laws but they did expose the contradictions in the system, upped the cost of government's attempt at legitimacy if the judgments were expressly reversed and made it more difficult to fashion an effective control scheme.

But what about the appeal court and the results brought about in these judgments? The judgments in both *Komani* and *Rikhoto* read as relatively formalistic, technical approaches to the law. There is nothing in the judgment authored by Judge Rumpff in *Komani* nor that written by Judge van Heerden in *Rikhoto* which indicate any judicial disapproval of the very system they were called upon to analyse. Abel notes correctly that 'the courts took no cognizance of moral, economic or political factors, resting their decisions exclusively on the narrowly legalistic ground that the regulations were *ultra vires* or misinterpreted.'[43]

That they approached the cases in this fashion is not surprising. Judges in South Africa, particularly during the dark years of apartheid, rarely articulated any normative premise upon which they based their judgments. But, as already discussed, the courts in these cases knew about the influx control system and its consequences. In *Komani*, Chaskalson had framed the case in the introduction to his address as concerning an egregious abuse of human rights.

The arguments raised went to the heart of the apartheid system, a point argued forcibly by government counsel. So, the judges who, as a collective Bench, had done very little to temper legislative or even executive excesses and who, through the results of these cases, fashioned a precedent that, before the cases were heard, most legal commentators thought impossible to achieve, must be taken to have appreciated the consequences of their judgments.

So why suddenly did they act in this fashion? Perhaps it may disappoint readers but this book does not, nor do the authors consider that they can, advance one, single, comprehensive reason for this process of adjudication. Some indications for an explanation are, however, possible. Arguably, no two influx control cases were ever previously litigated with the precision displayed by the legal teams in *Komani* and *Rikhoto,* nor was the appeal court ever confronted in these kinds of cases with the quality of advocacy presented by Arthur Chaskalson.[44] Most cases are not won on advocacy alone, but in the rare case it remains a powerful tool.

It should also not be forgotten that the very policy instrument of the pass laws was no longer accepted as an essential mechanism which government needed to deal with what it perceived to be the problems of urbanisation. As discussed above, by the time these cases came to court, Riekert had already produced his report about the need to reconsider aspects of policy. For example, he stated: 'The Commission is further satisfied that, although it will be possible ... to apply influx control more effectively than at present much of the bitterness and frustration caused by it can be eliminated.'[45] In similar fashion, Dr P J van der Merwe, Director-General of the Department of Manpower, said in 1979: 'It is hardly necessary to stress that the quality of life within black communities needs to be improved very substantially and very rapidly, in the interests of political and economic stability, the support for the free enterprise system by blacks, and economic growth and development.'[46]

The political and economic climate within which these cases were contested meant that the judges no longer operated within the age of racist certainty that existed throughout the 60s and until the Soweto uprisings of 1976. It is surely naïve to suggest that a judiciary is impervious to the existing public discourse, even in the case of those who lived in Bloemfontein in the late 1970s, where, without Internet access, email and with only the local newspapers and the SABC, they were so closeted from opposing thought.

In summary, a case was compellingly presented and argued. It raised troubling questions of a kind to which the political wisdom of the dominant party cannot supply any easy answers. Part of the ruling class advocated significant changes to the very system that was being discussed in court. The cases could be disposed of on relatively narrow, technical legal grounds. This may not be a full and complete explanation for these outcomes but all these considerations played a role in the eventual outcome.

Conclusion

Within slightly more than a decade of the *Komani* case being launched, the country had changed forever. Hence it is tempting, in the light of these subsequent dramatic developments, to reduce the importance of the litigation started when Veli Komani decided that the law should help him unite his family under one roof in the urban area where he lived and worked.

But, as has been illustrated in this chapter, these decisions hastened the end of a system which had cruelly governed the lives of black South Africans for almost a century. It made the task of the government more complex in its desire to revamp these legal controls, such changes creating, in turn, more favourable grounds for political resistance.

Perhaps of equal importance, cases such as *Komani* and *Rikhoto*, thanks to the tenacious principle of the litigants and the commitment, dedication and forensic brilliance of their lawyers, preserved more than a scintilla of the rule of law and thus its potential importance for democracy. That preservation was to prove important in the manner in which the country became a constitutional democracy during the following decade.

Endnotes

1 Influx control was governed by the Black Urban Areas Consolidation Act 25 of 1945; denationalisation by various pieces of legislation governing the homelands, such as the Status of Transkei Act 100 of 1976, the Status of Bophuthatswana Act 98 of 1977, the Status of Venda Act 107 of 1979, the Status of Ciskei Act 110 of 1981 and the labour bureaus in, terms of the Black Labour Act 67 of 1964.

2 Stephen Ellman 'Law and legitimacy in South Africa' (1995) *Law and Social Inquiry* 407, 441, and a transcript of an interview with Rikhotso conducted by Ellman (1994) kindly given by Ellman. We have used the spelling 'Rikhoto' when referring to the case as it is known by that name.

3 Figures provided by Michael Savage 'The imposition of Pass Laws on the African Population in South Africa 1916-1984' (1988) *African Affairs* 181.

4 Report of the Local Government Commission TP.7 (1922).

5 This term is borrowed from Hannah Arendt who, in her work *Eichmann in Jerusalem* (1963), argued that the great evil in societies like Nazi Germany was not committed necessarily by fanatics or psychopaths but by ordinary people who accepted the premises of their government's policy and who therefore conducted themselves with the attitude that their actions were normal and ordinary. We want to argue that this paradigm is applicable to the conduct of the administrators who are partly the subject of this chapter.

6 General Circular No 25, 1967 para 1.

7 The applicable law was s 10(1)(c) of the Black (Urban Areas) Consolidation Act 25 of 1945 which provided 'No Black shall remain for more than 72 hours in a prescribed area unless he produces proof in the manner prescribed that ...(c) such Black is the wife ... of any Black mentioned in para (a) or (b) of this subsection and after lawful entry into such prescribed area, ordinarily resides with that Black in such area.' As Mr Komani qualified under para (b) because he had been employed for more than 10 years by the same employer, his wife may have been excused for reading ss (c) as affording her a right to live with him.

8 That advocates, from time to time, represent clients with whom they disagree ideologically, is attributable to the taxi cab rule of the Bar—if available, an advocate must take the brief offered. In this way, unpopular causes can find legal representation. Whether the rule should apply also to the state is a more controversial question.

9 In fairness, there was precedent equating ordinary residence with lawful residence, although not necessarily pertaining to the legality of the housing regulations.

10 The Black Sash was founded in 1955, initially to campaign against the removal of coloured voters. See Chapter One. As apartheid extended its web of control, the Black Sash began a campaign against the pass laws. White women, to cite its National Director, Marcella Naidoo, in 2005, used the relative safety of their white classification to don symbolic black sashes as a symbol of mourning and protest against unjust laws. From 1955 onwards, the Black Sash played a brave and principled role as an important element of civil society, of which its advice offices were a critical component. The South African Institute of Race Relations was started in 1929.

11 Arthur Chaskalson interview (July 2007).

12 There is a point of jurisprudential curiosity here: some 15 years later, most of the Constitutional Court, under now Chief Justice Chaskalson in *Du Plessis v De Klerk* 1996 (3) SA 850 (CC), used the same approach of the limited state to decide that the new Constitution applied only to relations between the state and the individual, thus finally disposing of a controversy about the potential reach of the Constitution.

13 Budlender and Chaskalson interviews.

14 Cited by Richard Abel *Politics by Other Means: Law in the struggle against Apartheid* (1995) 27. This superb book contains a comprehensive account of these cases and accordingly we have inevitably drawn on its material.

15 Komani interview with Zackie Achmat in his film *Law and Freedom* (2005).

16 The hypocrisy of people like Koornhof, who so personified the cruel lack of integrity of the entire National Party enterprise (although Koornhof and his fellow traveller, Pik Botha, Minister of Foreign Affairs, were the exemplars of this approach), is shown in the comparison of his opposition to the *Komani* judgment with the following told to an American audience a year earlier: 'I detest the dompas. I declared war on the dompas. That thing must be ousted completely and totally out of my country and I have requested my officials to work on it.' *Time* (4 September 1987).

17 Abel *ibid* 31.

18 *Ibid.*

19 Note from Paul Kennedy to Charles Nupen (5 March 1983) LRC Papers in Cullen Library.

20 Page 21 of the typed judgment LRC papers.

21 Cited by Abel *ibid* 48.

22 The quote from *Rikhoto* appears, as does the explanation, in Stephen Ellmann 'Law and Legitimacy in South Africa' (1995) *Law and Social Inquiry* 407, 443.

23 Rikhotso told Ellmann of his confidence that the court in Bloemfontein would uphold his case. Ellman *ibid* 443.

24 Arthur Chaskalson 'The Right of Black Persons to Seek Employment and be Employed in the Republic of South Africa' (1984) *Acta Juridica* 33, 40.
25 Abel *ibid* 53.
26 Abel *ibid* 54.
27 Abel *ibid* 53.
28 *Hansard* 10 August 1983 col 10994.
29 Not that it should now be assumed that all whites have shrugged off this world view.
30 *Hansard* col 10988 (10 August 1983).
31 *Rand Daily Mail* (7 June 1983).
32 *Hansard* col 10991 (10 August 1983).
33 Quoted by Abel *ibid* 58.
34 *Black Affairs Administration Board, Western Cape and Another v Mthiya* 1985 (4) SA 754 (A).
35 Harold Rudolph 1985 *Annual Survey of South African Law* 35.
36 Abel *ibid* 61.
37 In some way, this makes the achievements of this litigation even more remarkable. Unlike the TAC litigation discussed in Chapter Seven, neither litigant could rely on civil society pressure to push his case. The combination of the political and the legal was significantly absent in these cases. It was rather the lawyers, Budlender and Nupen in particular, who refused to withdraw from the fight and bask in the glory of court victories. Their remarkable persistence in their dealings with a recalcitrant administration ensured that the orders granted by the Appeal Court would not simply be ignored in perpetuity.
38 Rikhotso interview (1994), which reflects his feeling of satisfaction against the odds. Copy of interview with author.
39 *Financial Mail* (1 February 1980).
40 Commission of Enquiry into legislation affecting the utilisation of manpower. RP32/1979—The Riekert Report.
41 See the analysis of D Davis and G Budlender 'Labour Law, Influx Control and Citizenship: The Emerging Policy Conflict' (1984) *Acta Juridica* 141. The government was also intent on using citizenship of the so-called independent homelands as a further means of control; making black South Africans citizens of the homelands, deportation and use of alien status were additional tools to maintain a core and periphery of workers.
42 For a comprehensive history of the United Democratic Front, see Jeremy Seekings *The UDF A Victory of the United Democratic Front in South Africa* (2000).
43 Abel *ibid* 63.
44 In an interview with the author, Geoff Budlender spoke in awe of the way Chaskalson confronted and then swung in his direction a hitherto hostile court.
45 Riekert Commission at paras 4.204 *(h)* and 4.280 *(h)*(ii).
46 P J van der Merwe *An Analysis of the Report of the Commission of Inquiry into Legislation Affecting the Utilization of Manpower* (1979) 45.

five

Exposing detention without trial

The National Party is prepared to accept responsibility for the policies that it adopted and for the actions taken by its office bearers in the implementation of those policies. It is however not prepared to accept responsibility for the criminal actions of a handful of operatives of the security forces of which the Party was not aware and which it never would have condoned.
F W de Klerk[1]

I was escorted to his office and told to strip naked. Told to put my penis on his desk. Then he took a policeman's baton and started to stroke it without ever taking his eyes off me, and then he raised the baton and brought it whacking down on my penis. After that he paused; he threw questions at me, then left me in agony. When he saw my agony subsiding, he made me stand against that desk and put my penis there again. But this time he did not hit it immediately. He picked up his baton, raised it, and waited for the expectation of pain to capture me before he hit. And then a step further. When my penis was on the table and his baton was raised, he moved his arm, little jerking movements in slight flickers as though it was going to come smashing down, but it didn't. He watched me flinch: I cringed with the pain that was as real as if his baton had struck. And so it went on, a slight movement of his arm as if to strike, but no strike, driving me to a point where I was almost begging him to do it, to get it over with. But he could see that coming too.
Mac Maharaj[2]

At the commencement of the state of emergency declared in 1986, the *Weekly Mail* (now the *Mail and Guardian*) published a photograph prominently on the front page of the newspaper which depicted a column of policemen armed with sjamboks and firearms, walking in formation down one of the main streets of downtown Johannesburg. The caption read: 'The country is now in their hands.'

This terrifying depiction of police power luminously captured the implications of the state of emergency. The police were the law, yet above and beyond the law. In truth, the creation of unaccountable police power had begun much earlier. Between 1960 and 1990, 80 000 South Africans were detained by the police without the benefit of a trial. During these three decades, South Africa had a parallel system of incarceration. Common law criminals, including murderers and rapists, were imprisoned after a conviction by a competent court. While many were arrested and then detained prior to the commencement of their trial, each had had the opportunity to approach a court for bail. Violent criminals were entitled to legal representation, although, in many cases, the inexperienced lawyers who were appointed to defend these murderers and rapists in terms of a *pro deo* system should have been mandated to carry health warnings for their clients, such was their lack of preparation for dealing with complex trials. But the trial took place in open court, and a conviction occurred after the presiding judicial officer had delivered a judgment setting out his or her reasons for both the conviction and the sentence. Once convicted, an accused possessed a right to lodge an appeal against the conviction and sentence.

By contrast, 80 000 detainees were incarcerated at the whim of a police officer. Courts were possessed of narrow powers to review these decisions. But even these powers were rarely exercised. All too often, courts committed jurisprudential suicide by limiting even the slim supervisory review powers which they possessed under the ordinary rules of common law. Detainees did not have the benefit of legal representatives who could argue that they had been

Detainees did not have the benefit of legal representatives who could argue that they had been detained illegally

detained illegally. The system allowed the police to incarcerate thousands of political opponents of the government. It is not surprising, therefore, that of the 80 000 who were detained 80 percent were released without any charge brought against them. Only 4 percent of detainees were ever convicted of any crime.[3]

The graphic description provided by Mac Maharaj of his mistreatment in detention was not an isolated exception. Torture was systematically used against detainees. The Truth and Reconciliation Commission heard that about 22 000 detainees had been tortured and physically assaulted during their period of detention. Some 73 detainees died during the period of detention.[4] For a long period, (white) South Africans were in denial about this parallel system of 'law' which was designed to crush legitimate political opposition to the apartheid regime. Many newspaper reports published research undertaken by various academics to inform the public of the nature and extent of police brutality.

It took a courageous, young district surgeon to force the country to confront the reality of this systematic process of political repression. This chapter is about the story of that doctor and the legal team who assisted her in exposing the reality behind detention without trial. As is revealed in this chapter, the sheer intensity of the system employed for almost 30 years is itself powerful proof against F W de Klerk's defence to the TRC that torture and death were the work of a few psychopaths who abused the criminal 'justice' system.

The first steps

Gilbert Marcus is today one of South Africa's leading senior counsel. During his career, he has won many victories which have advanced the cause of human rights in South Africa. But, in this case, it was a cameo role played by Marcus some 20 years before that began a process of litigation which culminated in the exposure of some of the most notorious police practices employed in apartheid South Africa.

In 1985, Marcus received a telephone call from a friend, Kathy Orr. She told him that her sister, Wendy, a district surgeon in Port Elizabeth, was in urgent need of legal advice about a matter of great public importance. Marcus intuited the problems that Wendy Orr might be facing as a district surgeon. He knew immediately whom she should consult and referred her accordingly: Halton Cheadle was then in his mid-30s. He had built a reputation as a leading labour law attorney in South Africa. As a result of working with a number of hugely talented and courageous lawyers, including Clive Thompson, Fink Haysom, John Brand, Martin Brassey and Ray Zondo, carefully planned litigation had ensured that a body of progressive labour law was under construction which would help the independent trade union movement create an industrial democracy in the midst of a racist autocracy.

Cheadle is one of the few lateral thinkers in the South African legal community. This gift, together with great charm and prodigious energy, ensured that he had the ability to launch a series of significant legal challenges against crucial 'legal' components of the apartheid state. But few, if any, of his cases could have been as daring as that which was to follow his meeting with Dr Orr. It brought into the public glare the very brutality that the government used to impose its undemocratic will upon any political opposition. To fully grasp the magnitude of this legally unfettered system of control, it is necessary to take a brief historical tour through its development.

The legal context of detention without trial

After World War II, the South African legal system became the subject of great international controversy, not only as a result of its race laws but also because of its security legislation. Indeed, it was not the racist nature of the South African legal system but its repressive security laws that first prompted the Security Council of the United Nations to order mandatory sanctions against the member state when it directly imposed an arms embargo on South Africa.[5] This decision followed the death in detention of a great South African political leader, Steven Bantu Biko, and a consequent security crackdown in 1977 in which 18 organisations and three newspapers were banned, 47 political leaders detained and a number of citizens subjected to various forms of restrictions. Biko became the 45th person to die while being held by the police in detention.

Biko became the 45th person to die while being held by the police in detention

Detention without trial had begun much earlier. In 1963, section 17 of the General Law Amendment Act of 1963, commonly known as the '90-day' clause, was introduced into the South African legal system. This provision authorised any commissioned police officer to arrest and detain in custody for periods of 90 days any person whom such officer suspected of having committed or being about to commit certain offences or being in possession of certain information. The detainee could then be held until the Commissioner of the South African Police had formed an opinion on whether he or she had satisfactorily answered all questions put during interrogation.

No one, save for a Magistrate, had the right to visit the detainee or had a right of access to the detainee without the permission of the Minister of Justice or a commissioned police officer. The detainee was effectively cut off from the outside world—he or she had no right to consult a lawyer or see family or friends.

Wide powers had been granted by Parliament to the executive to curb all forms of political opposition with the passing of the Suppression of Communism Act in 1950. But, even by these early 'standards' of unfettered executive contest, the 90-day clause introduced an entirely new dispensation. In a major article published in 1966, Professors Tony Matthews and RCL Albino[6] wrote:

> When parliament introduced the ninety-day clause, it brought something entirely alien into our legal system. The clause was foreign both in the spirit and traditions of South African law and to the western ideas of freedom and government which we inherited but which we have not treasured much in recent years. The origin of solitary confinement as a means of obtaining information and evidence is in itself an explanation of the alien taint it has in countries that know something of western tradition.

The cancer spread rapidly through the legal body. The courts appeared to encounter little legal or moral problem with these laws. In 1963, Albie Sachs, now a judge of the Constitutional Court, was detained under the 90-day clause. He brought an application to court to permit him and other detainees the same rights as awaiting trial prisoners, including rights to exercise and to have access to reading and writing materials. The Cape Supreme Court found in favour of Sachs. On appeal to the Appellate Division, Judge Ogilvie-Thompson determined that the purpose of detention without trial was to induce the detainee to speak. Thus he reasoned that a detainee like Sachs could not be equated with an awaiting trial prisoner. In any event, asked the judge, where would the boundary regarding a detainee's rights be drawn? He wrote: 'In the present case we are concerned with reading matter and writing materials; but is a detainee who in happier days habitually enjoyed champagne and cigars entitled as of right to continue to enjoy them during his detention?'[7]

The Steyn Court we encountered earlier in this book, and of which Ogilvie- Thompson was a key member, had again served the government well. The judiciary was complicit in the erosion of rights in that it willingly, with a few notable exceptions, placed no legal barriers in the way of such unfettered police power. Detainees were left increasingly to the non-existent mercy of the police. Judge Ogilvie-Thompson got his reward. He became Chief Justice after the retirement of Lucas Steyn in 1971.

By 1967, the period of 90-day detention had been extended to indefinite detention without trial[8]. The Terrorism Act was the ultimate authoritarian tool. The key provision in the Act was section 6 which empowered any commissioned officer above the rank of Lieutenant-Colonel to order, without warrant, the arrest and detention for interrogation of any person whom he believed had committed or intended to commit the offence of terrorism. The central phrase was 'offence of terrorism' to the extent that the police powers of detention flowed from a belief that a detainee had or was about to commit an act of terrorism.

He had caused a traffic jam when moving from one side of the road to another in order to sell a cake to a party supporter

The definition of terrorism was so wide that Tony Matthews suggested that 'without exaggeration the crime is so broad that there is hardly a person who had not at some time committed it. With the enactment of this Act we have arrived at the position that the authorities, if they are determined, could bring home a charge of terrorism against anyone who is *persona non grata* with them.'[9] Mathews illustrated the breadth of the definition of terrorism with the example of a senior police officer who could arrest and detain on an indefinite basis, the leader of the white opposition, De Villiers Graaff, himself ironically no more than a benign racist, because he had caused a traffic jam when moving from one side of the road to another in order to sell a cake to a party supporter who had arrived at the party's fundraising cake sale.

It was no exaggeration to say that the police were legally placed beyond any form of control or public accountability. Breyten Breytenbach captured their enormous power when he wrote:

> There is nothing, there is no power anywhere in the world that has any say over them. They can keep you forever, they can put their heavy hand on you, they can break you down, they may even go red in the face and really let rip.[10]

As noted, the Truth and Reconciliation Commission received more than over 22 000 statements from victims who alleged that they had been tortured by members of the security forces.[11] Sad as it is to now reflect, much of this would or could have been known to the white electorate who voluntarily voted the National Party into power over five decades. But, if white South Africa was engulfed in state of moral paralysis during the 1970s and 1980s, Wendy Orr was about to provide an antidote to this condition. It was she who provided the means by which the conditions in detention could be exposed in the courts.

People could have found out if they cared

Today, it is difficult to find any defender of the system, as is evident from F W de Klerk's remarks cited in the introduction to this chapter, or anyone who claims that he or she would have defended the system had they been placed in such knowledge. Yet, as noted, there was clear information available about these practices from the media and academic research, most of it ignored. But courts held a measure of legitimacy—once accepted by a judge, the allegations of torture were converted suddenly into a 'public truth'. The following is a short summary of the evidence that was available to the public. Before the Wendy Orr case, it had little effect in shaping public reaction.

The TRC made reference to the study released by a group of doctors who documented that, between September 1987 and March 1990, 94 per cent of a sample of detainees had claimed either physical or mental abuse. The study found that the beating of detainees was widespread and that half of those alleging physical abuse still showed evidence of the abuse on physical examination. An assessment of their psychological status found that 48 per cent of these detainees were psychologically dysfunctional.

It was consistently alleged over a 20-year period that detainees were subjected to the following forms of torture: various forms of suffocation including a 'wet bag over the head', forced electric shock, sexual torture, psychological torture, prolonged periods of solitary confinement, physical assault.

The TRC concludes, in the clinical style that characterises much of its report: 'It is accepted now that detention without trial allowed for the abuse of those held in custody, that torture and mal-treatment were widespread and that whilst officials of the former state were aware of what was happening, they did nothing about it.'[12]

As was evident from the early cases in the 1960s, the perpetuation of this monstrous machine was assisted in considerable measure by the judiciary. The TRC report observes:

> More distressing is the fact that many judges and magistrates continued to accept the testimony of detainees, despite the fact that most of them knew that the testimony had been obtained under interrogation and torture whilst in detention. In this way, the judiciary and the magistracy indirectly sanctioned this practice and, together with the leadership of the former apartheid state, must be half accountable for its action.[13]

In 1985, Don Foster, a professor in the Department of Psychology at the University of Cape Town, published a report on the treatment of a large sample of detainees in which he found that the vast majority had been subjected to the kind of torture techniques subsequently identified by the TRC. A vigorous publicity campaign was launched against this study, particularly in the pages of *Die Burger* and the *Cape Times*, by a number of academics, mainly from the University of Stellenbosch, who claimed that the report was unscientific and accordingly should not be trusted.

Professors Herman Crause, Diko van Zyl and Jacob van der Westhuizen[14] kept up a barrage of pseudo-academic abuse in the pages of the *Cape Times* and *Die Burger*, claiming that the study was 'unacceptable science' in that there was no control group (presumably, of detainees who were given champagne and cigars as opposed to the wet bag), the detainees in the sample remained anonymous and the conclusions were not tested with the police before publication of the report. In short, this was politics masquerading as science.

Retired Judge President of the Cape Supreme Court, Judge Helm van Zyl[15] joined the attack. For him, the report provided ready ammunition to the country's communist enemies. He demanded to know the identity of all the detainees interviewed. He insisted that the courts invariably offered all detainees protection. We can only presume that the judge would have been happy to have the identity of all these detainees exposed to the police so that they could be detained again, only to find the courts completely ineffective in the supervision of police power.

Dr André Schulman provided further support in numerous letters penned to the *Cape Times*. For example, he wrote:

> The effect of a 2.4 cm high front page headline announcing that the police subjected 83 percent of detainees to torture is to give stimulation and justification to those who want to commit real murder and torture on members of the police force and other 'collaborators' and to make the public less inclined to condemn them for these acts.
>
> Whether it is the scientific logic or the newspaper reporting which is at fault, a similarly prominent and emotive retraction is urgently needed.[16]

Brigadier Odendaal, a former Divisional Commissioner of Police, offered a quasi-official view:

> I have often been puzzled by some criminologists, because those I know haven't even seen the inside of a police cell, not to mention the slightest experience to what goes on in the front lines of the battle against crime. In comparison some of my men at Woodstock and other police stations can list a man's previous convictions just by looking into his face.[17]

White South Africans may have had their doubts about the nature of police conduct but the majority kept these to themselves. And the deaths continued. In the notorious John Vorster Square, the first death of a detainee took place in 1971. Achmat Timol died while in police custody. The police claimed that he had jumped from a window on the 10th floor of the building while being interrogated. Similar 'non-explanations' were provided for other deaths in detention in John Vorster Square. On 20 January 1977, Elomon Malele died. Police claimed that 'he had suddenly fallen down', hitting his head on a table which caused fatal brain injury. A month later, on 15 February 1977, Mathews Mojo Mabelane died. Police said his death was caused by an attempt to escape; before they could react, Mabelane was already 'halfway' through an open window. On 5 February 1987, trade unionist Dr Neil Aggett was found hanging in his cell after 70 days of detention.

As resistance to apartheid increased, so did the numbers of people who were detained without trial. In 1985, some 2 436 people were detained in terms of section 29 of the Internal Security Act (the revamped version of section 6 of the Terrorism Act). According to the Minister of Police, a total of 7 996 were detained from 21 July 1985 to 7 March 1986 in terms of regulations which had been promulgated under the Public Safety Act, that is emergency regulations which were passed during the intensification of political resistance in the second half of the 1980s.[18]

Wendy Orr: Preparing the case

When Wendy Orr met Halton Cheadle on 3 September 1985, she was 25 years old and had recently arrived in Port Elizabeth to work in the District Surgeon's office after completion of her medical studies at the University of Cape Town.

Prisoners who complained subsequent to an admission or transfer were required to be examined by a district surgeon

When he received the call from Marcus, Cheadle was already in Port Elizabeth acting in his capacity as a labour lawyer on behalf of the trade union movement. He had travelled to Port Elizabeth to deal with cases to be brought by trade unions before the local industrial court. It was probably because of his well-known role as a leading labour lawyer for the trade union movement that the security police in Port Elizabeth did not consider that there was anything untoward about his presence in Port Elizabeth. To the extent that they did show an interest, it was because they were desirous of gaining information about the proposed labour litigation. Had they known that the labour litigation was but a side show, they would surely have increased their surveillance.

Wendy Orr's knowledge about police brutality was itself a reflection of the bifurcated state of the South African's 'legal' system: lawless police activity existing side by side with intricate administrative regulations. In keeping with South Africa's bureaucratic adherence to laws and regulations, a prison regulation required that each prisoner be examined by a doctor on admission, transfer and release. Prisoners who complained subsequent to an admission or transfer were required to be examined by a district surgeon who was then obliged to record the complaint. When the complaint was of assault, the doctor was required to fill out a medical report and to complete certain progress reports on a 'prisoner's injury form'. During August 1985, Orr examined an average of some 20 new emergency detainees per day. All these cases were subject to the prison regulations.

On some days, Orr examined more than 200 detainees in a morning. It had become clear to her that, in the majority of cases when detainees complained that they had been assaulted, they presented symptoms consistent with their complaints.

Orr was not a politically active person while a medical student at the University of Cape Town. But the ethical dilemmas confronting a district surgeon in the heart of this emergency machine troubled her greatly. It was for this reason that she was desperate to consult a reliable lawyer. At their first meeting, she told Cheadle the entire story of her experience as a district surgeon in examining detainees. Cheadle realised immediately that, for the first time, reliable evidence could be placed before a court to prove the extent of police brutality in the heart of a system designed to perpetrate apartheid control.

Orr's observations had the potential to develop into a massive case. Sensibly, Cheadle advised Orr that if she made an affidavit documenting her experiences as a district surgeon, not only would she lose her job but she would be subjected to extensive state pressure and harassment. Her life would change dramatically and, not least, would probably be endangered.

She asked for time to consider her position. A week passed before she finally contacted Cheadle who had returned to Johannesburg. She was prepared to be party to litigation. This decision had been taken with a great measure of anxiety and after careful consultation with her family and Marcus.

Dr Orr's observations had the potential to develop into a massive case

A great problem with litigation of this nature concerns the procurement of evidence. How is an allegation of torture against the police to be proved? Normally, the case would turn on the word of the detainee against the 'official' voice of the police. A detainee would invariably be seen as an unreliable witness, in that, as a detainee, such a person was 'subversive' and would wish to bring the police into disrepute.

In a case where the applicant seeks an order which will prevent the continuation of conduct she alleges is unlawful, litigation takes the form of an application instead of a trial. The Court is provided with sworn statements, being affidavits deposed to by the contesting parties. Only in exceptional circumstances does a court have the benefit of oral evidence given by witnesses. To have a district surgeon depose to an affidavit was a major advantage to Cheadle and his legal team. But obstacles remained. True, Orr could depose to an affidavit, but without documentary evidence to support her assertions, the state could deny these allegations, which, if true to the form of the courts, might be enough to stave off any of the relief sought on behalf of detainees.

The state argument would be the usual one. Orr was yet another tool in the hands of the 'communist inspired onslaught' on the South African government. There was no independent proof to support the 'wild' allegations of a young and easily influenced district surgeon, no concrete evidence, hence no relief from the courts. That was the state's legal mantra and, for a long time, it had proved to be crushingly effective.

The Cheadle team then met with an amazing piece of luck. Orr's direct superior was Dr Ivan Lang. Lang was the assistant district surgeon for the area of Port Elizabeth. He had built up an 'impressive' record as a doctor who appeared to act more as a front for the security police than as a medical practitioner primarily concerned with the welfare of his patients and who rigorously adhered to the ethical responsibility of the medical profession. In September 1977, Lang had examined Steve Bantu Biko on a number of occasions. He had disregarded the savage beatings and the serious injuries sustained by Biko. Even though there were medical tests showing blood in the cerebrospinal fluid, Lang issued a certificate in which he stated: 'I found no evidence of any abnormality or pathology on the patient'.

Dr Lang's grossly unethical behaviour notwithstanding, the South African Medical and Dental Council exonerated him of unprofessional conduct, even in the face of massive protests from the medical faculties of the Universities of Cape Town and Witwatersrand. The pressure brought by some of these principled doctors finally bore fruit. In January 1984, the Supreme Court ordered the Medical and Dental Council to re-open its enquiry into the conduct of the doctors who had examined Biko before his death. In July 1985, the court found Dr Lang's superior, Benjamin Tucker, who had authorised the police to transport Biko 470 kilometres in the back of a Land Rover, when he was suffering from serious injury, guilty of improper and disgraceful conduct and suspended him for three months. The council's appalling inability to grasp the sheer magnitude of Dr Tucker's culpability meant that it suspended the three months' penalty for two years, knowing full well that Tucker was about to retire.

The pressure brought by some of these principled doctors finally bore fruit

Lang was found guilty of 'improper conduct' and was given a caution and a reprimand. But he was not about to take any further chances concerning his lack of medical oversight over the same police brutality as that which had caused the death of Steve Biko. To cover himself, Lang now wanted every medical history card of each detainee to be copied. He instructed Orr accordingly. This afforded her an unexpected opportunity to copy almost 300 medical cards twice, one for Lang and another for her attorney, Cheadle.

The forensic advantage of this piece of luck is illustrated in Orr's affidavit to which she deposed in support of the application that was to be brought before the court. The applicants sought an order preventing the police from assaulting or otherwise mishandling detainees. The dry legalese employed in her affidavit to justify the order sought proved more damning than any emotive condemnation of the police and prison authorities, together with Dr Lang and the medical authorities responsible for the health and welfare of detainees. The affidavit was truly a case of facts speaking for themselves.

In her affidavit, she said the following of the responsible medical authority:

> On 5 September 1985 I was present when Dr Lang phoned his superior Dr Krynauw. He is the regional director of the department of National Health in the Eastern Cape. Dr Lang informed Dr Krynauw that there were many detainees at St Albans who complained of police assault and asked him what he should do in this regard. After he had spoken to Dr Krynauw Dr Lang told me that Dr Krynauw had said that all we should do was to make copies of all yellow cards of the detainees who had complained of assault and to keep copies in case any of the detainees should institute civil action against the department of health. It seemed that Dr Krynauw was not at all concerned with the wellbeing of the detainees and that his only concern was to protect the department of health in the case of trouble.

Cheadle's team had the material to substantiate the allegations that were to be made by Orr. The photocopying and preparation of the affidavits of the various applicants, being a number of ex-detainees and, particularly that of Orr, proved to be a hazardous task. But with this independent evidence, the state would encounter great difficulty in contesting these allegations, although as we shall shortly see the photocopies were not about to be put to immediate use.

By now, the security police may well have been aware of Cheadle's presence. But only one incident caused alarm. A number of lawyers, as well as secretarial support, had assembled to work on the application. Port Elizabeth is a small town and it is not easy to blend anonymously into the surroundings, hence the anxiety of the legal team. One night, as they were having dinner at their hotel one of the members of the team returned to her hotel room to find papers and other possessions strewn over the floor of the hotel room. There was real anxiety that the security police had finally obtained some evidence of the impending application. Much to the relief of the team, they discovered that all the security police had taken were papers pertaining to the labour law litigation that had brought Cheadle to Port Elizabeth in the first place.

After this scare, the police did not appear until the night before the case was to be heard in court. Wim Trengove SC recalls, however, that a police Casspir had been parked outside the hotel occupied by the legal team on that night. No attempt was made by the occupants of the Casspir to enter the hotel.

Cheadle had the great foresight to brief Trengove. Today, Trengove is widely regarded as South Africa's finest barrister. In the mid 1980s, he had begun to build his formidable reputation. It was during this turbulent political period that Cheadle had first heard of Trengove and briefed him in the Kannemeyer Commission dealing with the massacre of members of the community in the Port Elizabeth/Uitenhage area. At this hearing, Trengove had also met Orr. It was during this inquiry that Cheadle and others like Haysom saw the forensic skill of Trengove. Trengove proved to be a devastating cross-examiner of the police witnesses. Haysom who, together with Cheadle, was part of the legal team in the Kannemeyer Commission and who later became President Nelson Mandela's legal counsel, loves to tell the story of Trengove in action at the Kannemeyer Commission. A police officer had testified at some length, articulating the usual denial of any police illegality. At about 12:40, the examination by the police lawyers ended. Judge Kannemeyer asked Trengove whether it would now be appropriate to take the luncheon adjournment. Trengove insisted that the Commission continue until 1 o'clock and that he be given the opportunity to begin his cross-examination. Within 20 minutes, Trengove, in his staccato questioning, had reduced the police officer to a lying wreck. As Haysom came out of the court, he overheard a police brigadier phoning headquarters to report on the morning's developments, saying: 'Ons is nou in groot kak.'

With the affidavits prepared, the lawyers could confidently launch an application to the Supreme Court. An application is made by way of a notice of motion accompanied by supporting affidavits and documentary evidence. A notice of motion sets out the relief the applicants seek in a case of this kind. In this case, an interim interdict was sought in which the police were to be restrained from assaulting or threatening to assault a number of people who were listed in the documentation, as well as any other person who was detained in terms of the emergency regulations and any person who in future would be detained in terms of the emergency regulations in the magisterial districts of Port Elizabeth and Uitenhage.

Thanks to the great legal skill and insight of the legal team into the process of launching these kinds of applications before a court, Orr's initial affidavit was not accompanied by any of the medical evidence in their possession. There was no need to risk an investigation into the manner in which copies of medical records had been acquired by the legal team. The affidavit simply documented her experience as a district surgeon in the Port Elizabeth area. It made no mention of the supporting medical records and files that were now in the possession of the legal team.

However, all Orr's allegations were sourced in the files that she had copied. While Cheadle was understandably reluctant to employ this evidence for fear of exposing Orr to the very treatment that was the subject of the application, her affidavit itself told an astonishing and detailed story of police brutality and incorporated material from the medical records.

In some 50 pages, she described the experiences of a range of detainees who suffered at the hands of their police interrogators. The following passages provide a flavour of the contents of her affidavit:

> A recent and rather bizarre case that comes to mind is that of Sicelo Gqobona whom I examined at St Albans prison on 18 September 1985. He was brought to the front of the queue of the sick parade that day because I

was told the police were in a hurry to take him to the Louis Le Grange police station for interrogation that day. He complained of an upset stomach. He said that his stomach was upset because he had drunk petrol a week before. When I checked his record, I noticed that he had been in detention at the time. I asked him why he had drunk petrol and where he had obtained it seeing that he was in detention at the time. He said that he was being interrogated by the security police at the Louis Le Grange police station. In the course of his interrogation I believe it was on Thursday 12 September 1985, they had forced him to drink petrol. He also said that they assaulted him, striking him in the face, and had trodden on his chest when he lay on the floor. By the time I examined him his lips were very swollen and he had small lacerations on the inside of his mouth.

Each case described in the affidavit took the reader a step closer to the heart of police brutality. Of another case, Orr writes:

> Of those detainees that I examined on 16 August 1985, one case particularly comes to mind. He was a young man whose name I was subsequently able to trace in the drug register as Mbulelo Joseph Sogoti. He had weals from his shoulders to his buttocks. There were so many weals that I could not count them. They were superimposed upon each other. His wounds were fresh and he was in great pain. He was brought in to me in a wheelchair. He could not speak but his friends who brought him told me that he had been assaulted by the police. I prescribed bed rest and an intra-muscular injection of Pethilorfan (a very potent pain killer) and anti-inflammatory drugs. Whenever it is prescribed, it has to be recorded in a drug register kept at the hospital. It was by that entry that I was able to trace this man's name.
>
> This case had a rather disturbing sequel. When I first examined the detainees, I specified that I required to see him again to review his case a few days later. He was, however, never brought to me again. I recently searched for a yellow card but found that it was missing. I then checked the prison register to see if I could find out what had happened to him. According to the prison register, he had not yet been discharged from prison. I asked to see him, but when his name was repeatedly called out there was no answer.

Later in her affidavit, Orr makes mention of the yellow medical cards that she had extracted and copied:

> [They] relate to the period from 22 July to 16 September 1985. There are 286 of them. As I explained above they are obviously incomplete and there must have been more complaints than those. But even taking it at 286 the number of complaints is astronomical compared with the frequency of complaints of assault ordinarily received in prison. For instance, a few days ago I gathered approximately 200 newly admitted ordinary prisoners (prisoners not being held under the emergency regulations). Of those prisoners only one had a complaint of assault. That proportion is typical of my experience in prison.

When the police read this affidavit, they would not have known that each allegation was supported by documentation, particularly medical cards which had been copied by Orr.

As already discussed, the evidence placed before the Court in this kind of case takes the form of an affidavit deposed to by the applicant, Wendy Orr, together with other supporting affidavits. The respondents, being the police, then had an opportunity to answer all the allegations by way of their own affidavit called the answering affidavit. The purpose of the answering affidavit is to ensure that the police can rebut the key allegations made by the applicant so that the Court is faced with such contested evidence that it cannot justify granting any legal relief sought by the applicant. A person mandated to depose to the answering affidavit on behalf of the police was thus required to state why the key allegations of the applicant had no basis either in fact or, arguably, in law.

Brigadier Schnetler, who deposed to the answering affidavit on behalf of the South African Police Services, might have thought that, without any objective evidence, Orr's allegations, together with confirmatory affidavits of detainees, would be dismissed by the Court as nothing more than bold, unsubstantiated allegations. The line taken by Schnetler was to argue that the version of conditions of detention contained in the affidavits deposed to by Orr and other applicants was based on hearsay, that is, not upon direct evidence or could not be substantiated by any documentary evidence. But the details of the individual cases set out in the Orr affidavit forced Schnetler to refer to the very medical records that he alleged would debunk Orr's claims of torture, but which, unbeknown to him, were already in the possession of Orr's lawyers.

This afforded Cheadle the opportunity of exploiting a rule of court procedure by which a party can demand copies of documents referred to by the opposition in their answering affidavit. In short, this rule of court means that, when Brigadier Schnetler referred to medical records he alleged would illustrate that Wendy Orr was not telling the truth, the applicants could then request copies of all these medical records so as to test the truth of the denial of the applicant's case.

After reading Orr's affidavit, together with that of Brigadier Schnetler, the Court was obliged to decide whether the rights of the various detainees, on all the evidence, were in jeopardy and, therefore, whether there was justification for an order preventing the police from the commission of assault or torture. Orr's evidence was obviously sufficient to persuade a court that there was a factual basis for the allegations made. The Court then granted what is referred to as an interim order, that is, an order preventing the police from acting illegally, pending a further date, at which hearing the Court would determine, on the evidence, whether a permanent order against the police should be granted.

In the meanwhile, Orr and those detainees who were joint applicants could obtain a court order permitting them to obtain copies of all the medical records to which Schnetler had made reference in his affidavit. Now they could copy all the records with the protection of the Court, as the Court had ordered that the applicant had a legal right to examine and copy any of the medical records referred to by Schnetler in his affidavit. Schnetler's defence was about to implode, for the Court could now be presented with documented proof to substantiate each and every allegation made by Orr in her initial affidavit. But we are running ahead of the chronology. We must return to the first application made to the Court.

In this case, the detainees' case was supported by a detailed affidavit from a district surgeon, whereas the police case consisted of a set of bland and bare denials made by Brigadier Schnetler. Small wonder that when the parties went before Judge Eksteen on 25 September 1985 there was no basis on which Mr Liebenberg, acting on behalf of the state, could oppose the relief being sought by the applicants.

The relief as formulated, of course, had to be drafted into a court order. Trengove understood well the potential of the legal system. He embarked upon an imaginative formulation of the draft order by inserting a paragraph into it to be presented to the Court, which draft Judge Eksteen duly granted. It provided that the officers in command of the St Albans and North End prisons in Port Elizabeth were instructed to read out the order to all detainees held at both prisons.

The officers in command of the two prisons duly complied with the order. They summoned all the prisoners and detainees into a central area so that the order could be read out aloud. To their amazement, detainees who had been effectively shut off from the outside world heard prison officers read out a court order which restrained any form of assault upon them for any reason. They cheered as the order was read out. Slowly, a change both in mood and in the power relationships occurred as the fairly lengthy order was read out to acclamation from the detainees and the consternation of the prison warders.

There was widespread press reaction to the court proceedings. The *Eastern Province Herald* of 26 September 1985 led with the story: 'Doctor claims "daily abuse of detainees"'. The *Cape Times* editorial of 26 September 1985 captured the mood:

> The police can no longer brush off allegations about their treatment of detainees. Evidence is mounting that detainees are being systematically assaulted or tortured. The University of Cape Town's Institute of Criminology found last month that 83 per cent of 176 former detainees had been assaulted and that physical torture of detainees was widespread. Without referring specifically to assault allegations, police denied that torture was used to obtain information from detainees. There have been numerous court cases recently in which detainees have alleged assault and brutality.

An article on this page today states the concerns of the relatives of those detained. Their views will only have been strengthened by the Supreme Court order granted in Port Elizabeth yesterday which restrained police from assaulting detainees in the Port Elizabeth and Uitenhage areas. An affidavit from a district surgeon backed by detailed allegations stated that detainees were systematically assaulted after arrest or during interrogation. The district surgeon stated that police were quite unrestrained and that the Departments of Prisons and Health seemed to have turned a blind eye to the situation.

These allegations are horrifying. They warrant the suspension of senior police officers in the Port Elizabeth area. Together with similar allegations from other parts of the country they warrant a judicial inquiry into the maltreatment of detainees. If the allegations are found to have substance, the Minister of Law and Order Mr Louis le Grange should resign at last.

The whole shoddy system of detention without trial which paves the way for such abuses should be scrapped. The present system on available evidence results in the physical injury and sometimes the deaths of people who are in the care of the State. It does incalculable harm to the image of the police and to the prospects of a negotiated peaceful settlement in this country. It is a system South Africa should never have adopted and which it cannot afford to retain.

The order granted by Judge Eksteen was, of course, of a temporary nature. It allowed the police to file further papers and to approach the Court in opposition to any final relief which might have been sought by applicants. Indeed, on 4 February 1986, the parties were back in front of Judge Jones. In preparation for the hearing before Judge Jones, Wim Trengove drafted heads of argument in which he noted: 'It is alarming that those assaults seem to have continued even after the interim order of the 25 September 1985.'

The police continued with their practice of systemic torture

Notwithstanding the interim order and the widespread publicity, the police continued with their practice of systemic torture.

By now, Cheadle and his team had gained access to the medical history cards, prison registers and various other documents housed in the prisons. Within a week, they had photocopied some 7 000 documents which would be annexed to a 68-page affidavit deposed to by Dr Orr. The police may not have complied with the interim order of 25 September 1985 but the further legal action now exposed, in more detail, the forms of conduct that had become almost standard practice among the police towards detainees.

Judge Jones was faced with a massive amount of evidence on paper. In this kind of case, a judge may have little option but to make an order that the disputes should be referred to oral evidence. This allows those witnesses who have deposed to contradictory affidavits to be cross-examined on their version of events. Judge Jones made such an order. This would have meant that various parties would be required to testify before the Court about the conditions under which they suffered at the hands of the police and to be cross-examined accordingly. The police witnesses would then be subjected to the withering cross-examination of Wim Trengove, never a pleasant prospect, particularly for police who, as the record of evidence revealed, had lied continuously throughout this litigation.

The interim order restraining the police from any misconduct was extended to 17 June 1986. By now, the State President had lifted the state of emergency, thus ending the emergency detentions. The applicants, therefore, withdrew their case but, in September 1986, Louis le Grange, the Minister of Law and Order, agreed to pay costs calculated at R22 262 000 without admitting any of the allegations. A year later, the police made a payment of R1.2 million to the victims of police violence and their families. Trengove recalls the joy of his clients at beating the oppressors. Even a local prostitute received R12 000 for police buckshot which hit her buttocks!

Conclusion

> I am pleased that the ex-detainees have received some form of compensa-
> tion for all they went through. However, I feel it would have been better
> had the case gone to court.
>
> None of the police involved has been disciplined ... I feel angry that
> there are still doctors such as Ivor Lang who have not been disciplined and
> are still a party to the whole system.   *Wendy Orr*[19]

The *Wendy Orr* case did not stop detentions or torture. A second state of emergency was declared on 12 June 1986. By the end of that year, about 25 000 people had been detained. During this period, a further 15 court applications were launched by 75 detainees regarding allegations of assault and torture. In 1987, a study by the National Medical and Dental Association (NAMDA) revealed that some 89 per cent of a sample of 131 detainees claimed to have been beaten with fists, hands, sjamboks, batons and other blunt instruments.[20]

In June 1987, NAMDA called for an urgent investigation into allegations made by detainees at East London's Fort Glamorgan Prison that there was a marked lack of medical treatment. Similar action was initiated by detainees at Diepkloof Prison, Johannesburg.[21]

The pattern of detention, torture and lack of integrity by the vast majority of district surgeons who 'administered' to detainees continued throughout the 1980s. The courts, save in a few notable cases, failed detainees miserably. The Appellate Division, during this period, supported the war against law by curbing any power of judicial review by which the police could have been held accountable.[22]

Viewed in this depressing light, the question arises as to the gains, if any, that flowed from the immensely courageous action of Wendy Orr and the imaginative litigation strategy that ensured the legal success of the applications she brought to court.

The *Wendy Orr* application illustrates the complexity of litigation of this nature. As Rick Abel observed in his careful study of the *Wendy Orr* case: 'The application reveals the enormous disparity in the power of South African voices. Black victims . . . have loudly denounced police violence for decades. They have little access to media or courts, however, and less credibility with white audiences.'[23]

It took a determined and courageous district surgeon, who was white, to make the courts listen to the cries of detainees who were overwhelmingly black. But once her voice had been given judicial approval, albeit in the form of limited legal relief against the police, the practice of police brutality could no longer be denied. It was all very well attacking the police on the basis of academic research produced by the UCT Institute of Criminology, studies which could be attributed to 'left-wing academics'. But, once a court considered these allegations so serious that a court order against the police was granted, a denial of the practice became far more problematic. The system had been exposed in a court and that was markedly more effective than academic research or reports in opposition newspapers.

It took a determined and courageous district surgeon, who was white, to make the courts listen to the cries of detainees who were overwhelmingly black

The manner in which the court orders were read to detainees shifted the power balance between captor and detainee. It emboldened others to use the courts to expose police brutality. Ultimately, the practice of detention continued for several more regrettable years. But the exposure of torture in the courts gave the evidence a new-found legitimacy. Significantly, the motley crew of pseudo-scientists, politicians masquerading as academics and white supremacists, for whom any means to protect white rule was justified, who had incessantly attacked the UCT report, fell silent as soon as the *Wendy Orr* case hit the press. Thereafter, no one had an excuse to use the defence 'we did not know what was done in our name'.

We can now return to F W de Klerk's submission to the TRC in May 1997. In keeping with the National Party's overall argument before the TRC, De Klerk contended that the torture of some 20 000 people over a 30-year period was nothing more than the work of aberrant police officers. There can be no doubt that many of the most notorious security police officers involved in the administration of the system were cruel psychopaths. To be sure, had Mother Teresa policed the system, torture and physical brutality may not have taken place. Those who worked as security policemen were unlikely to be blessed with truly generous dispositions, even if many completed their week of torturing detainees by attending church services on Sunday mornings. But the fault did not lie with a few psychopaths. The pattern of torture revealed a systemic practice over a 30-year period. It was known to anyone prepared to read the accounts of detainees, whether in newspapers or in academic research. It was obvious to anybody who took the trouble to examine the affidavit of Wendy Orr or the press reportage of the case. But the practice continued long after 1986.

The 'system' was the cause of the brutality. The 'system' was implemented and administered by the National Party. It is an insult to all of those who were brutalised by 30 years of detention without trial, in the manner described so compellingly by Mac Maharaj, to suggest that the sole cause of their suffering was a few aberrant psychopaths like 'Rooi Rus' Swanepoel.

Endnotes

1   Submission to the Truth and Reconciliation Commission (TRC) by F W de Klerk (14 May 1997).
2   Mac Maharaj describing his experience in detention while tortured by 'Rooi Rus' Swanepoel in Padraig O'Malley *Shades of Difference* (2007) 124.
3   *Truth and Reconciliation Commission Report* vol 4 p 201 paras 12-14.
4   *Ibid* para 14.
5   Resolutions 417 and 418 of October and November 1977.
6   'The Permanence of the Temporary' 1966 (83) *South African Law Journal* 16, 23.
7   *Rossouw v Sachs* 1964 (2) SA 551 (A) at 564.
8   Section 6 of the Terrorism Act 83 of 1967. The 90-day detention clause was suspended on 30 November 1964, only to be replaced in 1965 by a more widely drawn provision which authorised detention for 180 days. That, in turn, was replaced by the indefinite clause and s 6 of the Terrorism Act.
9   A S Mathews *Law, Order and Liberty in South Africa* (1971) 176.
10 Breyten Breytenbach *True Confessions of an Albino Terrorist* (1984) 19.
11 *Ibid* vol 6 section 5 chapter 2 p 618.
12 *Ibid* vol 6 section 5 chapter 2 p 621.
13 *Die Burger* (29 October 1985, 7 November 1985 and 11 November 1985).
14 *Die Burger* (8 November 1985).
15 *Cape Times* (24 September 1986).
16 *Cape Times* (8 November 1985).
17 *A Survey of South African Race Relations* (1985) 440-441.
18 *Eastern Province Herald* (7 June 1990).
19 *Survey of Race Relations* (1986) 830.
20 S Browde *The Treatment of Detainees* (Paper delivered at NAMDA national conference 4 April 1987)
21 M Rayner *Turning a Blind Eye: Medical Accountability and the Prevention of Torture in South Africa* (1987).
22 Nicholas Haysom and Clive Plaskett 'The War against Law: Judicial Activism and the Appellate Division' 1988 (4) *SAJHR* 303 .
23 Richard Abel *Politics by Other Means: Law in the Struggle against Apartheid 1980-1994* (1995) 257.

six

A bridge over our troubled waters?

(with apologies to Simon and Garfunkel)

The transition from apartheid to a constitutional democracy occurred, in part, through the use of law. It was also built in incremental stages, like individual bricks being laid, rather than as one major concrete span being manoeuvred into place.

This chapter looks at two aspects of this transition. The first is the legal transition from an era characterised by oppressive legislation to one framed in terms of a democratic rights-based Constitution, which took place through the mechanism of the interim Constitution. The transitional arrangements set out in the interim Constitution ensured that government would continue during the period leading up to the election of the first democratic government and that institutional integration would occur at all levels of government. Essentially, the transitional scheme foreshadowed the structures of the future South Africa. Most notable for our purposes was the creation of the Constitutional Court, an institution that was critical to transporting the society into an era of constitutional democracy.

The second aspect of the transition is the attacks that the transitional mechanisms, particularly the Constitutional Court and the Truth and Reconciliation Commission (TRC), suffered from both the left and the right wings. The left tested them with difficult cases, such as that brought by family members of anti-apartheid activists, including the family of Steve Bantu Biko, who challenged the TRC process, seeking their proverbial 'day in court'. That case highlighted the difficulty of efforts to reconcile the understandable urge for punishment and retribution with the necessary political reconciliation. A right-wing attack came in the form of the challenge to President Mandela's executive authority brought by the erstwhile doyen of South African rugby, Dr Louis Luyt.

The process towards democracy

The political transition to constitutional democracy[1] took place in highly managed stages. Often accompanied by fraught political moments and, unfortunately, occasionally spilling over into violence, the transition was also prominently marked by the use of law. Politics alone was insufficient; law was needed to accomplish the shift in political power and government.

The transition really began mid-year in 1989 when ANC leader Nelson Mandela met the then State President P W Botha in Victor Verster prison, near Paarl in the Cape. Mandela acknowledged that it was 'in the national interest' for the ANC and the government to meet urgently to negotiate for the country's political future.

Mandela acknowledged that it was 'in the national interest' for the ANC and the government to meet urgently

A month later, the ANC's lobbying efforts successfully ensured that the Organisation of African Unity and the United Nations adopted the Harare Declaration, setting out the basis for a transition to democracy and demanding that a representative and elected body draft South Africa's Constitution.

In September 1989, P W Botha was replaced as head of state by F W de Klerk. At the same time, civil society organised a defiance campaign through a new umbrella body, the Mass Democratic Movement (MDM), which grew out of the anti-apartheid organisation, the United Democratic Front, which had been formed in 1983. A month later, several ANC leaders were freed and, on 8 December, the Conference for a Democratic Future took place at which approximately 6 000 representatives of the MDM passed a resolution in favour of negotiation with the National Party government.

CODESA

Almost a year later, on 29 and 30 November 1990, the all-party preparatory meeting took place: 20 organisations and parties attended. The name of this forum was declared to be 'the Convention for a Democratic South Africa (CODESA)' and, critically important, it adopted the principle of 'sufficient consensus' as the decision-making mechanism during its proceedings to settle disagreements. Unfortunately, minutes before the end of the meeting, the Pan African Congress walked out—accusing the ANC of 'selling out'.

Notwithstanding, CODESA's first session on 20 and 21 December adopted a declaration of intent which all parties—except the IFP and the Bophuthatswana government—signed. The NP confirmed—for the first time—that it would accept an elected constituent assembly provided that that body also acted as an interim national government. In February 1992, the NP accepted the ANC's demand for an interim government and the principles that a new South Africa would seek to be non-racial, non-sexist and democratic. A CODESA working group produced an initial agreement on general constitutional principles against which the Constitution that was ultimately negotiated would be tested. This was an important step towards the role to be played by the Constitutional Court in certifying the final Constitution.

This agreement also settled the conflict between the ANC and the NP over how the political transition would be managed. While the ANC wanted the Constitution to be drafted and adopted *after* the first nationwide democratic election, the NP wanted it completed *before* the country's electorate went to the polls. In a masterstroke, agreement was reached that the parties would negotiate and adopt the principles against which the negotiated text would ultimately be evaluated. In this way, the constitutional principles constituted, in a sense, the first bridge over which the country travelled away from apartheid and towards a democratic constitutional state. Through this mechanism, the transition to a constitutional process was made possible.[2]

In March, the NP held an all-white referendum to test support for the negotiation process—and received overwhelming support for reform. In the same month, the ANC proposed a two-phase interim government: the first would consist of the formation of a Transitional Executive Council (TEC); the second would commence after the elections and consist of the interim government and constituent assembly. The TEC would be multiparty in form and function alongside the existing parliament. Sub-committees of the TEC, with executive powers, would be established for key areas of government.

The constitutional principles constituted, in a sense, the first bridge over which the country travelled away from apartheid and towards a democratic constitutional state

At the beginning of May, the parties headed for CODESA II, the second plenary session, where the ANC hoped to achieve agreement on the proposed two-phase interim government. CODESA met on 15 and 16 May, but stalled on the question of the size of a special majority—as opposed to a simple majority of 50 per cent plus 1 vote—required to adopt the final Constitution.

A massive setback occurred on 17 June, when more than 40 people were massacred during a march in Boipatong—a sign of the determined effort of reluctant and obstructionist groups to derail negotiations. Days later, ANC leaders met to discuss the massacre's implications: they reaffirmed a commitment to a negotiated settlement but broke off talks and accused the government of complicity in the attack. The ANC's tripartite alliance partners—the South African Communist Party and the Congress of South African Trade Unions—launched a mass-action campaign on 15 July. The ANC next sent a list of demands to De Klerk and, a few days later, the President responded by denying government involvement in the violence and refused to commit himself to majority rule. However, he also tried to reduce the political temperature by disbanding notorious battalions, banning dangerous weapons and agreeing to international monitoring.

Fishing for peace

At the beginning of September, the ANC chose its Secretary-General, Cyril Ramaphosa, to establish a channel of communication to replace bilateral meetings and to allow contact to continue. Ramaphosa and Roelf Meyer, his NP counterpart, promptly went trout fishing together.

The importance of this relationship to the ultimate success of the negotiations cannot be underestimated. In fact, it was even discussed in Canadian politics, as this quote from a speech during that country's parliamentary proceedings shows:

> I'd like to relate an anecdote that comes from Allister Sparks, who has written in the *New Yorker* about the silent revolution I spoke about earlier. He speaks of two young political men playing the same political position, but on opposite sides of the fence. The one on the white team was named Roelf Meyer, Deputy Minister of Constitutional Development. On the black team was Cyril Ramaphosa, Secretary General of the ANC and chief negotiator. Both men were invited by a mutual friend to do some fishing. Ramaphosa was an expert at fly fishing and offered to teach Meyer and his sons how to do it. Regrettably, as they were fly fishing, Meyer got a hook deeply imbedded in one of his fingers. The group returned home, where Ramaphosa's wife, who was a nurse, tried to remove the hook, without success. Finally Cyril intervened, seeing that Meyer was in some significant pain. 'Roelf,' he said, 'there is only one way to do this.' He poured him a glass of whisky and fetched a pair of pliers. He then took a firm grip on the hook and said: 'I've always wanted to hurt you Nats, but never as much as this.' And at that, Ramaphosa yanked the hook out. Meyer, relieved, looked up and muttered: 'Cyril, don't say I didn't trust you'.
>
> Although the post-election period will be difficult, and many changes to come pose even greater challenges for South Africa, the centripetal forces that have brought South Africa this far appear stronger than those that would cause it to fly apart. The inescapable mutual dependency of black and white South Africans is what holds them together. It is the lesson of the fish hook. May we all learn such a lesson. Nkosi sikelele Afrika. God bless Africa.[3]

Demonstrating the tenuous and volatile nature of the political climate at the time, on 7 September, soldiers in Bisho, Ciskei, opened fire on people who, as part of the mass-action campaign, were protesting against the homeland government. Many died but this tragedy did cause the return of both sides to the negotiating table.

On 26 September, the two parties agreed on a record of understanding, addressing details of the transition such as the make-up of a constitutional assembly, an interim government, political prisoners, hostels, dangerous weapons and mass action.

In the following months, the parties undertook bilateral negotiations and prepared for a planning conference to be held in March. On 4 and 5 March, the planning conference on negotiations was held at the World Trade Centre in Kempton Park, near Johannesburg. In the cavernous hall, far more suitable as a site for new model motor car launches but now reconfigured with dry-wall partitioning into offices and a negotiation chamber, delegates and advisors from

26 parties and organisations gathered initially to pass a resolution for the resumption of negotiations.

On 1 April, the Multiparty Negotiating Forum (MPNF) of 26 participants—including the PAC, the Conservative Party and the Afrikaner Volksunie—met, and successfully defined the issues to be dealt with at the multiparty negotiations.

Strains at the seams

Crisis loomed yet again on 10 April when Chris Hani, the SACP leader, was assassinated by right-wingers, Polish immigrant Janusz Walus and former Conservative Party MP, Clive Derby-Lewis. This tragedy prompted the ANC to call for negotiations to be speeded up.

In June, 27 April 1994 was chosen as the date for South Africa's first non-racial elections. The technical committee on constitutional matters was instructed to produce a transitional Constitution that set out the process and mechanics for the drafting and adoption of a final, democratic Constitution by an elected assembly.

On 25 June, Eugene Terre'Blanche and members of his Afrikaner Weerstandsbeweging stormed the World Trade Centre

Then on 25 June, Eugene Terre'Blanche and members of his Afrikaner Weerstandsbeweging stormed the World Trade Centre. The ill-fated 'invasion' demonstrated the right wing's resistance to the negotiations—and of the still-present threat of insurrection and civil war.

Tensions were also obvious from the IFP, which had proposed a federal Constitution which was rejected at the negotiations. Eventually, after months of preparation, a summit between Nelson Mandela and the Inkatha Freedom Party's (IFP) Mangosuthu Buthelezi took place to ease the IFP's concerns.

Three months later, the ANC and the NP reached agreement on a government of national unity, a provision for two Deputy Presidents, the required percentage to elect a Deputy President and the right to appoint cabinet posts. The NP abandoned its claim to a veto over the decisions of the cabinet.

On 16 November 1993, in a last-minute bilateral meeting between Nelson Mandela and F W de Klerk, agreement was reached on the final issues required to complete the interim Constitution—a deal known as the 'six-pack' agreement. The MPNF ratified the interim Constitution in the early hours of the morning of 18 November.

In the meantime, however, violence between IFP and ANC supporters on the East Rand escalated to the point of civil war. In March, Nelson Mandela and Mangosuthu Buthelezi agreed to international mediation over the status of KwaZulu but the agreement fell apart before mediation could even begin. Bomb blasts in central Johannesburg and, on March 28, the death of eight IFP marchers outside Shell House, the ANC's headquarters in the city, further increased the temperature in the political pressure cooker.

In the same month, Ciskei and Bophuthatswana collapsed under the pressure of internal discontent. Terre'Blanche's AWB rushed to the defence of Bophuthatswana's leader, Lucas Mangope—but his commandos were massacred. This folly was captured on television news in an almost cathartic moment: black soldiers executing white racist terrorists. The right-wing myth of racial superiority was exploded on the television screens of the nation. The dangers of insurrection prompted General Constand Viljoen to establish the Freedom Front (on the promise of consideration of a white homeland) and join the list of candidates on the ballot in the upcoming elections.

The right-wing myth of racial superiority was exploded on the television screens of the nation

Just days before the elections, agreement was reached through a Kenyan negotiator between all negotiating parties, including the IFP.

A landmark in history

South Africa's first non-racial election was contested on 27 April 1994. It produced 400 leaders in the National Assembly and 90 in the Senate. In terms of section 68(1) of the interim Constitution, a joint sitting of these bodies formed the Constitutional Assembly, established on 9 May. Nelson Mandela was inaugurated as democratic South Africa's first President on 10 May 1994.

The Constitutional Assembly worked within particular parameters towards the finalisation of a constitutional text. These constraints included the requirement of a two-thirds majority in favour for the adoption of the ultimate text, compliance with 34 constitutional principles agreed to in the interim Constitution and the adoption of a new Constitution within two years.

In June, the Constitutional Committee was established. This became the premier multiparty negotiating body in the Constitutional Assembly, led by Ramaphosa and Meyer.

By 22 April 1995, several sticking points remained: the death penalty, the lockout clause, the property clause, the appointment of judges and the attorney-general, language, local government, the question of proportional representation and the bar against members of parliament crossing the floor. But, on 8 May, the final text was adopted and, from 1 to 11 July, the Constitutional Court's certification hearing was held.

Smoothing out a wrinkled text

The certification process permitted any political parties represented in the Assembly to present arguments on whether or not the Constitution should be certified. This process—probably the largest hearing in South African legal history—involved at least 47 advocates representing 29 political parties, organisations and individuals. Among them were the ANC, the NP, the IFP, the Democratic Party, the Conservative Party and the African Christian Democratic Party. COSATU, Business South Africa, the SA Agricultural Union, the Human Rights Commission and the SA Institute of Race Relations were among the organisations that made submissions. The Court was required to test the text against the agreed 34 constitutional principles that had been negotiated early in the constitutional process and consider the arguments before it as to why it did, or did not, comply.

However, on 6 September, in the judgment *Ex parte Chairperson of the Constitutional Assembly: in re Certification of the Constitution of the Republic of South Africa 1996*, the Court unanimously rejected certain clauses and ruled that the text adopted in May 1996 could not be certified.

The draft of the Constitution failed in several respects to satisfy the conditions thrashed out in multiparty talks

The Court said the draft of the Constitution failed in several respects to satisfy the conditions thrashed out in multiparty talks. But it said the instances of non-compliance should present no significant obstacle to the formulation of a text that met these requirements. The Court pointed to the Constitution's failure to entrench agreed fundamental rights, its failure to protect the independence of watchdogs—including a Public Protector and an Auditor-General—and to the reduction of provincial autonomy.

The Constitutional Assembly had to reconsider the text, which it did, and accordingly passed a number of amendments in sufficient time that the Court would be able to certify the text that year.

On 7 October, the parties reached an agreement on all eight clauses that had been rejected by the Court. The Assembly approved, with only one vote against, an amended Constitution for submission to the Court on 11 October.

The amended version contained many changes: some dealt with the Court's reasons for rejection; others simply tightened up the text.

The Constitutional Court's second hearing began on 18 November. On 4 December, in *Certification of the Amended Text of the Constitution of The Republic of South Africa, 1996*, it granted its unanimous approval.

The judges found that the Constitutional Assembly had 'conscientiously' remedied the eight defective provisions. The Court also dismissed 16 objections from the DP, IFP and the province of KwaZulu-Natal, as well as the complaints of 18 people and interest groups.

The Court certified that the text complied with the constitutional principles and it duly became the Constitution of the Republic of South Africa. It was signed by Nelson Mandela, as President, in Sharpeville on 10 December 1996 and came into effect on 4 February 1997. And so, the chief design for the constitutional bridge was approved and adopted. Progress towards the society promised in the hard-fought text could now begin.

The Truth and Reconciliation Commission

Laudable though the creation of the Constitution was, there was much to be addressed that could not be settled in a legal document. The tragic and terrible abuses and brutal excesses of apartheid had to be confronted. After the adoption of the Constitution, the relatively bloodless political transition that followed was due, in large part, to the political decision to create a Truth and Reconciliation Commission (TRC). This would be the process through which South Africa would discover, explore, confront and acknowledge its awful past. The TRC and its aims were to become the second bridge the country needed to build.

The TRC and its aims were to become the second bridge the country needed to build

The Promotion of National Unity and Reconciliation Act 34 of 1995 provided for the creation of the TRC. The Commission would be appointed by the President in consultation with the Cabinet. The TRC was mandated to establish the complete picture of the gross violations of human rights committed between March 1960 (the time of the Sharpeville massacre) and 10 May 1994 by means of hearings and investigations that the Commission would undertake. It was also charged with facilitating the granting of amnesty, the recommendation of reparations to the victims of human rights abuses and the preparation of a report containing recommendations for measures to prevent any future violation of human rights.

The work of the TRC eventually included: '140 hearings across the country, with about 2 400 victims testifying and the names of some 27 000 recorded. The final tally was 21 519 victim statements containing evidence of 30 384 gross human rights violations. The commission made more than 15 000 findings before it passed the baton to the government to follow up on recommendations ranging from redress to retribution, in the form of further investigation and prosecution.'[4]

Critical to the entire process envisaged by the Act was the amnesty committee, staffed by three judges and two commissioners. It was empowered to consider applications for amnesty which it could grant if satisfied that the applicant had committed an act that constituted a gross violation of human rights, made full disclosure of all relevant and material facts and the act to which the application relates was 'an act associated with political objectives committed during the course of conflicts of the past'. In terms of section 20(7) of the Act, a person granted amnesty by the committee would not be criminally or civilly liable in respect of that act.

But the TRC process did not completely exclude the operation of the criminal justice system. Prosecutions of those who did not apply for amnesty, or who were refused it, would be possible. And, as we now know, several prosecutions did in fact take place. The most high-profile of these were the criminal prosecutions of apartheid apparatchik, Eugene de Kock ('Prime Evil') and former head of South Africa's chemical and biological warfare programme,

Dr Wouter Basson ('Dr Death'), and the plea bargain entered into by, among others, former Law and Order Minister, Adriaan Vlok, for the attempted murder of Rev Frank Chikane.

The different outcomes in the De Kock case (successful prosecution and conviction) and the Basson case (acquittal after a trial lasting 18 months) starkly outline the debate about which vehicle—a trial or the TRC hearings—ultimately revealed more of the details of the apartheid government's murderous methods. In essence, both processes search for the truth and strive to establish 'what happened'. The TRC linked this in its quasi-theological style, to forgiveness and cathartic confession, while, in general terms, retributive justice is the claimed goal of a trial. However, the TRC process has been criticised for producing a linear, 'just the bare facts' narrative that never grappled with or sought to explain the underlying pathologies and normative explanations for apartheid. As Christodoulidis put it: 'It failed to re-write collected memories as collective memory.'[5] Individual narratives were never fused into a collective account of a brutal past.

Posel and Simpson perceptively explain how this happened:

> The limits of the 'history' written by the TRC in turn inhibit its 'cathartic' and 'healing' qualities. With its powers of explanation stunted, the TRC cannot produce a consensus about *why* the terrible deeds of the past were committed. The increasingly familiar refrain among white South Africans that apartheid was merely a 'mistake' for which no one was responsible, that somehow the system propelled itself impersonally, may be one of the more ironic, unintended consequences of the TRC's rendition of the past.
>
> To the extent that the report does venture into historical explanation, its consequences may once again be deeply ironic. The report's only answer to the question of why the country was subjected to such a violent and abusive past is itself in need of explanation—the prevalence and intensity of racism. But in the absence of an explanation for racism itself, the report fails to suggest any plausible grounds for transcending the racism of the past. If racism was part of the warp and woof of South African society, how can it be undone? The fact that it is embedded in the social fabric is also a measure of its tenacity. If we do not understand the conditions under which racism was produced, reproduced and intensified in South Africa, taking account of its interconnections with other modes of power and inequality such as gender and class, how can we transcend it?[6]

In contrast, the trial records developed during the prosecutions of De Kock and Basson arguably offer more insight into the apartheid mindset. Taken together, of course, the TRC and parallel criminal proceedings have exposed our shameful past and made it increasingly difficult to claim the amnesia still so popular among white South Africans. The two trials require a brief examination.

De Kock

The 18 month-long criminal trial of De Kock, a 'marathon affair' in his words, starkly illustrates the implications of prosecuting apartheid's foot soldiers, or those who executed its plans, while a political solution was found to deal with the handover of power by their commanders. As he saw it, his trial was:

> ... two years of betrayal—first by the state that gave me my orders, and then by my friends who lined up to testify against me ....
>
> The state case ... turned out to be an attempt to find a scapegoat for the crimes of a repressive official apparatus whose tentacles reached right to the top—not only of the security forces, but also of the National Party government. I do not deny that I am guilty of the crimes, many of them horrible, of which I was accused. But I am not the only guilty one. The state chose to give indemnity from prosecution to many of my men simply so that a bulldozer of a case could be assembled against me—and in the process allow other men just as guilty as I to laugh in the face of justice.
>
> But we at Vlakplaas, and in the other covert units, are by no means the guiltiest of all. That dubious honour belongs to those who assembled us into the murderous forces that we became, *and which we were intended to be all along*. And most of them, the generals and the politicians, have got off scot-free.[7]

The De Kock trial commenced on 20 February 1995 and saw 87 witnesses testify for the state. The prosecutor was Deputy Attorney-General, Anton Ackermann, together with a special team of investigators. Judge Willem van der Merwe, later to become a national figure when he presided over the rape trial of Jacob Zuma, adjudicated, assisted by two assessors. The trial record eventually reached 12 000 typed pages. De Kock faced 121 charges, including murder, manslaughter and conspiracy to murder.[8] He was convicted on 89 of these, and sentenced to serve two life sentences, plus 212 years, all to run concurrently.

De Kock faced 121 charges, including murder, manslaughter and conspiracy to murder

As De Kock himself recognised, the trial was important for three reasons. First, it was 'the first time that South Africans were made aware of what we in the security forces had been ordered to do; anyone who paid attention to the proceedings quickly realized the culpability of the generals and the government'. Second, 'the way in which the state chose to prosecute and portray me—as a common criminal, not a political one—was significant'. And third, 'one has to recall that what is now common knowledge about me and C10 (De Kock's special police unit) was mere speculation before my trial. Many pieces of evidence, stories and events exploded, as they say, like bombshells.'[9]

With respect to the second of these, De Kock wrote that Ackermann had informed the Court that the trial was not a Nuremberg-type hearing. On the contrary, he told the Court, it was not political in nature but concerned criminality, and it would expose age-old sins: cold-blooded murder, theft, fraud and the perversion of justice.[10] One criticism of the trial was that it focused on 'purely individual criminal acts' rather than 'the question of structural and systemic crimes—the surrounding ideological/political philosophy, the setting up of Vlakplaas, and an administrative-executive system that directed De Kock ...'[11]

Belatedly, in March 1996, De Kock applied for amnesty to the TRC but was denied it. Out of 7 115 amnesty applications made to the TRC, 1 154 got the nod and a further 150 people were granted partial amnesty. But only 267 of these applicants were members of the South African security forces, and then, they were mostly police officers.[12]

The questions of guilt and remorse were not absent from De Kock's prosecution. Tellingly, De Kock's testimony in mitigation of sentence included the following statement: 'I cannot say how dirty one feels. Whatever we attempted in the interests of the country did not work. All we did was to injure people, to leave people with unforgivable pain, to leave behind children who will never know their parents. I sympathise with the victims as if they were my own children.'[13] Accepting this sentiment at face-value, and ignoring the self-serving circumstances in which it was made after his conviction, the trial leaves one with the uncomfortable but unavoidable conclusion that the TRC was neither the only, nor necessarily best-suited, vehicle to expose the truth about what was done in the name of apartheid, nor to achieve reconciliation.

'I cannot say how dirty one feels. Whatever we attempted in the interests of the country did not work'

Basson

Dr Wouter Basson, a cardiologist and the former head of South Africa's chemical and biological warfare (CBW) programme, named 'Dr Death' by the media, was prosecuted on 67 charges, including fraud, theft, drug possession and trafficking, as well as murder and conspiracy to murder. His prosecution was led by the same prosecutor, Anton Ackermann, who had headed De Kock's prosecution. Jaap Cilliers led the defence team. The trial began on 4 October 1999 and ended on 11 April 2002, following the testimony of 153 prosecution witnesses and a total of nearly 200 witnesses.

The trial record contains chilling testimony of assassinations through poisoning, painstaking research into lethal drug cocktails and the establishment of front companies through which millions of rands were channelled to fund, among other efforts, the notorious Project Coast. Basson was also linked to the infamous assassination attempts on the lives of Rev Frank Chikane and Dullah Omar. Despite the TRC's investigation into his activities and the CBW programme itself, and Basson appearing before the TRC hearings, Basson did not receive amnesty from that body but was criminally prosecuted.

However, this prosecution was a significant failure. It was severely hampered by the legal rulings and attitude to the case of presiding Judge Willie Hartzenberg. For starters, he refused to sit with assessors in the case. Usually, a judge can sit with two other people who act as a sounding board for his impressions and assist in reaching decisions. But here, Judge Hartzenberg, a highly competent and experienced judge, took the arguably surprising decision to sit alone, without assessors who, at the very least from the point of public perception, could have assisted and resulted in a more demographically representative court trying the case, where the charges went to the very heart of apartheid's darkness.

In the first blow to the case against Basson, Judge Hartzenberg dismissed the charges relating to conduct outside South Africa on jurisdictional grounds and found that Basson was covered by the 1989 Namibian amnesty that precluded prosecution of all security force members deployed to the South West Africa/Namibia bush war. This meant that Basson could not be prosecuted for six of the most serious charges against him. These included the murder of an estimated 200 SWAPO detainees injected with muscle relaxants before their bodies were thrown into the sea, a plan to murder administrator Peter Kalangula by smearing a toxic agent on the door handle of his car, and a plan to poison the water supply of SWAPO refugee camps located outside Windhoek with vibrio cholera.[14] Judge Hartzenberg also dismissed charges relating to the proposed murder of Ronnie Kasrils and Pallo Jordan while in exile in London, and the deaths of Gibson Mondlane in Mozambique and of Enoch 'Knox' Dlamini in Swaziland, in a rejection of the prosecution's argument that these plans were formed in South Africa.[15]

'There are several indications that the judge's attention might have wandered at times, or that he did not fully digest the significance of certain testimony'

The remaining charges were all ultimately dismissed. However, in his 1 453 page judgment, Judge Hartzenberg made several minor typographical and major factual errors revealing, in the view of his critics, a less than thorough, and not impartial, weighing and consideration of the voluminous evidence before him: 'Apart from a slew of incorrect names (both of companies involved in the fraud charges and individuals, including some witnesses) there are several indications that the judge's attention might have wandered at times, or that he did not fully digest the significance of certain testimony.'[16]

In fact, at one point during the trial, Judge Hartzenberg told an astonished courtroom that he was 'bored to death' with the presentation of evidence concerning financial dealings, fraud and theft. The acrimony between the Bench and the prosecution, who perceived bias in his approach to the trial, also escalated to unprecedented levels during the trial. This prompted a recusal application (which was rejected) and culminated in the unusual step of prosecutor Ackermann placing on the record the 'untoward malice and hostility' displayed by the judge during exchanges with counsel in chambers.[17]

In the end, Judge Hartzenberg's 'findings reinforced the perception—created by such failed legal exercises as the 1990 Harms Commission of Inquiry and the 1996 KwaMakhutha trial—that the top echelons of the former SADF appeared somehow to be above the law.[18] Coupled with the fact that the vast majority of CCB agents have still not been publicly named, that they have not been required to disclose details of their covert cross-border activities—or even all their operations inside South Africa—and that Project Coast's deepest and darkest secrets will almost never be revealed, Judge Willie Hartzenberg's findings have, unfortunately, done far more to shield than shame those who can never answer truthfully when asked, as inevitably they will be, "So what did you do in the war, Daddy?"[19]

At the inevitable international press conference that followed his acquittal, Basson began his personal public rehabilitation, coupled with a return to private practice in Pretoria. He argued that the millions spent on his prosecution could have been used to buy medicines that could save the lives of HIV-positive mothers and babies. Burger & Gould offer the following assessment: 'In the most public of all forums, with the eyes of the world's media on him, the man who was only too willing to exchange his surgical scrubs and scalpel for the cloak and dagger of apartheid's CBW spy, donned the mantle of human rights activist, appealing to the authorities in "our hard-gained democracy" to reconsider priorities, use available funds effectively for the "betterment" of the population, and decide what South Africans needed most: medicine or retribution.'[20]

'Project Coast's deepest and darkest secrets will almost never be revealed'

These cases certainly focused attention on the system's ability to deal with the past. The public disclosures that emerged from these trials brought South Africa closer to the truth of the systemic and calculated cruelty of the unparalleled system than had the seven TRC volumes.

Perhaps presciently and certainly understandably, the TRC mechanism did not meet with universal acclaim. This important bridge was attacked from the outset by litigants possessed of much moral authority who launched a gut-wrenching case.

The attack from the 'left'

In the case known in the law reports as that of the *Azanian Peoples Organisation (AZAPO) v The President of the Republic of South Africa*[21], the families of key anti-apartheid activists who were murdered by the apartheid regime, namely Steve Biko, Griffiths and Victoria Mxenge, and Dr and Mrs Fabian Ribeiro, together with AZAPO, brought an application to set aside section 20(7) of the Act that established the TRC, which precluded prosecution in favour of amnesty. The applicants argued that the state was obliged under international law to prosecute those responsible for gross human rights violations. As a result, section 20(7) constituted a breach of international law, both customary international law (the collective body of historic practices between states) and international treaties law. In this case, the Genocide Convention of 1948, the International Convention on the Suppression and Punishment of the Crime of Apartheid of 1973 and the Convention against Torture and Other Cruel

Inhuman or Degrading Treatment or Punishment of 1984 were all relevant instruments of international law on which the application relied.

The applicants also argued that section 22 of the interim Constitution supported their case. That section provided that every person had the right to have justiciable disputes heard by a court of law or, where appropriate, another independent impartial forum and that they had been denied that right. By operation of the Act, they could no longer approach a court seeking, for example, civil remedies such as damages or compensation arising out of the murder of their husbands, fathers, wives, daughters and sons.

The government's lawyers countered these legal submissions by arguing that the Act followed directly on the post-amble of the interim Constitution which provided as follows:

> This Constitution provides a historic bridge between the past of a deeply divided society characterized by strife, conflict, and untold suffering and injustice, and a future with the recognition of human rights, democracy and peaceful coexistence and development opportunities for all South Africans, irrespective of colour, race, class, belief or sex.
>
> In order to advance such reconciliation and reconstruction, amnesty shall be granted in respect of acts, omissions and offences associated with political objectives and committed in the course of the conflicts of the past. To this end, Parliament under this Constitution shall adopt a law determining a firm cut off date (which shall be a date after 8 October 1990 and before 6 December 1993) and providing for mechanisms, criteria and procedures, including tribunals, if any, through which such amnesty shall be dealt with at any time after the law has been passed.

The government's argument maintained that the Constitution itself envisaged a process of amnesty and that the Act had merely implemented this constitutional mandate. The Court was clearly confronted with a major moral dilemma. All the judges knew, or should have known, of the heroic sacrifices at issue. Many had personal acquaintances with the victims. To look these heroes' families in the eye and refuse the right to pursue a remedy against those who had murdered their loved ones in so callous and cynical fashion represented a judicial task designed to elicit considerable angst. This is evident from the majority judgment of Judge Mahomed, in which he wrote: 'Every decent human being must feel great discomfort in living with the consequences which might allow the perpetrators of evil acts to walk the streets of this land with impunity, protected in a freedom by an amnesty from constitutional attack but the circumstances in support of this case require carefully to be appreciated.'[22]

Our own interviews with those involved in the hearing confirm that the judges struggled with the dilemma posed by the case. Judge John Didcott, the judge with the most consistent human rights record of any member of the judiciary who had sat during the apartheid era, was even more than his usual pugnacious, probing self on the Bench. He tore into counsel for the government as he personally struggled to come to terms with the excruciating moral dilemma posed by the case and, in particular, the applicants.

The Court understood the problem of justice versus political settlement, and, in particular, the right of individuals to seek redress for the egregious harms they had suffered, against the political compromise designed to avoid a bloody revolution. To pick up again from the judgment of Judge Mahomed:

> The effect of an amnesty undoubtedly impacts upon very fundamental rights. All persons are entitled to the protection of the law against unlawful invasions of their right to life, their right to respect for and protection of dignity and their right not to be subject to torture of any kind. When those rights are invaded those aggrieved by such invasion have the right to obtain redress in the ordinary courts of law and those guilty of perpetrating such violations are answerable before such courts, both civilly and criminally. An amnesty to the wrongdoer effectively obliterates such rights.[23]

But the judge offered as justification the existence of the amnesty that enabled him to move beyond these problems and dismiss the application. The first response from the Bench represented a serious stretch of the judicial imagination:

> The families of those unlawfully tortured, maimed or traumatised become more empowered to discover the truth, the perpetrators become exposed to opportunities to obtain relief from the burden of a guilt or an anxiety they might be living with for many long years, the country begins the long and necessary process of healing the wounds of the past, transforming anger and grief into a mature understanding and creating the emotional and structural climate essential for the "reconciliation and reconstruction" which informs the very difficult and sometimes painful objectives of the amnesty articulated in the epilogue.[24]

One is entitled to wonder whether this approach leads to a diminution of the moral weight of the abuses of human rights conducted under and by the apartheid regime and its human instruments, crimes that are swept away on hopeful consequentialist speculation.[25]

The second justification offered by Judge Mahomed clearly revealed the pragmatism of the Court in coming to its conclusion:

> Even more crucially, but for a mechanism providing for amnesty, the 'historic bridge' itself might never be erected. For a successfully negotiated transition, the terms of the transition required not only the agreement of those victimised by abuse but also those threatened by the transition to a 'democratic society' based on freedom and equality. If the Constitution kept alive the prospect of continuous retaliation and revenge, the agreement of those threatened by its implementation might never have been forthcoming and, if it had, the bridge itself would have remained wobbly and insecure, threatened by fear from some and anger from others.[26]

The Court had a clear understanding of its central role in the construction and preservation of the bridge.

The attack from the 'right'

The TRC was not the only new institution to face a legal attack. The country's first democratically elected President and the newly created Constitutional Court were the next to come under fire—this time, from the right of the political spectrum.

For many in South Africa, particularly from the white community, rugby is a religion. It is thus not a matter in which interference by government is welcome. However, the issue of non-racialism in rugby has been consistently on the political agenda since 1994. In 1997, President Mandela appointed a commission to investigate the management of the internal affairs of the South African Rugby Football Union (SARFU). The rugby union went to court seeking to invalidate this decision.

Two key arguments were raised in support of the application. Firstly, there was the allegation that President Mandela had failed to invite SARFU to give its views regarding the purpose of the commission, given the existence of an agreement which was intended to resolve government's concerns about the management and internal affairs of SARFU. Secondly, the question arose as to whether the President had not abdicated the responsibility to appoint a commission to the Minister of Sport, Steve Tshwete, and hence failed to appreciate that a Presidential commission remained his sole responsibility.

The issue of non-racialism in rugby has been consistently on the political agenda since 1994

The application was heard in front of an extremely conservative judge, Judge William de Villiers, a man who early in his career had sought the exclusion of the present Deputy Chief Justice, Dikgang Moseneke, from the Pretoria Bar. In an unprecedented move, the judge decided that President Mandela should be summoned to give evidence before the Court. So it was that more than 40 years after the *Rivonia* trial, President Mandela found himself once again in the witness box in a Pretoria court.

The case was clearly an attempt by the 'old guard' to fight back against the very core institutions that underpinned the newly established constitutional democracy. An eminent senior counsel reported that he was in the Pretoria High Court robing room when the announcement came through that the judge had summoned President Mandela to give evidence. A huge roar of approval broke out from the assembled ranks of the Pretoria Bar: their man was giving it to this newly appointed President.

It is worth pausing to consider the remarkable decision by the President to testify, when a claim of executive privilege (or the claim that a sitting member of the executive branch of government could not be compelled to testify) may have successfully avoided that spectacle. Interviews with those involved in the case confirm that President Mandela was determined to demonstrate his belief that no one was above the law, that the law should be obeyed and that executive power should be held accountable through processes such as judicial oversight or consideration by the courts of the reasonableness of the executive's conduct.

But Dr Luyt's own account[27] of President Mandela's testimony reveals the deep acrimony and political manoeuvering that pervaded the proceedings:

> Preferring to take the word 'stand' to its literal extreme, he refused a seat and stood up for the duration of his testimony. Observers in the business of myth-building described this as a gesture of respect for the court. I believe, however, that he did so to demonstrate his authority over the man seated on the bench. Mandela's refusal to use the customary 'Lordship' in addressing Mr Justice de Villiers and referring to him simply as 'Judge' supports this contention.
>
> . . .
>
> Referring to our questioning of the validity of his affidavit, which had prompted Justice de Villiers to subpoena him, Mandela told the court: 'I would never have imagined that Louis would be so insensitive, so ungrateful to say when I gave my affidavit [that] I was lying. Dr Luyt is a pitiless dictator. No leader can stand up to him. You cannot talk of democracy.'

By the end of the proceedings, Judge de Villiers had, astonishingly, found that not only had the President failed to invite SARFU to make its views known prior to the calling of the commission, but that the President's evidence in this regard could not be believed. In making a credibility finding against him, he also found that the President had abdicated his responsibility for the appointment of this commission. Inevitably, the case went on appeal to the Constitutional Court. Ultimately, that court overturned all the grounds on which Judge de Villiers had found for SARFU.

Far more significant, however, was the attack then launched by Dr Luyt on the Constitutional Court itself. He claimed that he had 'a reasonable apprehension that every member of the Constitutional Court will be biased against him'. He thus brought an application for the recusal of five of its members, namely Justices Chaskalson, Langa, Kriegler, Sachs and Yacoob. He claimed that, 'after careful deliberation', he had decided not to include the other judges expressly in his application but to leave it to the conscience of each individual member of the Court whether they should sit in the case. The scope of the recusal application was significant. If Dr Luyt had been able to ensure that there were fewer than eight members of the Court who could sit, no appeal would have been possible because the necessary *quorum* of the Court is eight judges.

The recusal application had much broader implications for the Constitutional Court's role in the new constitutional order. The stakes were high indeed. As one commentator noted: 'If allegations of past political affiliation and personal indebtedness by reason of appointment to the court were to hold sway, the Constitutional Court would effectively be paralysed. In virtually every case, the government is a litigant. Hence, it could always be argued that the kinds of factors raised by Dr Luyt would preclude a fair trial. The recusal application, therefore, was calculated to undermine the very status of the Constitutional Court as an institution.'[28]

Interestingly, and rather ironically in the light of subsequent attacks upon the judiciary, the same type of claim—that the appointees to the Court would be reliable ANC sympathisers—was made at the time by certain political commentators of different political positions. For example, historian R W Johnson, the ex-Oxford don, alleged that 'the government can "count on the sympathies of a large majority" of the court.'[29] The respected progressive political analyst Steven Friedman asked: 'What happens to democracy when the right issues are raised by the wrong people?'[30] Friedman's argument was that 'serious questions' needed to be asked about the Constitutional Court's 'enthusiasm (or lack of it) for aiding citizens if doing so might cause offence to the majority party.'[31]

The specific grounds on which recusal of individual judges were sought were essentially of two types: that the judge in question was politically affiliated with the ANC and/or had personal relationships with office-bearers in the new executive. Luyt alleged[32] that Justice Sachs had held a position of leadership in the African National Congress and that Justices Langa and Yacoob had been members of the ANC. But all these judges had severed their ties with the ANC immediately upon their appointment to the Court. Dr Luyt alleged that, in addition to his party affiliation, Justice Langa's status as founder member of the Release Mandela Committee in Natal, his role as an adviser during the talks that led to the Groote Schuur and Pretoria Minutes, and his attendance at a 'personal dinner with President Mandela at his house' were grounds for recusal.

Luyt alleged that Justice Sachs had held a position of leadership in the African National Congress

As to Justice Kriegler, Dr Luyt alleged, *inter alia*, that there appeared to be animosity between him and his attorney, that their own 'fairly close relationship in the course of which he on numerous occasions attended rugby matches at Ellis Park as my guest' had apparently ended and that perceived sarcasm in his questioning at an earlier hearing in the appeal caused concerns of bias.

Dr Luyt also raised questions about Justice Chaskalson's representation of President Mandela at the *Rivonia* trial, and of his former wife on various occasions; his role as adviser to the ANC during the constitutional negotiations; President Mandela's attendance at the wedding of Justice Chaskalson's son; and a dinner he attended which was held in honour of Justice Chaskalson upon his departure from the Legal Resources Centre, which he had served with great distinction.

The flavour of Luyt's objections is captured in his truly appalling attack upon Justice Sachs, the basis of which is set out in the judgment of the Court:

> Perhaps the most inappropriate allegation made in the whole of this unfortunate application is that relating to the severe injuries which Justice Sachs suffered in Maputo in the hands of South African security forces. As is well known, Justice Sachs lost his right arm and sight in one eye in consequence of a bomb placed under his car. The allegation that Justice Sachs would by reason thereof be biased against the fourth respondent or in favour of the President reflects adversely on those who make that allegation and provides no basis for its recusal. That is a tasteless allegation which is rejected. The less said about it the better.[33]

The recusal application failed, a result which Dr Luyt described, in his inimitable way, as 'about as surprising as hearing that the All Blacks had beaten Japan'.[34]

But this case was critical for another reason as well. It revealed the anxiety that this new Constitution, with its lofty ambition for a non-racial, non-sexist and truly free society, would penetrate far into the intimate personal sphere of South African citizens. This reach would mean the critical analysis of personal areas such as language, religion, sexual orientation, marriage, and, yes, even sport. As Dr Luyt saw it, 'the government continues to march relentlessly towards greater control of every facet of our lives'.[35] A more recent example, confirming that the same anxiety has not dissipated with time, is the controversy and subsequent complaints of human rights violations that followed the Forum for Black Journalists' exclusion of white journalists from an off-the-record briefing by ANC President, Jacob Zuma.

The *SARFU* case also held fundamental implications for the Court, its legitimacy and the outcome of the main attack on the President of the Republic. It is trite that legitimacy and credibility are the main currency of any court and that the highest court in the land must be held to the highest ethical standards, and be unimpeachable, in order to have any real (moral) authority. The appearance of bias is fatal to a court's authority and a society's acceptance of its decisions.

The perception of the highest court as biased, whether in favour of a political party or incumbent government or political faction, and not as impartial and loyal only to the values and principles of our constitutional democracy, holds deeply troubling consequences, particularly for a critical institution in our democracy. It is clear that the mere establishment of the Constitutional Court and its operation has alone been insufficient to lift itself into legitimacy in the minds of South Africans. A study conducted in the 1990s by James Gibson found empirical support for this view:

> In most established political systems (and especially in the United States), courts draw far more loyalty from ordinary citizens than do parliaments. Parliaments are often tainted with all the unsavory business of democratic politics—compromise, partisanship, log-rolling, and so on—that people find

displeasing . . . Courts, on the other hand, usually shroud their proceedings in secrecy, presenting a public image of solemnity, dignity, and reasoned and impartial decision making. Nothing could be more different from the way in which parliaments are typically portrayed (for example, as having notorious and unruly question periods). That the South African Constitutional Court attracts no more loyalty than the Parliament suggests that the Court has been unable to differentiate itself, that the image of the institution as doing something quite different from the other branches of government, and in a different way, has not yet penetrated the consciousness of the South African mass public. Failure to establish itself as a strictly legal institution has impeded the growth of the legitimacy of the Constitutional Court.[36]

This failure to set the Constitutional Court, as an institution, above politics, removed from the fickle and capricious nature of that arena, has provided the licence for the now widespread attacks on the Court and the broader judiciary in the fraught political climate of 2008. Public support for an institution whose role is unknown to, and therefore unappreciated by, most South Africans simply cannot be expected. But it is critical to the success of our constitutional democracy. As Chief Justice Langa said in a speech given nearly 10 years ago:

> The integrity of the judiciary is fundamental to peace, justice and security in any country. This imposes a heavy responsibility on judges and magistrates to function in a manner that sustains such integrity. Judges are accountable. They do not work in secret or behind some bush. They have to give reasons for their judgments and these are available for scrutiny and analysis by higher courts and by the public . . .
>
> But a good judge needs appropriate judicial space within which to work. In the exercise of our judicial function, we are answerable only to the Constitution and the Law. An environment must exist wherein the judges can dispense justice impartially, without fear or favour. That then requires that government and the public respect the independence and integrity of the bench. . . .[37]

It is to part of the record of the Court that we must now turn, and in particular to three cases where it faced the burden of dealing with the need for transformation.

Endnotes

1   We draw heavily on the most useful information and narrative set out on the Constitutional Court's own website, http://www.constitutionalcourt.org.za (visited 30 June 2008). See also the comprehensive account offered by A Sparks *Tomorrow is Another Country—The Inside Story of South Africa's Road to Change* (1996).

2   See R Spitz and M Chaskalson. *The Politics of Transition: A Hdden History of South Africa's Negotiated Settlement* (2000) chapter 6.

3   From *Hansard*, private members' statements of Legislative Assembly of British Columbia, Member G Brewin, p 10 209, 1994 Legislative Session: 3rd Session, 35th Parliament, Friday April 22, 1994 Morning Sitting vol 14 no 13. The full story is to be found in Sparks *ibid*.

4   Chiara Carter 'Is the TRC threatening to become a cold case?' *Independent Newspapers* (8 April 2008).

5   E A Christodoulidis 'Truth and Reconciliation as Risks' 2000 (9) *Social and Legal Studies* 179-201 quoted in K Van Marle 'Law's Time, Particularity and Slowness', 2003 *South African Journal of Human Rights* 245.

6   D Posel & G Simpson (eds) *Commissioning the Past* (W.U.P.) (2002) 168.

7   E De Kock and J Gordin *A Long Night's Damage: Working for the Apartheid State* (Contra) (1998) 249.

8   *Ibid* 250.

9   *Ibid* 251.

10 *Ibid* 252.

11 Pumla Gobodo-Madikizela *A Human Being Died That Night: A South African Woman Confronts the Legacy of Apartheid* 61.

12 Chiara Carter 'Is the TRC threatening to become a cold case?' *Independent Newspapers* (8 April 2008).

13 De Kock and Gordin *ibid* 274-275.

14 M Burger and C Gould *Secrets and Lies* (2002) 191.

15 *Ibid* 191.

16 *Ibid* 192.

17 *Ibid* 191.

18 This perception increased over the next decade as many ordinary citizens, as is evidenced by reaction to newspapers and radio talk shows, complain about the law's bias some 15 years into non-racial democracy.

19 *Ibid* 218–219.

20 *Ibid* 188.

21 1996 (8) BCLR 1015 (CC)

22 At 1027.

23 At 1028.

24 At 1029.

25 See in this regard Kader Asmal, Louise Asmal and Ronald Suresh Roberts *Reconciliation through Justice* (1996).

26 At 1028.

27 Dr Louis Luyt *Walking Proud* (2003) 267, 299.

28 'The Administration of Justice' *1999 Annual Survey of South African Law* 779.

29 *Ibid* citing R W Johnson in the *London Review of Books* vol 21 no 19 Letters 30 September 1999.

30 *Business Day* (17 May 1999).

31 'The Administration of Justice' *1999 Annual Survey of South African Law* 781.

32 1999 (4) SA 147 (CC) paras 15–5.

33 1999 (4) SA 147 (CC) para 97.

34 *Ibid* 309.

35 *Ibid* 309.

36 James Gibson *Overcoming Apartheid: Can Truth Reconcile a Divided Nation?* (2004) 304.

37 'Defending Democracy' *Sunday Tribune* (23 September 1999).

seven

A break with the past,
a view of the future

L ife and death. An eye for an eye. State-sanctioned murder. A necessary deterrent. Cruel and inhuman punishment. Few legal issues promote as passionate or divisive a debate as that surrounding the use of the death penalty. Scan the letters to the editors of South Africa's newspapers on any given day and invariably there will be a call for the reintroduction of the death penalty to 'deal with' the prevalence of violent crime in this country. Politicians and the public alike regularly make public appeals for a referendum on the issue. To these people, the death penalty is an essential crime-fighting weapon that has become unavailable since the abolition of capital punishment by the Constitutional Court in a judgment delivered on 6 June 1995.

The Court's decision holds significance for South Africa beyond the issues of crime and punishment. As seen in the preceding chapters, certain lawsuits transcend their facts and assume an importance far beyond the immediate dispute because of their significance for society at large. *State v Makwanyane* was such a case. Not only was it the first case chosen for hearing by the new Constitutional Court, but *Makwanyane* represented a foundational moment, a line drawn in the sands of South Africa's history marking the start of a new legal era.

The Court's judgment embodies this dramatic change. Unusually, each of the 11 judges wrote a judgment concurring with the main judgment written by the President of the Court, Arthur Chaskalson. Each judge set out reasons for supporting the decision to abolish the death penalty. These judgments are striking in how they differ from most court judgments which laboriously recount the facts of the case to be decided. Here, the details and factual background as to how its protagonists—Themba Makwanyane and Mavusa Mchunu—came to be sentenced to death are all but absent. These men appear to be irrelevant to the decision, appearing only fleetingly in Justice Chaskalson's main judgment. Their stories and role in the case are dealt with in a meaningful way only by Justice O'Regan. Prior to 1994, it is likely that these men would have ended their lives on the gallows. Neither Makwanyane nor Mchunu are sympathetic figures. They were callous murderers convicted of a quadruple homicide from a botched cash heist ambush and robbery in which Volkskas Bank employees Cornelius Havenga, 22, and Petrus Pretorius, 63, and police officers Matthys Thompson, 23, and Robert Goddard, 22, were all shot dead.[1]

The importance of so-called social impact litigation in the new constitutional era is well demonstrated by the litigation process in this case. Renowned senior advocates Wim Trengove and Gilbert Marcus were approached by the Bar Council and accepted the case as a vehicle to challenge the constitutionality of the death penalty.[2] A plaintiff was needed—someone sentenced to death under the old penal system. The Department of Correctional Services was contacted and the names of prisoners under a death sentence were requested. These happened to be Makwanyane and Mchunu. By this bureaucratic coincidence, these men gave their names to one of the most important cases in post-apartheid South Africa. They never even met the lawyers who would argue to spare their lives prior to the hearing of the appeal, and remain incarcerated in prison where they are serving life sentences for these crimes.

The 11 judges themselves bore the clear mark of the new society under construction—most had fought long and hard for the end of apartheid. Some had been intimately involved in the drafting of the Constitution, *The 11 judges themselves bore the clear mark of the new society under construction* including the 'right to life' clause, and negotiations for South Africa's transition to a constitutional democracy. In fact, 5 of the 11 were on the public record as abolitionists and none were on the record in favour of capital punishment[3], making the job of counsel arguing for the retention of the death penalty a truly uphill battle.

This was confirmed at the hearing by an intervention by Acting Judge Sydney Kentridge—the legendary senior counsel, widely regarded as the finest lawyer never to have become Chief Justice of South Africa, who, among his many important cases, led the team on behalf of the Biko family at the inquest into the death in detention of struggle leader Steve Bantu Biko. He interrupted his colleagues' barrage of questions from the bench to request that the retentionist camp's counsel be heard 'in your own words and in your own time'. This was an unsubtle judicial hint to his colleagues, Ismael Mahomed and John Didcott, to afford counsel a chance to develop his argument. The two remained relatively silent for a few minutes.

Kentridge admitted in an interview with the authors that he and some of his fellow justices did not find the case as easy as one may expect. Primarily, this was because counsel for the retentionists raised some thoughtful arguments, described below, that required careful consideration and deliberation before they could be rejected. But the case was also difficult because of the Court's awareness of the political stakes and the importance of its treatment of the death penalty in building a new South Africa.

These stakes were confirmed on the day before the hearings commenced. The Court's first president, Arthur Chaskalson, informed the audience that attended the opening ceremony of the Court that the first case to be heard by the Court concerned the vital question of whether the state had the right to take the life of a convicted person. In his speech in which he officially opened the Constitutional Court, the first democratically elected president, Nelson Mandela, had noted that, the last time he had been in a court was to find out whether he and his co-accused in the *Rivonia* trial would be sentenced to death. The significance of the decision three decades earlier to imprison, rather than execute, Mandela was surely not lost on those in attendance. Mandela then went on to say 'Today I rise not as an accused but on behalf of the people of South Africa, to inaugurate a court South Africa has never had, a court on which hinges the future of our democracy.'

But before we return to this landmark case, it is necessary to embark on a brief excursion through the history of capital punishment.

History of the death penalty[4]

The question of capital punishment has bedevilled most societies. Capital punishment is as old as human history and has seen the convicted beheaded, forced to walk the plank, burnt at the stake, crushed by heavy stones, mauled by ferocious beasts, crucified, drawn and quartered, disembowelled and dismembered. To achieve this ultimate penalty, modern states have used the guillotine, noose and gallows, firing squad, electric chair and lethal injection.

In 1752, British judges could order posthumous tarring and chaining of corpses to increase the horror for onlookers, apparently hoping to enhance the claimed deterrent effect on potential wrongdoers. In 1783, James Boswell proposed that 'convicts should be hanged without hoods that the distortions may be seen'. In an ideal world, he argued, criminals would have their heads publicly smashed open with an iron mallet, before being jugulated with a machete and hacked apart with an axe. He noted that attendance at public executions by criminals was for enjoyment, not deterrence. Even debtors were liable to end their days for nothing more than indebtedness: after 60 days in prison, their failure to repay their creditors was punishable by execution or enslavement, at the election of the creditor. In fact, if a debtor owed more than one creditor, he could apportion the debt among the creditors by having them collectively tear him limb from limb. In Roman penal law, an individual who had killed his parents was beaten with rods until blood was drawn, then was drowned in a sack containing a dog, a cock, a monkey and a snake.

Attendance at public executions by criminals was for enjoyment, not deterrence

Public executions were common until the 19th century, when politicians became concerned that, on one hand, raucous ritual would lead to its becoming unpopular, and, on the other, 'popular disgust' would soon lead 'to the entire abolition of capital punishment'. Hangings then took place behind prison walls and away from public viewing—arguably increasing its popular support because the physical horrors of execution were no longer witnessed by the public.

Prussia was the first European state to end public executions, relocating beheadings away from public view in 1851. Russia and the Austro-Hungarian Empire next abolished the death penalty.

As gory as is this history of capital punishment and as widespread as was the practice, there is another trend that can be identified—the abolition of capital punishment as societies develop and democratise. With the notable exception of the United States, where the appetite for executions can be explained, at least in part, as the product of that country's religious and puritanical past and resulting religious and conservative world views, the death penalty has been abolished throughout the world in the last century. By the end of 2007, 91 countries had abolished the death penalty for all crimes. A further 44 countries have abolished it in practice.

Even in those countries that retain the death penalty, the circumstances in which it is available have been reduced and circumscribed, as in its abolition for minors or mentally ill offenders. When coupled with the rise in forensic technology, such as DNA testing, that frequently clears convicted prisoners on death row through the diligent efforts of law students and public interest attorneys worldwide, qualms about the use of the death penalty are common.

Justification

The trend to abolition notwithstanding, the death penalty retains significant popular support. The 'hang 'em high' lobby apart, there are rational justifications presented for its retention. Two main arguments have been used to justify the capital punishment of criminals. First is the principle of retribution—embodied in popular discourse in the idea of 'an eye for an eye'—which essentially institutionalises and legitimises the desire for vengeance and revenge against criminals. Proponents argue that the accuseds' own actions 'brought this on themselves'. Hence retributive justice promotes a theory that proportionate punishment is morally acceptable as a response to crime. Only a proportional response to a crime represents just punishment.

Retributive justice promotes a theory that proportionate punishment is morally acceptable as a response to crime

Critics of this argument suggest that it requires the state to sink to the level of criminals and makes the state 'no better than them'. Retribution, obviously, precludes the possibility of an individual's rehabilitation during his incarceration, given his death.

Second, advocates of the death penalty claim that it is a deterrent to future criminal activity. While heavily disputed, this argument boils down to 'if they know they might die for it, they might not do it'. However, extensive studies around the world have demonstrated that the availability of the death penalty has little or no conclusive deterrent effect on criminal activity.[5] Even if one were to accept the deterrent effect of the death penalty, it begs the question of whether an alternative punishment—such as life imprisonment—would not serve as an equally effective deterrent.[6]

Clearly, the most vexing problem with the administration of capital punishment is the irreversibility of the death penalty in the event that the conviction was the result of an error. A study in 2000 by researchers at Columbia University of 5 800 capital convictions from 1973 to 1995 found serious errors in 68 per cent of them.[7] The horror of an innocent man or woman executed for a crime he or she did not commit means that even supporters of the death penalty can only conscionably hope that it is carried out in the absence of any reasonable doubt as to the guilt of the accused.

South Africa

Historically, the death penalty was part of the law governing South Africa from the days of its control by the Dutch East India Company. Executions were public affairs and were often accompanied by disembowelling, dismemberment or 'breaking' on a wheel when the body was stretched from opposite sides. In fact, the executioner received separate payments for such additional services—8 rixdalers for decapitation or hanging, 12 for breaking limbs, 6 for strangling, 2 for scorching, 6 for quartering and hanging up the pieces and 4 for chopping off a hand.[8] One wonders how this scale of payment for these gruesome services was determined! By the end of the 18th century such 'accessory torture' had been abolished, although public execution was still practised until late in the 19th century.[9]

Executions were public affairs and were often accompanied by disembowelling, dismemberment or 'breaking' on a wheel

The Criminal Procedure and Evidence Act 31 of 1917 provided for a mandatory sentence of death, except where the perpetrator was younger than 16 or was a woman who had murdered her newborn child. The courts could exercise mercy, however, and this resulted in a reprieve for many.[10] Later, during apartheid, the death penalty was available to punish a wide range of offences, including murder, robbery and housebreaking with aggravating circumstances, sabotage, 'undergoing training or obtaining information abroad to further communism, and furthering economic and social change in South Africa by violent means', 'participation in terroristic activities', kidnapping and child-stealing, and rape.[11]

By the late 1980s, when South Africa suffered under repeated states of emergency, the Society for the Abolition of the Death Penalty, Lawyers for Human Rights and other civil society organisations challenged the death penalty and urged reform. Government repeatedly affirmed its commitment to the death penalty but indicated it was 'receptive' to proposals to reform capital punishment. Minister of Justice, Kobie Coetzee, in remarks to Parliament on 27 April 1989 (five years to the day before the historic elections ending apartheid) identified reforms for consideration, including abolition of the mandatory sentence for murder, creating an automatic right of appeal to the Appellate Division once a capital sentence was passed, and some extension to a judge's sentencing discretion.

Needless to say, black South Africans suffered the harshest consequences of the apartheid state's imposition of death penalty. Judicial bias played a significant role in a number of cases. For example, between 1947 and 1966, no white offender convicted of the rape of black women was executed. In damning contrast, 122 black offenders convicted of the rape of white women were hanged during the same period of time.[12] This racial bias was often exacerbated by the accuseds' poverty, resulting in inadequate legal representation for capital cases. Accordingly, the death penalty's arbitrary imposition was often the result of ineffective counsel, overeager prosecution, judges willing to ignore irregularities in evidence and a lack of procedural safeguards.

The total number of executions in South Africa for the 10-year period between 1980 and 1989 was 1 219

During the nearly eight decades in which statistics were maintained, 4 226 executions occurred in South Africa. In the 57 years between 1911 and 1968, 2 323 executions (an average of 40 per year) took place. However, in the 20-year period between 1968 and 1988, 1 904 people were executed (an average of 95 per year). In 1987 alone, the largest annual number ever hanged, 164 people were executed.[13] The total number of executions in South Africa for the 10-year period between 1980 and 1989 was 1 219. During the same period, the total number of death sentences handed down in South Africa (excluding Transkei, Bophuthatswana, Venda and Ciskei) was 1 842.

By the early 1990s, the death penalty was restricted to the crimes of murder, treason committed in wartime, robbery with aggravating circumstances, kidnapping, child-stealing and rape. It was discretionary, not mandatory, and could be imposed only when the judge was satisfied that 'the sentence of death is the proper sentence', following a consideration of any facts in mitigation or aggravation of sentence.[14]

As demonstrated in academic studies[15], the discretionary nature of the death sentence meant that 'the personal disposition towards capital punishment of the individual judges 'played a critical role in whether, in cases where the death sentence was a competent verdict, it was imposed'.[16] The highly problematic consequence of this finding was that the identity of the judge presiding over a capital trial was a major factor in whether a conviction would carry capital punishment. As Angus and Grant framed the issue:

> [j]udges are not *automata* and we do not suggest that they ought to make decisions mechanically. It is, therefore, inevitable that personal attitudes will play a role in judicial decision-making and result in differences in sentencing. But, where life and death are at stake, such inconsistency cannot be tolerated.[17]

This discretion, and its inconsistent result, was vigorously defended by the Deputy Judge President of the Transvaal Provincial Division at the time, Judge David Curlewis. In correspondence responding to the Angus and Grant study, Curlewis stated:

> Only an *ignoramus*, or a person with little regard for the truth would deny [that judicial attitudes towards the death penalty play a material role in imposing or not imposing that sentence]. . . .
>
> The above fact does not lead to people who do not deserve to die being sentenced to death; it leads to people who should be sentenced to death escaping the death penalty. . . .
>
> Let me make my meaning plain. A person who deserved to hang was more likely to get the death sentence from me or my ilk than (at random) my brothers Roux, MacArthur, Van Schalkwyk, Nestadt, Goldstone or Gordon. The reason is that these judges are at heart abolitionists for one reason or another.
>
> There's nothing wrong with this. After all, the present Chief Justice is an abolitionist, and beliefs are to be respected. But obviously, and for that reason, they cannot be sound on the imposition of the death penalty.
>
> The answer to this problem (until the Government does away with the death sentence) will be clear to the authors: for the good of the community and for the peace of mind of such judges, they should not sit on capital cases.[18]

Curlewis argued notwithstanding that this was an unsatisfactory state of affairs, given how highly the legal system prizes predictability and certainty.

As apartheid came to its final chapter, the imposition of the death penalty became a highly politicised issue. This is best exemplified by the case of *State v Safatsa and Others*,[19] known more commonly as the 'Sharpeville Six'. Six people were each sentenced to death for the murder of the Deputy Mayor of Lekoa by a mob. Judge Human imposed the death penalty on the six defendants despite the acceptance that none of their actions had causally contributed to the death of the victim.

However, the doctrine of common purpose—according to which, if two or more people, having a common purpose to commit a crime, act together in order to achieve that purpose, the conduct of each of them in the execution of that purpose is imputed to all the others[20]—was used to cure this otherwise fatal deficiency in the evidence presented by the prosecution. These sentences were upheld by the Appellate Division and the pending executions attracted an international campaign for clemency, supported by calls for sanctions if the executions took place. Initially, the government obdurately supported the decision of the Appellate Division. Deputy Minister of Information, Dr 'Slim'

Stoffel van der Merwe[21], stated that 'to hang and imprison a criminal does have a demonstrative effect, namely that crime is punished'.[22] The government eventually bowed to this political pressure. The six were saved from the gallows by presidential reprieve, but not before South Africa's judiciary and system of 'justice' took substantial flack, enduring criticism and international scorn. The negative perceptions of the highest court at the time, the Appellate Division, were captured in the following criticism of the appellate judgment in a work devoted to the case: 'The cost of this narrow judgement was potentially incalculable ... The cries for justice would henceforth only be answered where property rights were at stake. Life and liberty would count for nothing. And the worst was that this retreat was not forced upon the court by a dictator.'[23]

A moratorium on the carrying out of the death sentence was announced by then State President, F W de Klerk, on 2 February 1990

So it was that the escalation in executions in the 1980s coincided with the political turmoil engulfing the country at the same time and, when welcome political change came, the death penalty was not unaffected.

First, a moratorium on the carrying out of the death sentence was announced by then State President, F W de Klerk, on 2 February 1990, in his watershed speech of that day. Specifically, all executions were suspended and every sentence of death passed but not yet executed was to be reviewed. The import of this radical change to the punitive regime in South Africa, and its appropriate announcement in one of the most important political speeches in our history, was explained thus by Etienne Mureinik[24]:

> A leader committed to breaking that cycle [of systematic racial oppression and execution] could have found no better way to start than by suspending the hangman. Had we continued to treat it as routine to break human necks in batches of seven, the season of violence would have had to linger. Every hanging has proclaimed the value of violence, and every hanging has affirmed the contempt for the personhood of people upon which apartheid depends. It has become impossible in this country to pledge peace and humanity without noticing the role of the death system, and undertaking to do something about it.
>
> These are the reasons why the death penalty announcements are a central part of the President's opening-of-Parliament speech. Their presence in the speech is an important component of what imparts to it the quality of vision.[25]

Second, death row prisoners were afforded an automatic right to appeal to the Appellate Division. This was a significant change since any litigant, including people sentenced to death by a trial court, would otherwise have to request or apply for leave or permission to appeal. Now, there was a right of appeal. As Mureinik describes, this was significant not only because it recognised the unique position of such persons but also because it 'acknowledges ... that the entire approach to punishment for murder has until now been erroneous'.[26]

Finally, the death penalty was to be limited to 'extreme cases'. This too recognised that the use of capital punishment in South Africa had exceeded all justification and was disproportionate to any acceptable rationale.

The gallows were last in operation on 14 November 1989 and it is a tragic fact that executions took place but months before the moratorium hardened into reprieve and reprieve into abolition.[27]

For many opponents of apartheid, the execution of Eastern Cape ANC leader Vuyisele Mini in 1964 made it clear that the death penalty was for the use of overt, political purposes. Its suspension, and then ultimate abolition, was another step towards the establishment of a constitutional democracy and the recognition of every person's dignity and humanity. It was therefore an issue that would inevitably confront the negotiators for a new Constitution.

The gallows were last in operation on 14 November 1989

Death penalty and a constitutional South Africa

During the Convention for a Democratic South Africa (CODESA), negotiators from political parties representing all South Africans convened. Delegations from across the governmental and political spectrum began negotiating the creation and design of a transitional government and the first representative democratic state for all South Africans. The issue of the death penalty was understandably fraught and controversial. In fact, despite countless days of discussion and several draft provisions, no consensus could be reached by these political negotiators on whether the death penalty would continue into the new South Africa.

The interim Constitution provided for a right to life. This unqualified formulation was the result of the multi-party negotiations at CODESA, but also showed how the negotiators could not agree on the question of the death penalty and decided instead to leave the issue up to the new Constitutional Court. In contrast, other bills of rights often qualified the right to deal with capital punishment, abortion or euthanasia, creating the textual space in which to permit, or prohibit, each of these. But South Africa's right to life was wholly unqualified and therefore gave no guidance on whether it could be limited to allow for the imposition of the death penalty.

Critical to an understanding of how the Constitutional Court resolved the question of the death penalty in particular, and to constitutional litigation generally, is a grasp of the workings of the so-called limitations clause. Every right enshrined in the Constitution could be limited by a law of general application (in other words, something that was not a mere political policy statement but a properly enacted piece of legislation or rule of the common law). Any legal limitation of a constitutional right requires proof from the State that such a limitation was justified. A limitation was only permissible under the interim Constitution's limitations clause to the extent that it was reasonable and justifiable in an open and democratic society based on freedom and equality and did not negate the essential content of the right in question. In other words, a court was required to make a two-stage enquiry. First, is the right in question limited by the conduct at issue? Second, is this limitation justified? The constitutional debate about the death penalty turned less on an answer to the question of whether the death penalty breached the right to life; the key issue was whether it could be properly justified.

So it was that, when the tall, angular, balding figure of senior counsel Wim Trengove rose in mid-February 1995 to address the Constitutional Court in its first case, the issue could not have been more stark. Life or death. Or, more precisely, whether the South African government would continue to impose the death penalty—by hanging by the neck until dead—on criminals convicted of the most serious crimes.

From 15 to 17 February 1995, the new Constitutional Court heard argument regarding the constitutionality of the death penalty. The precarious and novel nature of this new apex court was reflected in the temporary nature of the court's accommodation in an office complex in Braamfontein. Since the Constitution Hill precinct was not yet under construction, the Court was housed in a rather inauspicious venue. The argument was held in a corporate auditorium without the traditional wood-panelled walls of a courtroom. There were no grand staircases leading to a 'legal palace'. The teams of distinguished counsel took the lift to the second floor, sandwiched between the first floor housing corporate offices of American Express and the third floor occupied by a firm of attorneys.

Counsel even confessed to a palpable sense of nervousness on both sides

The importance of the moment cannot be underestimated and the novelty and unprecedented nature of the proceedings cannot be exaggerated. Counsel even confessed to a palpable sense of nervousness on both sides—both from themselves and the Bench—at this first hearing. There was no precedent for any of the new court's procedure—what robes the judges would wear, what order they would sit in on the bench, how they would be addressed by counsel or even what the procedure would be for organising oral argument.

In fact, the 11 judges held a meeting to discuss these elementary practical and logistical details. At this meeting, they decided to be addressed as 'Justice so-and-so', as in the American judicial tradition, instead of the traditional, and gendered, 'm' Lord' or 'm' Lady' still used today to address judges in many High Courts. On the question of how the judges should be seated, they decided against seniority—which would have placed Richard Goldstone first. Laurie Ackermann's wise, if self-serving, suggestion to sit in alphabetical order was also rejected, as was arranging themselves by chronological age. In the end, the judges decided that they would not sit in any particular order—although the Chief Justice would sit in the centre, with his deputy to his right. In hearings held today in the court building atop Constitution Hill in Braamfontein, the same holds true. The Chief Justice sits centred, flanked by the Deputy Chief Justice to his right, and the remaining members of the bench arranged in no set order on either side of them.

The judges also chose unisex robes embodying equality. Their robes are green and are therefore strikingly distinct from the English-styled black robes worn by judges in the civil courts or red when dealing with criminal matters. Unlike the robes of senior counsel, the Justices' gowns are not made of silk (which provides the colloquial term for a senior counsel) to symbolise the fact that not all of the judges are drawn from the ranks of silks. Unlike the vast majority of judicial appointments drawn exclusively from the ranks of senior counsel, the first court included three professors of law.

The parties to the case themselves embodied the changing political dispensation: the applicants, represented by Wim Trengove, and the national government, represented by veteran human rights advocate, George Bizos SC, were both in favour of the abolition of the death penalty. It was the Attorney-General of the Witwatersrand, represented by Klaus von Lieres und Wilkau SC, that argued for its retention. Several *amici curiae* (or friends of the court), representing viewpoints including those of abolitionist civil society organisations, the police and the Black Lawyers' Association, also argued to assist the Court in deciding this most contentious of issues.

The main argument advanced by the abolitionist parties was that the death penalty violated sections 9 (the right to life) and 11 (the right to be free from cruel, inhuman and degrading punishment) of the interim Constitution's Bill of Rights.

As the President of the Court summarised in his judgment:

> The principal arguments advanced by counsel for the accused in support of their contention that the imposition of the death penalty for murder is a 'cruel, inhuman or degrading punishment', were that the death sentence is an affront to human dignity, is inconsistent with the unqualified right to life entrenched in the Constitution, cannot be corrected in case of error or enforced in a manner that is not arbitrary, and that it negates the essential content of the right to life and the other rights that flow from it. The Attorney General argued that the death penalty is recognised as a legitimate form of punishment in many parts of the world, it is a deterrent to violent crime, it meets society's need for adequate retribution for heinous offences, and it is regarded by South African society as an acceptable form of punishment. He asserted that it is, therefore, not cruel, inhuman or degrading within the meaning of s 11(2) of the Constitution.[28]

Press reports of the day covered the retentionist position accurately:

> The camp fighting for the death penalty includes the SAPS and the State, represented by Witwatersrand Attorney-General Klaus von Lieres. They are supported by a private citizen, retired civil engineer Ian Glauber, who has formulated a well-considered, multi-pronged argument.

Glauber posits that murder committed as a result of emotional distress should be separated from murder committed by criminals who have no personal, emotional or psychological links with their victims. The latter, he says, deserve mandatory death sentences. He also disputes the claim that the death penalty fails as a deterrent, saying only the most brazen and stupid would not be deterred by such a fate. Glauber further argues that the primary objective of the Constitution is to protect the fundamental right to life of the innocent victim and not the perpetrator. On the irrevocability of the death sentence, he says that given the laws of evidence and conduct of the process, particularly capital cases, there tends to be an extreme unlikelihood of an innocent person being erroneously convicted. Glauber says that references in the Bible and Koran to death penalties repudiates claims that it is against the word of God.[29]

Both the judges and counsel were probing the scope and limits of constitutional litigation, in particular, testing to what extent public opinion could inform the debate around the meaning of a constitutional right. The Court was having none of this populist discourse. It was determined to set out as clearly as possible its conception of the Constitution, the rule of law and the role of the Constitutional Court in its interpretation and administration without bowing to popular views.

Newspaper reports at the time recorded some of the comments from the Bench:

White-haired and bearded with penetrating eyes, Natal judge, John Didcott, is terrier-like in trying to tear apart the pro-death sentence arguments. Justice Didcott snaps that he does not see why the Constitutional Court should have to pay attention to public opinion, however strong, and which may be 'ill-informed' or 'based on a fallacious belief'. Besides, says the judge, paying attention to public opinion is the job of the legislature and not the judiciary, which is there [to] interpret existing laws.[30]

The judges did not entirely hide their differences from the public gaze. At one point, Justice Albie Sachs, who had been a somewhat controversial appointment,[31] asked his first question of George Bizos. Before Bizos could say a word in response, both Justices Didcott and Mahomed fired questions at the bemused Bizos, Justice Didcott telling him not to answer Justice Sachs's question which, in his view, was hardly relevant. Bizos was reduced to asking the presiding judge, 'Who, Justice Chaskalson, must I answer first?'

As Von Lieres returned to the argument of the significance of public opinion, citing pro-capital punishment sentiments expressed to constitutional assembly chairman, Cyril Ramaphosa, at a meeting in the Cape, he drew an outburst from Justice Johann Kriegler, to 'play the ball and not the man', arguing that 'one incident in Paarl does not a national public opinion make'.[32]

Even Bizos, on behalf of the government, canvassed the pro-retention public opinion. In his typically colourful way, he read from newspaper clippings and letters to the nation's editors with such catchphrases as 'Hang 'em high!' He too was admonished from the bench that these references were irrelevant to the case before the Court. Unusually for the tenacious Bizos, who is not one to allow judges to disturb his particular flow of argument, he quickly changed tack.

In response to these submissions, the Court carefully explained in its judgment the critical difference between its role and that of the legislature, or Parliament. It is worth quoting the main judgment at length on this point:

> The Attorney General argued that what is cruel, inhuman or degrading depends to a large extent upon contemporary attitudes within society, and that South African society does not regard the death sentence for extreme cases of murder as a cruel, inhuman or degrading form of punishment. It was disputed whether public opinion, properly informed of the different considerations, would in fact favour the death penalty. I am, however, prepared to assume that it does and that the majority of South Africans agree that the death sentence should be imposed in extreme cases of murder. The question before us, however, is not what the majority of South Africans believe a proper sentence for murder should be. It is whether the Constitution allows the sentence.
>
> Public opinion may have some relevance to the enquiry, but in itself, it is no substitute for the duty vested in the Courts to interpret the Constitution and to uphold its provisions without fear or favour. If public opinion were to be decisive, there would be no need for constitutional adjudication. The protection of rights could then be left to Parliament, which has a mandate from the public, and is answerable to the public for the way its mandate is exercised, but this would be a return to parliamentary sovereignty, and a retreat from the new legal order established by the 1993 Constitution. By the same token the issue of the constitutionality of capital punishment cannot be referred to a referendum, in which a majority view would prevail over the wishes of any minority. The very reason for establishing the new legal order, and for vesting the power of judicial review of all legislation in the courts, was to protect the rights of minorities and others who cannot protect their rights adequately through the democratic process. Those who are entitled to claim this protection include the social outcasts and marginalised people of our society. It is only if there is a willingness to protect the worst and the weakest amongst us, that all of us can be secure that our own rights will be protected.
>
> This Court cannot allow itself to be diverted from its duty to act as an independent arbiter of the Constitution by making choices on the basis that they will find favour with the public.[33]

The judgment

The judgment issued by the Constitutional Court struck down the death penalty in South Africa. It also announced that things would never be the same in South Africa and proclaimed the new normative view grounded in the Constitution. The judgment was influenced by the personal and cultural backgrounds and experiences of the judges, by the acceptance of traditionally

African concepts such as *ubuntu* and by the Court's recognition that this judgment would describe and set the course for the new South African constitutional democracy. George Bizos captured the importance of the Court's impressive judgments when he observed that the decision had been taken to strike down a central component of the country's penal regime after an application by two accused who 'were almost beyond redemption'.[34]

The judgment is significant for its engagement with and reliance on comparative law—by canvassing the state of law in countries around the world. The judgment is also striking for its rejection of public opinion on the death penalty—an assertion of the Court of a constitutional project that rejects being bound by the inevitable fluctuations of such opinion.

Arguably, the most powerful case for the retention of the death penalty is the deterrence argument—that criminals would be deterred from committing crimes if they carried the death penalty. Yet, this relies on three assumptions for its power, none of which survived the careful scrutiny of Justice Chaskalson, who authored the main judgment. First is the assumption that those who are criminally inclined will pause and change their intended criminal course of action because of the possibility that the gallows will exact retribution. This ascribes a degree of rationality to the depraved that is, unfortunately, unwarranted.

Given South Africa's truly dismal performance at detecting, apprehending and prosecuting criminals, the sentencing stage is usually never reached

Second, before capital punishment is imposed, a criminal must be detected, apprehended, successfully prosecuted and linked to the crime and a court (and usually an appellate court as well) must satisfy itself that the death penalty is warranted. Thus, even when the death penalty was available as punishment for a particular category of offence, it was not always imposed by the court. Given South Africa's truly dismal performance at detecting, apprehending and prosecuting criminals, the sentencing stage is usually never reached. Thus, a criminal is unlikely to be deterred by the possible punishment, when the likelihood is that the essential prosecutorial steps to the gallows will never be taken.

Finally, the deterrence argument assumes that a criminal will be deterred by nothing less than the death penalty. It therefore seems as if death penalty proponents assume that the alternative to the death penalty is no punishment at all or punishment which can never deter. The Court's decision repeatedly makes clear, however, that the alternative to capital punishment is a term of life or long-term imprisonment. Clearly, a rational person would be similarly deterred from criminal conduct by the prospect of decades in the hospitality of the Department of Correctional Services, in prison conditions that are truly dire.

The Court therefore chose to assert its authority and unique role in the South African legal system with this most controversial of issues. It seized this opportunity to define the new constitutional order in a bold stroke. The judges' appreciation of the historic moment is clear throughout the judgment. Its tone shows that the new court and the society it would help create was a very clear break with the apartheid past where state power was abused in the worst possible way by depriving its citizens of their humanity, dignity, personhood and life itself. This sentiment was captured in Justice Didcott's judgment when he stated, quite simply, that 'the wanton killing must stop before it makes a mockery of the civilised, humane and compassionate society to which the nation aspires and has constitutionally pledged itself'. The judgment also describes the nation-building and transformational project then underway in the country.

The Court held that the constitutional prohibition on cruel, inhuman and degrading punishment must be construed in the historical context of the Constitution, as well as in light of other related fundamental rights provisions in the Constitution, specifically the rights to life, dignity and equality. The right to be free from cruel, inhuman and degrading punishment must also be realised in a way which secures the full measure of its protection for individuals.

The Court also recognised the political context that placed the question of capital punishment before it and acknowledged that it had been the subject of vigorous, though inconclusive, debate during the multi-party negotiating process. This failure to resolve the issue in the drafting process led to the 'Solomonic solution' that deliberately left the determination of the constitutionality of the death penalty to the Constitutional Court. Rather than being an abdication by the negotiators, it was a recognition of the limitations of multi-party negotiations and that this decision should be left to an institution fluent in the new South Africa's language of human rights.

Interestingly, while many of the judgments mentioned *ubuntu* and its inherent respect for each person's humanity and dignity, only the judgment of Justice Sachs dealt in any meaningful way with the question of how the death penalty was treated under African vernacular, or customary, law. Justice Sachs discovered that 'the materials suggest that amongst the Cape Nguni, the death penalty was practically confined to cases of suspected witchcraft, and was normally spontaneously carried out after accusation by the diviners. Soga says that the death penalty was never imposed, the reasoning being as follows: "Why sacrifice a second life for one already lost?" [35] Summary execution sometimes followed assaults on wives of chiefs or other aggravated cases, but were otherwise unknown, most criminal conduct was usually dealt with out of the property of the accused and "offences" were considered to be against the community or tribe rather than the individual, and punishment of a constructive or corrective nature was administered for disturbing the balance of tribal life.'[36]

Justice Sachs was the only judge who tried to anchor the rejection of capital punishment in any norm or bedrock principle, such as **ubuntu.**

Justice Sachs was the only judge who tried to anchor the rejection of capital punishment in any norm or bedrock principle, such as *ubuntu*. This is important since the other arguments (deterrence, retribution) are all consequentialist in nature, meaning that the death penalty should be declared unlawful because all justifications offered for its existence cannot be sustained. However, for example, if a new method of execution that did not constitute cruel, inhuman or degrading punishment was conceived, that basis for attacking the death penalty might then fail. Similarly, if new scientific study confirmed unequivocally the deterrent effect of the death penalty, that argument would also have to fail.

Given this reasoning of the Court, the question of the legality of the death penalty could be revisited in the future if further and better justification can be produced. Only a foundational, moral basis to reject capital punishment as abhorrent and hence contrary to a defined norm, standard or value that could not be revised would escape this fate. Justice Sachs's consideration of the issue in African vernacular law, and his reach towards a foundational value that rejects capital punishment, is therefore critical. It offers a possibility of rejection of the death penalty which is immune from impugned or contested scientific data. Accordingly, Justice Sachs found that the vernacular law's 'rational and humane adjudicatory approach is entirely consistent with and re-enforcing of the fundamental rights enshrined in our Constitution'.[37]

Reaction

Public reaction was divided, as expected. For example, Rabbi David Hoffman of the Progressive Jewish Congregation said he was 'very sad' for the families of victims of prisoners on death row, and asked: 'Is this decision really compassionate for the innocent and the victims of crime in our society?'[38] *Angry letters flooded into the nation's newspapers,* complaining that 'it seems that the right to life only applies to those who are found guilty of murder. It certainly does not apply to the law-abiding citizen or the victim'.[39]

Yet other South Africans cautiously welcomed the decision but demanded that such criminals 'must serve the longest possible sentences ranging from life imprisonment, without parole, during which period they must be trained to serve their fellow man and woman and in particular the victim's dependents. . . . In this way they would relieve the state of the financial burden which many misguided advocates of the death penalty consider cause enough to end their— the perpetrators'—lives'.[40]

At the time, Gauteng Premier, Tokyo Sexwale, seemed to share the view of many analysts who claim that the futility of life for prisoners serving life imprisonment (lacking, as it does, any hope of release, incentive for good behaviour or prospect of rehabilitation) is worse than being killed by the state when he said that he hoped Communist Party chief Chris Hani's killers—Polish immigrant Janusz Walus and former Conservative Party MP Clive Derby-Lewis—who were then two of the more famous death row inmates 'would grow thin with worry' in prison. 'In their porridge and in their coffee, they must see nothing but Comrade Hani's face'. Mr Sexwale added that it had been suggested to him that the two be hanged in public in the 80 000 seat FNB stadium outside Johannesburg.[41]

'In their porridge and in their coffee, they must see nothing but Comrade Hani's face'

The then Justice Minister, the late Dullah Omar, an outspoken death penalty abolitionist, assured 'a nation crying out for the death penalty that if prisoners were spared the gallows by the Court, they could spend the rest of their lives behind bars—with no remissions of sentence.'[42]

The retirement of South Africa's last hangman and his assistant was reported on 8 June 1995, following the scrapping of the death penalty by the Constitutional Court. Both men had been on full pay since the last executions in 1989 and were pensioners by the time of the decision that ended their livelihood. At the time, 453 prisoners were on death row. Bizos SC was appointed to spearhead the review of their sentences and lead the process of determining each of their fates.

On the question of what to do with these prisoners, then Deputy President, F W de Klerk, called for clemency to be granted to them, because 'the slate must be cleaned' and thereby 'focus the debate on whether we want to have this in future, in a country where there is a high incidence of crime'.[43]

The Constitutional Court ordered that the death sentences of these prisoners had to be set aside and substituted with appropriate alternative sentences. Two years later, Parliament passed a law providing for such substitution. On 25 May 2005, the Constitutional Court was called on to pronounce on the constitutional validity of that law and expressed its dismay that, 10 years later, 62 people remained under the sentence of death. The Court therefore extended its supervisory jurisdiction and began a process wherein a series of reports were filed with the Court, detailing extensively the status of the process and offering explanations and reasons for the continuing delay of substituted sentences. Each report occasioned a judgment from the Court—issuing further supervisory orders. So it was that, by 15 September 2005, 40 people were still on death row, but that number was reduced to 28 by 7 November, 9 by 15 February 2006 and the process was completed by 28 July 2006. Sentences were typically substituted with life or long terms of imprisonment.

This successful use of the Court's supervisory powers showed the opportunity lurking in future cases to press political and social progress. The added weight of the Court's supervision increased the political momentum to address the problem. As we turn to consider the strategic lawyering of the Treatment Action Campaign in the next chapter, the potential for the judicial branch to oversee the implementation of policy required by the Constitution will arise again.

Conclusion

Through *Makwanyane*, the new South Africa's democratic will was exerted in a significant and profound new way. Like the cases during the apartheid regime described in the first portion of the book, *Makwanyane* provides a clear indication of the power of law and the role of courts in shaping a country and society. In contrast to the apartheid courts, however, it also shows the Constitutional Court as a constructive instrument, articulating and creating a new relationship between the state and its citizens.

One thing is clear from *Makwanyane*: a constitutionally-sourced process of litigation, argument and decision could result in an outcome unimaginable but a few years before, when apartheid seemed a permanent feature of South African society. *Makwanyane* also showed that the individual and personal histories and experiences of the judges who decided it were a factor in the final decision. In this case, all of the judges had a clear and common understanding of the role played by the death penalty in apartheid South Africa. The judges understood their bridge-building role, thereby offering the possibility of courts being as dynamic and reflective of their political context as any other institution of government. The appointment of outstanding jurists with constitutional imagination had made an immediate impact.

The further importance of the decision was its rejection of majoritarian rule, or at least popular opinion, in favour of fidelity to the enumerated constitutional principles and values, regardless of their popularity with the broader society. The Court rose to enforce law and assert constitutional values despite the lack of popular support for such a decision.

Tellingly, though, the fact that one subsection providing for the death penalty as a competent punishment for treason committed in wartime remains on the statute books demonstrates that the issue of the death penalty may well be revisited at some time in the future. For this reason, the consequentialist nature of most of the reasons advanced by the Court for its decision in *Makwanyane* is troubling, since they do not provide a complete and permanent answer to the question of why capital punishment should be prohibited in South Africa's constitutional state.

It is obvious that the death penalty is the starkest exercise of power that a government has to regulate its citizens' lives

It is obvious that the death penalty is the starkest exercise of power that a government has to regulate its citizens' lives—by literally depriving them of life. If one also accepts that the courts embody the morality and social *mores* or norms of a society and that particular community's view of justice, then how courts deal with the criminal defendant accused of the very worst and most repugnant crimes is an illustration of that society's view of itself. It also points to the possibility of rendering state sovereignty accountable to values which are not within the reach of transient power. The first judicial act in building South Africa's transformed society was performed by the Constitutional Court in a decision on a fundamental question for any just government: the range of state power over a citizen—that is, when will it deprive a person of life? Viewed in this way, the judgments in *Makwanyane* represent a sizeable part of the foundations upon which the constitutional bridge must be erected.

Endnotes

1 SATV coverage reproduced by Zackie Achmat *Law & Freedom* programme (2005)
2 Author's interview with Trengove SC and Marcus SC.
3 *Weekly Mail* 17-23 February 1995 13.
4 See Sadak Atkadari *The Trial: A History from Socrates to OJ Simpson* (2005).
5 See the following for a detailed discussion of the applicable studies and the evidence against the deterrence argument: Jeffrey Fagan 'Death and Deterrence Redux: Science, Law and Causal Reasoning on Capital Punishment' 2006 (4), *Ohio Journal of Criminal Law* 255; John Donahue and Justin Wolfers 'The Use and Abuse of Empirical Evidence in the Death Penalty Debate' 2005 (5) *Stanford Law Review* 791. See also heads of argument in *Makwayane* at 57 *et seq.*
6 To indulge in wishful thinking for a moment, it seems that the greatest deterrents to criminal activity are both increasing the likelihood that a criminal will be captured and successfully prosecuted by the police and justice system, and addressing the socio-economic sources of crime.
7 CBS News (12 June 2000). See also Hugo Bedau *The Death Penalty in America* (1997).
8 Heads at 29 n74 Kahn 'The Death Penalty in SA' (1970) 33 *THRHR* 108, 109.
9 Heads at 29 n75 and n76; Kahn 'The Death Penalty in SA' (1970) 33 *THRHR* 108, 109-111; Devenish (1992) 1 *SACJ* 1, 7.
10 Heads at 30 n78 and n79.
11 Heads at 30-31 n81-n85.
12 Heads at 44; Van Niekerk 'Hanged by the Neck until you are Dead' (1969) 86 *SALJ* 457 and (1970) 87 *SALJ* 60.
13 Statistics from *Journal of Criminal Justice* (1989) 251-253.
14 Heads at 31.
15 Such as 'Sentencing in Capital Cases in the Transvaal Provincial Division and Witwatersrand Local Division: 1987-1989' by L Angus and E Grant 1991 (7) *SAJHR* 50.
16 *Ibid* 69.
17 *Ibid* 69.
18 *Ibid* 229 and 230.
19 1988 (1) SA 868 (A).

20 Snyman *Criminal Law* 4 ed 260.
21 There were two Stoffel van der Merwes in the Cabinet, one referred to as 'Slim' Stoffel and the other as 'Dom' Stoffel (the Minister of Home Affairs).
22 *Pretoria News* 17 March 1988.
23 Peter Parker and Joyce Mokhesi-Parker *In the Shadow of Sharpeville: Apartheid and Criminal Justice* (1998).
24 E Mureinik 1990 (6) *SAJHR* vii.
25 *Ibid* ix.
26 *Ibid* ix.
27 To paraphrase Mureinik *ibid* x.
28 At para 27.
29 Helen Grange 'A Matter of Life and Death' *Cape Argus* (17 February 1995).
30 Brendan Seery 'It could be the OJ trial without the blood' *Weekend Argus* (18/19 February 1995).
31 *Annual Survey of SA Law* (1994) 721-726.
32 Id.
33 At paras 87-89.
34 Interview with Zackie Achmat (2005).
35 At para 377 of the judgment.
36 At para 376 of the judgment.
37 At para 382 of the judgment.
38 *Cape Times* (8 June 1995).
39 *Cape Argus* (9 June 1995).
40 *Ibid*.
41 Roger Friedman 'Their Lives Hang by a Thread on Death Row' *Weekend Argus* (18/19 February 1995).
42 Friedman *ibid*.
43 Brian Stuart 'FW: Give Clemency to All on Death Row' The *Citizen* (17 February 1995).

eight

Activism, denialism, socio-economic rights and beetroot

> We cannot afford to allow the AIDS epidemic to ruin the realisation of our dreams. Existing statistics indicate that we are still at the beginning of the AIDS epidemic in our country. Unattended, however, this will result in untold damage and suffering by the end of the century.[1]
>
> Etienne Mureinik (1992)

The South African government's policy choices on HIV/AIDS have been arguably the most controversial part of its watch over the country over the past decade. That these choices landed up in court was inevitable. That the resulting legal war was waged over innovative constitutional clauses which the ANC ensured were part of the Constitution was perhaps a greater historical irony.

The inclusion of socio-economic rights in the Constitution, such as access to adequate housing, healthcare services, sufficient food and water and social security, was the subject of intense debate during the constitutional drafting process. Legal academics joined the fray as is evident from the debate that was intensely contested, in particular, in the pages of the *South African Journal of Human Rights*.

The debate essentially grappled with the unease generated by permitting an unelected judiciary to grant socio-economic rights to litigants weighed against leaving their realisation to, arguably, the greater unpredictability of political struggle. Essentially, if these rights are included in the Constitution, they are then justiciable (subject to judicial processes) and their holders can approach courts for relief based on the constitutional text itself. Opponents of this view argued that these rights should rather be established by the political processes of mobilisation, lobbying and legislative and executive action. They held that society cannot have judges running the country and making key distributional decisions in place of the elected and executive representatives of the people.

However, the former view won out and socio-economic rights were included in the Constitution. In a hugely influential article written in 1992, Etienne Mureinik spoke of the importance of courts being able to review policy choices rather than make them, using an argument that was rather prescient: 'A court might likewise intervene if the annual budget appropriated funds to build a replica of St Peter's, or perhaps a nuclear submarine, before the rights of education promised by the constitution had been delivered.'[2]

As this chapter shows, these rights may not have been successfully employed to challenge the purchase of submarines but they were used to challenge the government's response to the HIV/AIDS epidemic that is devastating South Africa.

Denialism and dissident science[3]

More than five million people live with HIV in South Africa.[4] As in other parts of the world, it was first identified in the white homosexual community, but was later discovered among black South Africans, and is now present throughout South African society and in all communities.[5]

Following the unbanning of the ANC, consultation between government and other health officials resulted in the formation of the National AIDS Convention of South Africa (NACOSA) in 1992. An eight-member drafting team, including two of the women to hold the post of Health Minister after apartheid, Nkosazana Dlamini-Zuma and Manto Tshabalala-Msimang, produced a National AIDS Plan a year later.[6] This was adopted by the Government of National Unity in 1994.[7] However, despite this promising beginning, national AIDS policy faltered during the Mandela presidency, sacrificed to other goals such as restructuring the healthcare system and emphasising basic or primary healthcare services.[8]

'Measured minute-by-minute during his presidency, Mandela probably spent more time with the Spice Girls and Michael Jackson than he did raising the AIDS issue with the South African public'

President Mandela made his first major public statement about AIDS only three years into his presidential term, and then to an international audience in Davos. Hein Marais powerfully summarises the position: 'Measured minute-by-minute during his presidency, Mandela probably spent more time with the Spice Girls and Michael Jackson than he did raising the AIDS issue with the South African public.' In an interview with the BBC, Mandela later admitted that he had faced resistance from audiences when he mentioned AIDS and that he had been warned that to talk about it might lose him the next election: 'I wanted to win and I didn't talk about AIDS.'

Xolela Mangcu attributes Mandela's omission 'mainly to the fact that Mandela found it awkward to talk about sexual issues, and was apparently discouraged from doing so by members of his own party'.[9] Regardless of its explanation, this failure of Mandela's political leadership at a time when HIV infection was rising sharply in South Africa has drawn criticism from Edwin Cameron, South Africa's AIDS activist judge: 'He more than anyone else could through his enormous stature have reached into the minds and behaviour of young people . . . A message from this man of saint-like, in some ways god-like, stature would have been effective. He didn't do it. In 199 ways he was our country's saviour. In the 200th way, he was not.'[10]

Health Minister Dlamini-Zuma made other mistakes. There was the Sarafina II scandal where European Union funding was allocated to, and wasted on, a play intended to raise AIDS awareness. A furore broke out around government support for Virodene, a claimed antiviral medication made from antifreeze, or dimethylformamide, which resulted in the purging and mass resignation of Medicines Control Council staff.[11]

By 1998, the Health Minister further undermined the government's response to HIV/AIDS by suspending projects aimed at preventing HIV transmission from mother to child (mother-to-child transmission prevention or MTCTP) through the use of antiretroviral (ARV) treatment.[12]

With Thabo Mbeki's elevation to the office of President, the South African government's HIV/AIDS policy veered increasingly off course, abandoning internationally accepted science and heading into the dark terrain of AIDS denialism. Most notable was the government's disputing that HIV causes AIDS. But the government was also reluctant to accept that antiretroviral drug treatment worked and dismissed offers of assistance from the pharmaceutical companies, in the form of price reductions or generic drug production.[13]

'The world's biggest killer and the greatest cause of ill-health and suffering across the globe, including South Africa, is extreme poverty'

The inclusion of so-called denialist scientists[14] on the Presidential AIDS Advisory Panel drew heavy criticism. In his typically acerbic style, the cartoonist Zapiro captured the madness of providing such a platform to these views in a cartoon published on 16 March 2000, showing the Mad Hatter announcing to 'President Mbeki's Select Advisory Panel of International AIDS Experts'— consisting of Dr Strangelove, The Nutty Professor, Dr Jekyll, Dr Seuss, the Pool Doctor, Dr Doolittle, Dr Alban, Professor Calculus and Dr Khumalo—that 'There is no causal link between HIV and AIDS'.

Mbeki's denialism was crisply summarised in his comments to the 2000 International AIDS Conference held in Durban. He told the assembled scientists, activists and medical professionals: 'The world's biggest killer and the greatest cause of ill-health and suffering across the globe, including South Africa, is extreme poverty.'[15] In later public statements, Mbeki questioned Parliament: 'How does a virus cause a syndrome? It cannot really, truly. I think it is incorrect from everything I have read to say immune deficiency is acquired exclusively from a virus.'[16] He repeated this view in newspaper articles and interviews locally and internationally. When *Time* magazine pressed him on whether he would acknowledge a link between the HI virus and AIDS, he replied: 'This is precisely where the problem starts. No, I'm saying that you cannot attribute immune deficiency solely and exclusively to a virus.'[17]

The Health Minister, who was now Tshabalala-Msimang, attracted controversy of her own, claiming that HIV had been scientifically engineered by the world's ruling elite to reverse the explosive population growth of the mid-

20th century.[18] She also urged AIDS sufferers to consume beetroot, garlic, lemon, olive oil and African potatoes to boost their immune system.[19]

The Mbeki government asserted that the white and, to use the government's term, 'Western' attitudes to its embrace of so-called denialism were racist. This point of view was captured in a document said to bear Mbeki's electronic signature, but believed to be authored by Peter Mokaba, which trumpeted:

> Regardless of the fact that the scientific proof is hard to come by, nevertheless the conviction has taken firm hold that sub-Saharan Africa will surely be wiped out by an HIV/AIDS pandemic unless, most important of all, we access anti-retroviral drugs. This urgent and insistent call is made by some of the friends of the Africans, who are intent that the Africans must be saved from a plague worse than the Black Death of many centuries ago. For their part, the Africans believe this story, as told by their friends. They too shout the message that—yes, indeed, we are as they say we are! Yes, we are sex-crazy! Yes, we are diseased! Yes, we spread the deadly HI Virus through our uncontrolled heterosexual sex! In this regard, yes, we are different from the US and Western Europe! Yes, we, the men, abuse women and the girl-child with gay abandon! Yes, among us rape is endemic because of our culture! Yes, we do believe that sleeping with young virgins will cure us of AIDS! Yes, as a result of all this, we are threatened with destruction by the HIV/AIDS pandemic! Yes, what we need, and cannot afford, because we are poor, are condoms and anti-retroviral drugs! Help![20]

In a letter dated 4 September 2006 and addressed to President Mbeki, 82 concerned HIV scientists, with prestigious credentials from across the world, captured the poverty of the government's response to the epidemic and the danger of the AIDS denialist view:

> To deny that HIV causes AIDS is farcical in the face of the scientific evidence; to promote ineffective, immoral policies on HIV/AIDS endangers lives; to have as Health Minister a person who now has no international respect is an embarrassment to the South African government. We therefore call for the immediate removal of Dr Tshabalala-Msimang as Minister of Health, and for an end to the disastrous, pseudo-scientific policies that have characterised the South African government's response to HIV/AIDS.

The final word on the governmental failure to address HIV/AIDS goes to Stephen Lewis, the United Nations Special Envoy for HIV/AIDS in Africa who concluded the 2006 AIDS conference in Toronto by saying:

> South Africa is the unkindest cut of all. It is the only country in Africa, amongst all the countries I have traversed in the last five years, whose government is still obtuse, dilatory and negligent about rolling out treatment. It is the only country in Africa whose government continues to propound theories more worthy of a lunatic fringe than of a concerned and compassionate state. Between six and eight hundred people a day die of

AIDS in South Africa. The government has a lot to atone for. I'm of the opinion that they can never achieve redemption.[21]

Clearly, it is well beyond the scope of this chapter to document the many shifts, details and developments that have marked South Africa's HIV/AIDS policy. What the preceding pages hope to do, however, is show how politicised HIV/AIDS treatment became and how divided views were between government and AIDS experts that treatment reached an impasse. Something had to give to break the deadlock

Campaigning for treatment

Leading the opposition to the government's response to the issue was the Treatment Action Campaign (TAC), founded on World AIDS Day, 10 December 1998. At its head was Zackie Achmat, who cut his political teeth as a community organiser in Mitchells Plain and later in the Marxist Workers' Tendency, a pro-poor socialist faction of the ANC. Achmat lives openly with HIV.

The TAC began as a part of the government-sponsored National Association of People Living With HIV/AIDS (NAPWA). In the hope of greater effectiveness, it broke away the next year to become an independent organisation.

Among the TAC's stated objectives[22] are to promote and sponsor legislation to ensure equal access to social services for and equal treatment of all people with HIV/AIDS. To this end, the TAC will challenge, by means of litigation, lobbying, advocacy and all forms of legitimate social mobilisation, any barrier or obstacle, including unfair discrimination, that limits access to treatment for HIV/AIDS in the private and public sector.

Lobbying and education were complemented by strategic litigation

Achmat confirmed in an interview with the authors that the TAC consciously and deliberately chose to pursue parallel strategies of law and politics to achieve its objectives. Thus, mobilisation, lobbying and education were complemented by strategic litigation. This litigation was also tailored to focus on narrow issues. This approach not only exploits the spaces available for change, but also creates the political and social conditions necessary for change. This context-creating political work needs to come before, during and after the institution of any related litigation because the launching of a case without this supporting political work would be dangerous. The TAC chose to campaign around the MTCTP issue 'not simply as a medical problem, but a human rights issue . . .'[23]

The case

A single dose of antiretroviral treatment, such as the drug Nevirapine, given to HIV-positive mothers is an essential aspect of preventing the further spread of HIV. According to *Pregnancy and HIV/AIDS: A PRACTICAL GUIDE*, issued by the TAC and the AIDS Law Project in July 2001:

> ... [a]t least 30 of every 100 HIV positive pregnant women in South Africa will transmit HIV to their babies. This is called mother to child transmission. It mostly happens during delivery, but may also occur while the baby is in the womb or after birth during breastfeeding.[24] The Nevirapine prevention regime consists of a single dose of 200mg given at the onset of labour, and one dose of 0.6mls Nevirapine syrup is given to the newborn within 72 hours of birth.[25] Where medically indicated, it can drastically reduce and all but immunise the infant against transmission of the HI virus. By 1998, it was estimated that up to 70 000 HIV-positive babies were born every year, with resultant increases in infant mortality rates.[26]

Between 1999 and 2001, the TAC held a series of meetings with both Ministers of Health to press for the provision of ARVs. It mobilised demonstrations, delivered a 50 000 signatory petition to the President and ran campaigns calling on the manufacturers of the required drugs to reduce their price. At first, these efforts were relatively well received and prompted government action. For example, the Gauteng Health Department moved aggressively to establish five sites at which MTCTP programmes were introduced.[27] However, as the grip of so-called AIDS denialism tightened and the pseudoscience of AIDS dissidents gained traction within the executive, the government's policy and action on MTCTP came off the rails. The Health Minister and President publicly aired views that the toxicity and possible side-effects of antiretroviral drugs were reasons to avoid their use.[28] As Heywood explains:

> Thus on 5 April 2000 the Minister of Health, Dr Tshabalala-Msimang, made a speech to Parliament that had all the hallmarks of 'dissidentese'. Raising reasonable concerns about a number of deaths of adults on therapeutic drug trials that appeared to be associated with daily Nevirapine use as part of a combination of anti-retroviral drugs, she confused these deaths with use of the same medicine for preventing intra-partum HIV transmission—despite the knowledge that it requires only one dose to mother and child and the fact that there were no reported adverse safety events concerning its use in MTCT.[29]

Over the next few months, the government seemed to accept Nevirapine in the light of encouraging clinical trials in Uganda. In response, the TAC backed off from its demands, pending the outcome of a local trial.[30] However, the government's next steps—notably, President Mbeki's failure to mention HIV as a specific challenge facing Africa in his opening speech to the International AIDS Conference held in Durban during July 2000 and the government's decline of an offer of five years' free supply of Nevirapine from its manufacturer—made it clear that waiting for political resolutions was probably going to be futile.[31]

The TAC again contemplated legal action to force access to the necessary treatment for MTCTP. It was joined in its drive for MTCTP action by, among others, Save Our Babies, a campaign of pediatricians founded by Drs Haroon Salojee and Ashraf Coovadia.

Following the formal registration of Nevirapine with the Medicines Control Council for MTCTP purposes on 18 April 2001, the TAC assembled its legal team of Geoff Budlender, attorney and Director of the Legal Resources Centre Constitutional Litigation Unit, and advocates Gilbert Marcus SC and Bongani Majola.[32]

The TAC's first letter of demand was sent to the Minister of Health and the nine provincial MECs for Health, seeking explanations for the failure to make treatment available throughout the country's public health sector. At the time, ARV provision was limited to two pilot sites per province, one urban and one rural. These pilot sites provided a comprehensive complementary programme which included counselling, information and education around related and critical issues such as breastfeeding. The effect of the programme structure was that, if a patient went to one of the two pilot sites, ARVs could be obtained. But if a patient was unable to access one of these sites—either because she could not physically go to them or she could not afford the cost of private healthcare and had to resort to the public system outside of these sites— she would be denied this critical treatment.

While it is obviously more desirable to have drug treatment bolstered by the other aspects of the programme, it is plainly undesirable to deny necessary drugs altogether.

Tellingly, the nine provinces differed drastically on their ARV rollouts. For example, while eight of the provinces claimed that their efforts were restricted to the pilot sites, the Western Cape planned to roll out to 100 per cent of the province's healthcare facilities. As Heywood explained:

> This early disjuncture between the provinces was to be the undoing of the government's legal case. By offering an example of what could be done, it created a moral pressure on other provinces to extend their programmes beyond the artificial boundaries of the pilot sites. Hereafter a divergence [occurred], sometimes openly, sometimes covertly, between those provinces who saw it as part of their constitutional duty to expand prevention programmes, and those who apparently did not.[33]

While the government responded to the TAC's concerns about the structure of the pilot programmes by reiterating its concerns about drug safety and efficacy and the need for further research, the TAC, joined by other organisations in civil society, challenged the reasonableness of this policy in an application filed in

August 2001. The respondents in the application were the Minister of Health and the provincial health MECs. The Western Cape was later dropped from the case, given its approach to the ARV rollout.

Two issues in one

There were essentially two issues in the case, which are related to each other as a result of the structure of the Bill of Rights. The first issue was government's overarching duty under sections 7(2) ('The state must respect, protect, promote and fulfil the rights in the Bill of Rights') and 8(1) ('The Bill of Rights applies to all law, and binds the legislature, the executive, the judiciary and all organs of state') to implement the rights expressly guaranteed in the Bill of Rights including specific healthcare rights. These were the right of every citizen to public healthcare and the right of children to be afforded special protection. These rights are expressed in sections 27 ('Everyone has the right to have access to... healthcare services, including reproductive healthcare ... The state must take reasonable legislative and other measures, within its available resources, to achieve the progressive realisation of each of these rights') and 28 ('Every child has the right ... to basic nutrition, shelter, basic healthcare services and social services').

This umbrella duty then gives rise to the second issue arising out of these provisions: whether government is constitutionally obliged to plan and implement an effective, comprehensive and progressive programme for the prevention of mother-to-child transmission of HIV throughout the country.

The government opposed the application on two grounds—that the relief sought was unaffordable and that Nevirapine posed health risks which required further research. While admitting that the drug had been registered with the Medicines Control Council for MTCTP purposes, the government's legal papers were peppered with doubts about its safety and raised the prospect of drug resistance in the future, which would be 'catastrophic for public health'.[34] The government also raised the flag of impossibility by arguing that Nevirapine was most effective when provided as part of a counselling, testing and educational programme in particular focused on breastfeeding practices (to prevent HIV transmission through breastfeeding) and ensuring access to infant milk formula, but that such a programme was impossible due to resource constraints.[35]

The government's legal papers were peppered with doubts

In response, the TAC filed replying papers replete with expert affidavits tackling the government's representation of the scientific evidence regarding Nevirapine's safety and resistance, as well as further evidence of the health department's budgetary and resource capacity to roll out its provision.

The clear appreciation by both sides of the high political stakes of the TAC's challenge to the government's public health policy on MTCTP were confirmed by counsel in interviews, as was the high level of acrimony between the parties. The possibility of political interference in the case was also raised. The South African Human Rights Commission applied to be an *amicus curiae*, or friend of the court, in the TAC case. This followed the Commission's investigation of a complaint filed by Dr Costa Gazi, a doctor from the Eastern Cape, who accused the Minister of Health of manslaughter for failing to provide MTCTP measures. However, the Commission abruptly withdrew its application to assist the Court. Subsequent media reports revealed allegations that the government's senior counsel had contacted the Commission's chairperson, Barney Pityana, and that the president's legal adviser had approached another member of the Commission to discuss its involvement in the case. According to these reports, an internal discussion resulted in a 5-4 vote to withdraw from the case. The Commission denied that political pressure caused its change of heart and stated that 'the decision to withdraw was based on the fact that we had nothing new or additional to contribute to the TAC case'.[36]

Judge Botha in the High Court

The application was heard in the charged atmosphere of rallies and marches organised by the TAC, building up to an all-night vigil by approximately 600 TAC volunteers outside the courthouse. The hearing itself was packed with TAC members, journalists, medical professionals and members of the public curious about this most high profile of cases.[37]

The application was heard in the charged atmosphere of rallies and marches organised by the TAC

The judge who heard the case was Chris Botha, ironically the son of a true apartheid idealogue and former Minister of Bantu Affairs. Yet this personal background was no obstacle to Judge Botha's capacity for progressive judgment. In his judgment issued on 14 December 2001 he found in favour of the TAC and decided that the government's policy on MTCTP was not reasonable. Judge Botha required that Nevirapine be provided when its prescription was medically indicated and ordered that the government was under a duty to both develop and implement an effective, comprehensive, national programme to prevent or reduce mother-to-child transmission of HIV.

The judgment was both praised and attacked. The *Sunday Times* published an editorial noting that '[t]he outcome shows that even strongly dominant political opinion cannot stand in the way of a Constitution that is supreme. Every child born free of HIV as a result of this week's decision will be living proof of the wisdom our society showed in opting for this form of democracy.'[38] But some legal academics argued that the judgment overstepped the line between the judiciary and executive. This criticism boiled down to a claim that 'government policy is a political creature and this is why it is governments that make policy, not judges. The remedy for unpopular government policy should rightfully be political, not legal.'[39]

This line of argument was relied on by the Minister when she announced the filing of an application for leave to appeal directly to the Constitutional Court on 18 December 2001, seeking clarification of the jurisdictional boundaries between executive policy-making and judicial review. At the same time, the TAC's lawyers launched an application to execute the part of the judgment that ordered that Nevirapine be made available where capacity to do so exists, arguing that further delay came at the unacceptable cost of newborn lives. Ordinarily, the initiation of appellate proceedings suspends the operation of any court order. However, the TAC argued that the implementation of the court's order before the appeals were finalised could save 10 newborn lives a day.[40] The government did not deny this claim.

However, the TAC argued that the implementation of the court's order before the appeals were finalised could save 10 newborn lives a day

Politically, provincial unity on the issue began to splinter after the judgment, with the premiers of Gauteng and KwaZulu-Natal announcing expansion of their MTCTP programmes.[41] This was echoed in President Mbeki's opening of Parliament speech, and later interviews, when he indicated that 'provinces with the resources to extend the programme should not be delayed by provinces that did not have the resources'.[42] However, the Health Minister distanced herself from these statements and was christened 'Dr No' by *The Star* newspaper in response.[43]

On 1 March 2002, the government's application for leave to appeal and the TAC's application for an execution order were heard by Judge Botha. Ten days later, he ruled in favour of the TAC, finding himself 'unable to formulate a motivation for tolerating preventable deaths for the sake of sparing the [government] prejudice that can not amount to more than organisational inconvenience'.[44]

The government then sought leave to appeal the decision on the execution order to the Constitutional Court. This application was again heard by Judge Botha, who refused leave to appeal. In response, the government sought leave to appeal directly from the Constitutional Court. Heywood argues that this was 'a failure of legal strategy' because, 'although the legal issues that the Constitutional Court had to decide were narrow, and different from those it would consider in the appeal, these could not be approached without consideration of the actual issues, including the rationality of the MTCT policy. The result was that the government itself created a situation that allowed the issues to be aired in the highest court in the land, a month before the dates set for the full appeal.'[45]

Heywood reports that:

> ... [d]uring the hearing, the Constitutional Court judges frequently
> appeared to be at a loss as to why government was so fiercely opposed to the
> execution order. In answer to a question from Chief Justice Chaskalson
> about how infants would suffer from being provided [with] a potentially life
> saving drug, the government's advocate, Marumo Moerane SC, referred to
> 'drug resistance'. When asked by Justice Madala whether government had
> documented any adverse events resulting from the use of Nevirapine in the
> past 11 months, Moerane answered 'no'. Yet, when Justice O'Regan later
> asked precisely what harm would be caused by the execution of the order,
> his answer was that there was 'potential for great, great harm'.[46] On 4 April,
> the Constitutional Court refused the government's application for leave to
> appeal against the order of execution and prompted the headline 'YES, you
> will, Dr No'.[47]

The Minister, for her part, made regrettable comments to the media in which
she indicated that she may not abide by the Court's decision, apparently
claiming that new information on the drug's safety required caution. In a
television interview with SABC News on 24 March 2002, she was asked
whether she would be prepared to follow the Court's decision. To this
she replied:

> *Minister:* My own view is that the judiciary cannot prescribe from the
> bench—and that we have a regulatory authority in this country that is
> interacting with the regulatory authority FDA of the USA and I think we
> must allow them to assist us in reaching conclusions.
> *Interviewer:* Mmm, so you think it's inappropriate that this is in court, but
> nevertheless it's there. Will you stand by whatever the Court decides?
> *Minister:* No, I think the court and the judiciary must also listen to the
> regulatory authority, both of this country and the regulatory authority of
> the US.
> *Interviewer:* So you're saying no?
> *Minister:* I say no. I am saying no.[48]

The Minister of Justice at the time, Penuell Maduna, rushed to assure a startled
public that 'we have no intention of circumventing the courts . . .We stand ready
to abide by the final decision of the courts on the execution order.'[49] But the
Health Minister's remarks underscored the discomfort apparently felt by the
executive about the judiciary's oversight role. They also exposed the contours of
their resulting challenge to the separation of executive, legislative and judicial
powers structured by the Constitution.

The Constitutional Court hearing

At the time of the hearing in the Constitutional Court, the posture of the matter
had changed in significant ways from when it was before the lower court.
Government accepted that something more had to be done to roll out the

treatment programme, the allocated budget was increased accordingly, and three provinces were already at 100 per cent coverage in their rollouts. One has to wonder why the government then persisted in the appeal. The Health Minister had backed down politically and appeared to have conceded the flaws in the policy, given the adjustments made to it. However, persist in the appeal the government did.

The atmosphere at the hearing was tense. Counsel for the Government, Marumo Moerane SC, spoke to us of the emotional judges who gave him a hostile hearing. It was plain that politics had percolated through the Court's walls and informed the Constitutional Court's view of the appeal.

It was plain that politics had percolated through the Court's walls It also was clear that the judges were not unaffected by the broader context in which its decision would be received. This was a major challenge to the executive of the Republic. Yet the Court appeared emboldened to take on the executive branch knowing that public opinion, including international opinion, was against its policy.

There was also palpable tension between the legal teams. The matter had been characterised by a lack of cooperation and a strategic approach that saw every possible technical or procedural point being taken. This all served merely to delay and frustrate the matter's progress, and increased its cost.

As an aside, one of the toughest strategic choices faced by legal teams in such high-stakes and high-profile cases is simply which battles to fight. While technical or procedural arguments may whittle down the case or gain some tactical advantage, they are often not taken up so as not to blur the focus on the main issue(s) in the case. So, adversaries will often agree to condone some non-compliance with the rules of procedure by the other side so as to get the matter heard in the most focused way.

Obviously, fatal flaws cannot be ignored. But, often, given the client's desire to litigate the issue in the full glare of publicity and exploit the political moment of a public hearing before a court, encrusting the case with unnecessary legal points obscures the 'real issue' or the 'big picture'. The lawyers, therefore, need to understand the client's agenda with the litigation because such cases are rarely just about the law. The TAC legal team spoke of the government legal team adopting a singularly obstructive, technical approach. It appeared that the 'big picture' was not uppermost on their agenda.

The atmosphere inside the Court's walls was only heightened by the TAC's decision to mobilise. 'Stand Up For Your Rights' marches took place in Johannesburg, Cape Town and Durban on the first day of argument, 2 May 2002. In the first, more than 5 000 people marched to the Constitutional Court. The Court was also packed with HIV/AIDS activists and health workers and the media had the hearing well covered.[50]

The Constitutional Court judgment

On 5 July 2002, three months after the hearing, judgment was handed down by 'the court'. Contrary to its practice of identifying the judge or judges who authored a judgment in which other members of the bench concur, this time the Constitutional Court handed down its unanimous judgment authored by 'the Court', as it did in other politicised cases such as the *Schabir Shaik* appeal. This was plainly an assertion of its role in executive oversight and demonstrated the judges' appreciation for the critical political importance of their decision. Turning to the government's policy and executive pronouncements, the judgment found that the policy did not pass constitutional muster, in that it failed to ensure reasonable access to healthcare services in a way that reasonably took account of competing pressing social needs.

It is a somewhat unusual judgment since it covers the science and medicine of HIV/AIDS, ARVs and treatment options in a considerable amount of scientific detail. This was a bold move given the AIDS denialism that polluted the corridors of power at the highest level. In most judgments, the recounting of the relevant facts is usually fairly uncontroversial and merely a necessary part of explaining the later reasoning of the Court when it applies the law to the particular set of facts. While parties to litigation often have competing versions of the facts, by the time the matter reaches an apex court, the facts are *Here, the simple act of recounting the science in question was a political act* often fairly settled. Their interpretation and significance is where the contest will remain. But here, the simple act of recounting the science in question was a political act. Accepting mainstream scientific explanations and theories on HIV/AIDS and the options available for its treatment meant a rejection of denialism, scientific dissidence and alternative views of the epidemic's cause, progress and required treatment.

The tone of the judgment reveals that this case was a no brainer on the factual issues. It also represented a deliberate assertion of the Court's institutional integrity and the mechanism of justiciability through which questions of executive policy were susceptible to judicial review and evaluation. But the Court was not about to run head-first at the executive edifice. Instead, it developed its own conception of deference to the executive.

The Constitutional Court's deference to the executive's powers seeks to marry the mandate of the text with the political realities confronting the 'weakest arm of government'. In other words, the Court outlines the acceptable approach to the questions in the case but allows the executive to determine how to follow this approach.

The Court's interpretation of so-called socio-economic rights was developed in a series of cases that arose before the TAC case. First, in *Soobramoney*[51] and, later, in *Grootboom*,[52] the Constitutional Court developed the requirements that government policy must be reasonable, tackle the plight of the most vulnerable first and navigate a course between reasonable measures and available resources.

This 'reasonableness' approach was chosen in preference to the so-called 'minimum core' conception of such rights. The latter view would require a court to determine the minimum content, or minimum core, of each right and then evaluate the government's policy to ensure that this was satisfied. However, this approach ignores the resources and other constraints on government and requires the Court to set policy, rather than allow it to be set by other branches of government. This strays outside the usual court's expertise.

Politically, the 'minimum core' approach is problematic because it is so definitive and prescriptive. In contrast, the 'reasonableness' approach allows government to decide on the nitty-gritty content of a policy and its implementation, and requires only that this be reasonable in light of the factors to be considered and the other demands on government's resources. To an important extent, it also recognises the weakness of a state which has battled to transform from one serving a few million whites to a democratic state which caters for the needs of the whole population of the country.

So, the Court recognised that its pronouncements on policy had budgetary and political consequences and hence the polycentric nature of such decisions. It also accepted that 'besides the pandemic, the state faces huge demands in relation to access to education, land, housing, healthcare, food, water and social security. These are the socio-economic rights entrenched in the Constitution, and the state is obliged to take reasonable legislative and other measures within its available resources to achieve the progressive realisation of each of them. In the light of our history, this is an extraordinarily difficult task.'

In its judgment[53], the Constitutional Court defined itself out of the policy-making process by stating that 'Courts are ill-suited to adjudicate upon issues where court orders could have multiple social and economic consequences for the community. The Constitution contemplates *This is the grime* rather a restrained and focused role for the courts, namely, to *and guts of* require the state to take measures to meet its constitutional *political process or,* obligations and to subject the reasonableness of these measures to *rather, what* evaluation. Such determinations of reasonableness may in fact have *happens when* budgetary implications, but are not in themselves directed at *political policy goes* rearranging budgets. In this way the judicial, legislative and *wrong* executive functions achieve appropriate constitutional balance.'

The Court's judgment therefore reads far more pragmatically than some of its other judgments. Gone are the lofty ambitions and idealistic tones of *Makwanyane*. This is the grime and guts of political process or, rather, what happens when political policy goes wrong.

Public opinion

The judgment raises the question of whether there can be a legal victory in such a case without political pressure framing the issues. Put another way, was this case a slam dunk for the Constitutional Court because the government had already accepted—or been forced to accept—that its policy must change under sustained critical political pressure from the TAC, the media, international commentators and other members of civil society?

Overall, the government's capitulation stands in welcome contrast to the historical governmental response in *Harris* to the Appellate Division's rejection of its policy choices. While the Health Minister's ill-advised comments that she would not abide by the decision of the Court may reveal an insider's view of where power should lie, ultimately the government yielded when it was clear that its policy was indefensible.

Another interesting comparison is how, in this case, the Court was bolstered by public support for its position, whereas, in *Makwanyane*, the Court discounted public opinion that ran contrary to the stance it wished to adopt. This interplay between public opinion and the Court's decision-making reveals that the bench is not isolated from politics and popular views. But, instead, it chooses when to follow and when to resist prevailing opinion. This awareness of political context, as well as consciousness of how their decisions will be received, explains, to some degree, the Court's general reticence and incremental approach. It is then left to apex courts to take radical steps on pressing issues.

A weak remedy

Despite its assertiveness in finding the government's policy unreasonable, the Constitutional Court was not as bold as Judge Botha when it came to the remedy ordered. The question was whether, in addition to declaring the policy unreasonable, the Court would also exercise its supervisory jurisdiction—through a structural interdict which would require regular reportbacks on progress in line with the Court's judgment. The order made by Judge Botha included a structural interdict requiring the appellants to revise their policy and to submit the revised policy to the Court to enable it to satisfy itself that the policy was consistent with the Constitution. The Constitutional Court rejected this remedy, although it required immediate action by government. And it displayed some sense of irony, or some might consider even a sense of humour, sarcasm or naïveté when it stated that '[t]he government has always respected and executed orders of this Court. There is no reason to believe that it will not do so in the present case.'[54]

Two explanations present themselves for the Court's refusal of the structural interdict and constraining itself to a pronouncement on constitutional validity. First, the political winds had shifted and the policy had been revised, making court supervision less necessary, although contempt proceedings were called for in December 2002 against the Health Minister and MEC for Health in Mpumalanga. The judgment acknowledged that 'During the course of these proceedings the state's policy has evolved and is no longer as rigid as it was when the proceedings commenced.'[55]

Second, the Court was ultimately reluctant to wade into matters of so-called polycentric policy-making. Recognising that the demands on government were diverse and immense and that the effect of the Court's order could be to divert resources away from other areas pressing for attention, the Court left such decisions to the policy-makers.

In argument, counsel for the government raised issues pertaining to the separation of powers, which are relevant to explaining the Court's remedial choice in two respects. First, the government urged deference by the courts to decisions taken by the executive concerning the formulation of its policies. And, second, the government argued that a limited order was most appropriate where a court finds that the executive has failed to comply with its constitutional obligations. In the judgment, the Court appears to have accepted the import of the second argument but found, in the first, that deference must yield to justiciability. In the words of the judgment, '[i]n so far as [judicial oversight] constitutes an intrusion into the domain of the executive, that is an intrusion mandated by the Constitution itself'. The Court therefore recognised the principle of separation of powers but only as it is in play with the supremacy of the constitutional role of the court.

The TAC case made clear that government was accountable, to the courts, to the Constitution and, through both of these, to the citizenry it serves. But it also revealed the weakness of litigation in achieving political and social goals. Delay, expense and often imperfect outcomes accompany litigation. This is why it is seldom successfully used in isolation from politics. In the crisp words of Geoff Budlender, TAC's attorney in the case, the judgment was 'simply the conclusion of a battle that TAC had already won outside the courts, but with the skilful use of the courts as part of a broader struggle'.[56]

Endnotes

1   Etienne Mureinik 'Beyond a Charter of Luxuries; Economic Rights in the Constitution' (1992) *SAJHR* 465-472.
2   The authors are heavily indebted to Nicoli Nattrass's comprehensive, exhaustively researched and referenced work *Mortal Combat* for the historical and empirical facts surrounding the HIV/AIDS epidemic in South Africa and the governmental response thereto.
3   Nattrass 'Letter to President Mbeki from Concerned HIV Scientists' (4 September 2006) 197.

4   Nattrass *ibid* 38-39.

5   Nattrass *ibid* 9.

6   Nattrass *ibid* 40.

7   Nattrass *ibid* 40.

8   Xolela Mangcu *To the brink: The State of Democracy in South Africa* (2008) at 50.

9   Nattrass *ibid* 40-41.

10 Natrrass *ibid* 41-44.

11 Nattrass *ibid* 44-60.

12 We use the term 'MTCTP', aware that it also appears as 'MTCT' in some of the relevant recent literature.

13 The term 'denialist' was coined by the TAC and is used here to show the power of its characterisation of the government's policies and the way in which this framed the MTCTP issue.

14 Mangcu *ibid* 56.

15 Mangcu *ibid* 56.

16 Mangcu *ibid* 56

17 Nattrass *ibid* 75.

18 Nattrass *ibid* 107, 113.

19 Nattrass *ibid* 88.

20 Mangcu *ibid* 57.

21 www.tac.org.za, last visited 4 January 2008.

22 Mangcu *ibid* 62.

23 www.tac.org.za/Documents/Literacy/mtctguid.rtf, last visited 29 January 2008.

24 *Ibid.*

25 M Heywood 'Preventing Mother-to-child HIV Transmission in South Africa: Background, Strategies and Outcomes of the Treatment Action Campaign Case against the Minister of Health' 2003 (19) *SAJHR* 278-280.

26 Heywood *ibid* 281.

27 Heywood *ibid* 281-285.

28 Heywood *ibid* 284.

29 Heywood *ibid* 285.

30 Heywood *ibid* 286.

31 Heywood *ibid* 286-289.

32 Heywood *ibid* 292.

33 Dr A Ntsaluba answering affidavit 658, 665, 705, 816; Heywood *ibid* 296.

34 Heywood *ibid* 297.

35 Heywood *ibid* 299-300; 'HRC has nothing new to add' *Mail & Guardian* (23 November 2001).

36 Heywood 300-301.

37 'Thanks to our Constitution' *Sunday Times* (16 December 2001); Heywood *ibid* 301.

38 Hopkins K 'Shattering the Divide When Judges Go Too Far' (March 2002) *De Rebus* 23-6; Heywood *ibid* 301.

39 Heywood *ibid* 304.

40 Address by Premier Shilowa at opening of Gauteng provincial legislature (http://www.gpg.gov.za/docs/sp/2002/sp0218.html); Heywood *ibid* 303.

41 *Newshour* SABC 3 (10 February 2002); Heywood *ibid* 303.

42 Heywood *ibid* 304.

43 *TAC v Minister of Health* TPD Case No 21182/2001 (8 March 2002) 12-13; Heywood p 305.

44 Heywood *ibid* 306-307.

45 Heywood *ibid* 307.

46 *The Star* (5 April 2002); Heywood *ibid* 307.

47 'More damage control after Manto says No' *The Star* (25 March 2002).

48 Ministry of Health media statement (27 March 2002).

49 Heywood *ibid* 310.

50 At para 38.

51 1998 (12) BCLR 1696 (CC).

52 2000 (11) BCLR 1169 (CC).

53 At para 129.

54 Heywood *ibid* 315.

55 At para 118.

56 G Budlender 'A Paper Dog with Real Teeth' *Mail & Guardian* (12 July 2002); Heywood *ibid* 314.

nine

A special relationship[1]

'Family, good friends, cigarettes and anger'

— Alix Carmichele
(when asked what sustained her in her 13-year fight for justice)[2]

Carol Burgers, her partner and children, were all holidaying in Plettenberg Bay. On Sunday, 6 August 1995, they decided to enjoy a walk along the beach at the secluded town of Knoetzie. Known as a tranquil and beautiful small hamlet, Knoetzie is an isolated spot, 12 kilometres from Knysna, *en route* to another popular holidaymakers' paradise, Plettenberg Bay. To get there, one winds down a dirt road which passes through the forests that mark the area, until one is alongside the beach. A handful of homes, only two of which are used by year-round residents, are the sum total of Knoetzie.

Burgers's group was startled to see a woman rushing towards the beach, bleeding and clutching her left arm. They initially thought she had been bitten by a dog. They rushed to help her, and Alix Carmichele told them that she had been attacked by a man named Francois Coetzee. She also announced that he was out on a pending rape charge and that her close friend, Julie Gosling, had repeatedly urged the police to apprehend Francois because he was a danger to the community. Gosling arrived shortly thereafter, and saw Alix sitting, covered in blood. About two hours later, an ambulance arrived to treat Alix's injuries.

Francois surrendered to the police after the attack. Unfortunately, this was not the first time he had attacked women in the area. These events prompted litigation, lasting more than a decade, to secure recognition of the constitutionally mandated duty of the state to prevent violence against women.

Francois Coetzee, 21 years old in 1995, was unemployed and lived with his mother in Knoetzie. Born in Knysna, he was the eldest of six children. His father, Daniel, left the family when Francois was nine years old. Annie Coetzee, his mother, worked as a domestic worker for Julie Gosling. Gosling edited a local Knysna classified newspaper called *Action Ads* and was occasionally assisted in the business by Annie.

Francois was a troubled child. Court records show how, as an early adolescent, his mother became aware that he was accused of molesting young girls. Hoping that there was some medication available that could control these urges, she consulted the family doctor about her son's behaviour. She was told that he was too young for any medication. Given what would follow, one can only wonder what tragedy could have been averted had there been earlier intervention to address Francois's inappropriate urges.

Beverly Claasen

Francois's grandmother lived in Hornlee, in Knysna. Next door, with her parents, lived Beverly Claasen, who was 25 years old in June 1994 when Francois climbed through her bedroom window and into bed with the sleeping Beverly. He touched her on her legs and waist, and pulled her panties down. He later acknowledged at trial that his 'leg and hands were not where they should have been' and claimed that he was looking for somewhere to sleep, and that he thought he was outside his grandmother's house. Beverly woke up and screamed, scaring Francois so that he leapt back through the bedroom window.

At the subsequent trial, Francois was convicted of housebreaking and indecent assault. The Magistrate found that he should not be sent to prison, taking into account that this was Francois's first conviction, and that he was a young man who had testified in mitigation of sentence that he wished to finish his matric and further his studies at the University of the Western Cape. The magistrate found that Francois might have been drunk on the night in question, but that he was nevertheless responsible for his actions. He was, therefore, sentenced to 18 months' imprisonment, suspended for four years, and to a fine of R600 or six months' imprisonment plus 12 months' imprisonment suspended for four years. His mother paid the R600 fine, and he was never incarcerated.

Eurena Terblanche

Nearly a year later, in March 1995, he attempted to rape and murder another of his neighbours, Eurena Terblanche, who was 17 years old at the time. Eurena was in matric at Knysna Secondary School, along with Francois. He sang in the choir with her brother and they knew each other from school; Francois had played dominoes at Eurena's house. On the night of Friday, 3 March, a dance was held at the Hornlee Hotel which Francois and Eurena both attended. He offered to walk her home, and she accepted because she knew him.

As subsequent evidence would show, on the walk home, he persuaded Eurena to accompany him on a detour, claiming he wanted to visit a friend of his. Initially reluctant, Eurena agreed. A little further on, he stopped and asked her what she was going to give him in return for walking her home. Eurena thought he was kidding with her, and laughed it off. Francois tried to kiss her and wrestled with her when she resisted him. Francois then grabbed her by the neck, kicked her legs out from under her and threw her into the long grass alongside the dirt footpath. He then punched her, kicked her and sat on top of her. She struggled throughout, but eventually passed out after Francois kept hitting, kicking and throttling her. He told her to shut up and, during the attack, he said that he wanted to kill her.

When she woke up, Eurena felt wet between her legs. She was wearing only a t-shirt, and her denim pants and shirt were lying next to her. But her panties were not there. Her arms were pressed underneath her and her legs were a little open. At the time she had passed out, she had been fully clothed.

Eurena fled to the home of people she knew and told them about the attack. Together with other neighbours, she returned home to her mother, Doreen. The police were called and Doreen told them Francois had raped her daughter. The police reported that Francois was already in custody, having been arrested at the Hornlee Hotel. Francois had apparently returned to the hotel where he asked hotel employees to call the police because he had murdered a girl. They disbelieved him but did call the police who arrested him for being under the influence.

Eurena fled to the home of people she knew and told them about the attack

Eurena was examined by a district surgeon and then met with the police to provide a statement about the attack. Her mother told the police about Francois's earlier conviction for the attack on Beverly, which the duty officer noted in the investigation diary, thinking it may be relevant to the question of bail.

Following further interviews with Eurena, and an inspection of the crime scene, the investigating officer handed over the file to the prosecutor handling Francois's appearance in court on Monday, 6 March. The investigating officer appears to have made no effort to ascertain the details of Francois's earlier conviction, and recommended that he be released on a warning. The prosecutor followed this recommendation. Francois was released on a warning, whereupon he returned to live with his mother in Knoetzie.

More warnings

A day or two later, Doreen Terblanche, Eurena's mother, visited her friend, Julie Gosling, because she knew that Gosling employed Francois's mother in her home and business. She told Gosling of the attack on her daughter and of Francois's earlier conviction for the attack on Beverly Claasen.

Distressed at this news, Gosling went to see the police to question why Francois had been released on a warning when it seemed reasonable to predict that he would commit a similar crime again. It was just a matter of time. She was told to discuss her concerns about his release with the senior public prosecutor,

Dian Louw, whom Gosling knew. Gosling told Louw that she was afraid that Francois would attack again. But Louw told her that there was nothing that could be done—until he broke the law again.

Francois's own mother was concerned about her son repeating his criminal conduct, and feared that he may harm himself. She discussed these fears with a relative of hers, who was also a sergeant in the police service, when he gave her a lift home. When they arrived in Knoetzie, they discovered that Francois had in fact attempted suicide. He had tried to hang himself with his necktie, and then drank all the pills in the house before slashing his wrists. He was rushed to hospital and treated, after which he returned to Knoetzie and his mother. Francois tried to commit suicide three times following his attack on Eurena.

The next day, Francois was interviewed by prosecutor Louw. He admitted that from the time he was 10 years old, he had suffered uncontrolled sexual urges. He had molested his cousin, would masturbate after becoming aroused on seeing women in bathing suits and otherwise masturbated frequently. Louw noted his previous conviction and recorded his sense that, when he attacked women 'it was as if a supernatural force got hold of him and he then committed a deed which he is not even aware of. His friends had started calling him "the ghost". He requested that he be sent to Valkenburg. He asked that he should not be kept in jail before he is sentenced.'

He was accordingly charged, and pleaded not guilty

Francois was referred to Valkenburg for 30 days' observation of his mental health. He returned to Knysna for a court appearance on 18 April 1995, where a report was handed up concluding that, despite a troubled past, Francois was mentally fit to stand trial. He was accordingly charged, and pleaded not guilty. The case was postponed for hearing in early May. Again, the presiding magistrate was not informed of Francois's earlier conviction and he was released on his own recognizance and warned to appear in court at the next hearing.

Alix Carmichele

While out awaiting trial, Francois attacked again. As would emerge in later legal proceedings, one morning towards the end of June 1995, Alix Carmichele, a freelance photographer from Knysna and close friend of Julie, awoke after spending the night at Julie's home to find Francois 'snooping around the house' and 'trying to push the window open.' Alix confronted Francois, who told her he was looking for Julie. Shaken, Alix called Julie and told her what had happened. Julie replied that Francois's explanation was unbelievable because he could plainly see that her car was not at the house. At Alix's request, Julie went to the Knysna charge office and reported the incident. Again, she was referred to prosecutor Louw.

Julie reportedly told Louw 'you've got to do something about this guy, there must be some law to protect society ... she said to me that there was nothing she could do and I remember this so distinctly because she put a peppermint in her mouth and she said "Oh, but that court stinks" and that is what she said and she said "her hands were tied".'

On 2 August 1995, Julie and Alix again raised their fears about Francois with Louw when she visited the *Action Ads* office in Knysna. Louw again claimed to be powerless to do anything about him. Until he broke the law again.

Four days later, on Sunday, 6 August 1995, as the Burgers were enjoying their walk on Knoetzie's beach, Alix arrived at Julie's home in the late morning. She had arranged to meet Julie there for a braai. Alix noticed an open window at the house, which was unusual because Julie was fastidious about locking up her home. Alix let herself into the house and went to play with Julie's dogs on the outside deck. Approximately 10 or 15 minutes later, she went back into the house to use the bathroom.

As she later told the police in her statement: 'As I was walking towards the bathroom, a man who I recognized as Francois Coetzee jumped out in front of me. He held a pick handle above his head. He struck me once on the head and I fell onto my knees. The blows that followed were directed at my head and face, and that is when I lifted my left arm to protect myself ... he struck me once again with the pick handle. I noted that he reached for a knife, which he had between his teeth and in his mouth. He spoke to me, calling me by my name and ordering me to turn around onto my stomach. That is when I noticed my left arm hanging uselessly and quite obviously broken ... He threatened to count to three. The knife was still in his mouth and he shouted at me through clenched teeth ... he dragged me by my clothes into the passage, still holding the pick handle and the knife.... By this stage, I was lying on my left side, when he suddenly threw the pick handle to his right into the passage and took the knife from his mouth. Standing over me, astride my body, he stabbed me with the knife. He lunged at me forcefully, stabbing at my heart region, on my left breast. The blade of the knife bent as it hit my breast bone and the blade buckled. I knew he intended to murder me by the crazed look in his eyes, therefore I kicked out at him with both my legs. He seemed surprised. He fell back and I tried to grab the pick handle, but I realized he was recovering quickly so I made a dash for the already open double doors ... Holding my broken arm, I dashed through the doors leading out to the deck and ran out onto the beach, towards people.'

'He struck me once again with the pick handle'

On 11 September 1995, Francois represented himself at the trial on charges relating to Eurena. After emotional testimony from both Eurena and Francois, he was found guilty of the attempted rape of Eurena and sentenced to seven years' imprisonment.

On 13 December 1995, Francois stood trial for the attack on Alix. He was convicted of attempted murder and housebreaking in the Knysna regional court and was sentenced to an effective term of imprisonment of twelve and a half years. He was incarcerated in Malmesbury prison. Francois told the inspector who accompanied him back to Knysna from his stint for observation at Valkenburg that he knew that he had 'done something wrong'. He told him that he was reading the Bible, that he knew that he would receive a jail sentence and that he had decided that he was going to study while he was in jail. In a depressing later development, Francois violently assaulted a female warden in Malmesbury prison in 2006.

Round one

Alix later described to a journalist how 'with each operation (to mend the broken bones in her arm), I became more angry. I asked myself why it happened to me. It didn't have to happen to me; if only the police and prosecutors had done their jobs properly.'[3] She was introduced to Perino Pama, a UCT graduate who had moved to Knysna, and retained him to launch a lawsuit aimed at holding the state accountable for its failure to prevent Francois's attack on her. Like other cases in this book, the *Carmichele* case would be the product of the extraordinary good fortune of having a determined litigant meet a committed attorney, willing to fund the case without payment, and up for the fight that would drag on for years and years. As Alix herself recognised and described in media reports, the same system that failed her, also failed to protect a desperate, lost soul from himself. Despite handing himself over after attacking his second victim, telling the prosecutor he could not control himself around women and attempting to commit suicide while out on a warning, the state let Francois Coetzee go free. 'A grave injustice has been done to Francois,' Alix says. 'Perhaps if they'd heeded his calls for help, he could've been rehabilitated. Now he'll spend most of his youth in jail. It's a wasted life.'[4]

Carmichele instituted proceedings in the Cape High Court for damages against the Minister for Safety and Security and the Minister of Justice and Constitutional Development. She claimed that members of the South African Police Service and the public prosecutors at Knysna had negligently failed to comply with a legal duty they owed to her to take steps to prevent Francois from causing her harm. Carmichele initially claimed R177 315.49 for her medical expenses, lost income and other damages.

When the trial started on 4 September 1997, Alix was represented by advocates Terry Price, an experienced member of the Port Elizabeth Bar whose previous career as a police officer and prosecutor was invaluable, and Deon Erasmus. 'Fef' le Roux SC, a seasoned counsel from the Cape Bar, and his junior, Ranjan Jaga, acted for the State. Judge Dylan Chetty presided. He was appointed to the Cape High Court after a successful career as a silk, or senior counsel, in the Eastern Cape, and earned himself a well-deserved reputation as a thoughtful, careful and hardworking jurist.

Procedurally, the issues of liability (was the state responsible for the attack on Carmichele) and damages (if so, how much was she entitled to as compensation) in the case had been separated. This meant that they would be determined in stages. Without a finding as to liability, there would be no need to lead evidence establishing damages.

Alix's case opened with evidence from the sergeant who received Eurena Terblanche's report of her attack, and noted Francois's previous conviction for the Claasen assault, thinking that it may be important to the prosecutor for bail purposes. The next witness was Doreen Terblanche, who confirmed that she had advised the police when reporting the attack on Eurena that this was Francois's second attack on a local woman. She also testified that she had told the police this because she did not want Francois released from custody. After he had been released, Francois went around to the Terblanche home. Doreen told him she did not want him there and called the police; he ran away. When the police arrived, she told them that if he ever set foot on her property again she would 'burn him until he was well-done' and how unhappy she was that he was not in custody.

The prosecutors had not made him aware of Francois's prior criminal conduct

Magistrate Kevin von Bratt from Knysna, who had released Francois after the attack on Eurena and who had referred him to Valkenburg for observation, took the witness stand next. He confirmed that the prosecutors had not made him aware of Francois's prior criminal conduct. Tellingly, he also confessed that the enactment of the Interim Constitution had shifted the approach to bail from a burden on an accused person to convince the court of his entitlement to bail, to an emphasis on the personal freedom of the individual. The practical effect of the new constitutional regime was that accused persons were released from custody more easily and readily.

Annie Coetzee, Francois's mother, then testified. She described how the attack on Alix was the culmination of her son's tragic life and how she had thought for a long time that 'there must be something wrong with him if he does these things.' She confirmed that he was known to her neighbours and employer in Knoetzie, and that he had sometimes assisted Gosling with chores, such as carrying firewood and batteries in winter, around her home.

Alix Carmichele told the Court that she knew about Francois's problematic personal history and his earlier attacks on local women. She confirmed that she felt threatened by him, despite his slight build, and that both she and her friend, Gosling, has spoken to the prosecutor, Louw, about him and their fears that he was a danger to them. Alix also described the attack itself and her belief that Francois wanted to rape her during the vicious assault.

In an unusual development, Carmichele's attorney in the case, Perino Pama, was next up to testify. Pama was a necessary witness in order to introduce the handwritten notes made by Dian Louw, the prosecutor, as evidence in the trial. The awkwardness of this case, arising in the insular setting of Knoetzie and Knysna, was only confirmed by the fact that Pama and Louw personally knew each other socially from living in their small Garden Route community. Pama, however, reports that Louw never had a bitter word for him concerning the case and he was determined to make the case about how the system had failed Alix, rather than about one prosecutor's shortcomings.

As an aside, Louw has since left the law and is now a skilled body stress release practitioner. One can only speculate that the reflection on her career in the law, with all its attendant and inevitable stress, caused by the case may have prompted her to change her life's work.

At the close of *Carmichele's* case, the State moved to dismiss her claim. On 1 November 1997, Judge Chetty granted this application, in what is known as absolution from the instance, meaning a finding, which has the effect of ending the trial, that there was no evidence from which a court could reasonably find that the police and prosecutors had acted wrongfully. In addition to dismissing the case, he ordered her to pay the legal costs (including the costs of two counsel) incurred by the State.

Carmichele had failed to convince the Court that it was reasonable to expect that the state should have prevented the harm caused to her

Carmichele had failed to convince the Court that it was reasonable to expect that the state should have prevented the harm caused to her by Francois; or, that it was under a duty to do so. This enquiry into the reasonableness of the state's action considers the convictions of the community, or the collective moral and social norms and standards observed and expected by our society of its members. These convictions are embodied, in the first instance, in the Constitution. In particular, an individual's constitutional right to safety and security of his or her person is implicated. Of course, here, the state's 'action' was in fact its inaction, or an omission, to act on the warnings received about Francois. In the words of Alix's attorney, Pama, '[o]ne is generally speaking entitled in law to 'mind one's own business', but this does not apply to the state. It is not entitled to mind its own business. Its very purpose is to mind the business of others.'

If Alix could establish that the state negligently failed to prevent the harm caused to her, the question of the suitable remedy would then arise: the 'so what?' question. As a victim of violent crime, Alix was in a unique position when compared to other victims. For example, imagine that a bureaucrat fails to perform some duty which causes one financial loss. The remedy is to compensate for that loss with a payment equivalent to the amount due if the bureaucrat had done his or her duty. As a victim of crime, Alix cannot have her body restored to its pre-assault state. But she can be compensated financially for the loss or damages suffered. These would include her medical expenses and lost income. This remedial solution would serve to create an incentive for the state to ensure that its functionaries perform their duties satisfactorily. It also distributes the burden of the loss resulting from the incident across the community, rather than having to be borne by the crime victim alone.

Relevant to this question of liability is whether Alix needed to establish that there was a 'special relationship' between herself and the state, giving rise to a particular risk against which she, in particular, should be guarded. While one could see that the repeated complaints about Francois established some sense of a relationship, and a direct one at that, between all these people, ultimately no special relationship was needed. In other cases, municipalities were held liable for potholes in their sidewalks into which pedestrians had fallen, resulting in injury and for preventing rocks from falling onto roadways. In none of these cases was a 'special relationship' between the state and the pedestrian/roaduser required. Alix argued that hers was a case analogous to these scenarios. To the extent that a 'special relationship' was required, there was such a relationship between women and the state, given that the former required the assistance and resources of the latter to protect them against violent sexual predators.

Alix needed to establish that there was a 'special relationship' between herself and the State

Judge Chetty noted that neither Alix nor Julie had laid a charge of trespassing against Francois from the earlier incident when he was snooping around the Gosling residence, and emphasised Magistrate von Bratt's testimony that accused persons were regularly being released on bail at the time. Relying on English case law, which is beyond the scope of this chapter to debate, Judge Chetty found that the state had not acted unreasonably or unlawfully and dismissed the case. Round One to the state.

Round two

Three weeks later, Alix applied for leave to appeal Judge Chetty's judgment to the Appellate Division (now called the Supreme Court of Appeal) in Bloemfontein. Judge Chetty granted her leave to appeal, but that appeal was also dismissed, again with costs. It was now 2-0 to the state.

The only issue considered by the Court in Bloemfontein was 'whether the failure on the part of [the state] to ensure that Francois was not allowed out on bail or a warning, but incarcerated pending his trial, constituted a breach of a legal duty owed' to Alix. Advocate Andrew Breitenbach, assisted by Advocate Terry Price, argued the appeal for Alix; the same legal team represented the state. Breitenbach is today a junior counsel of some seniority, on the cusp of taking silk, who has written several thoughtful articles in the area of administrative law in South African academic journals. He is a highly respected public lawyer and once he was on brief, it was clear that the SCA was going to be confronted with sophisticated constitutional arguments relating to the need to develop this area of law to grant relief to victims like Alix.

Interviews confirm that the legal team knew that politics would enter into this stage of the case. Not only was the case throwing the spotlight on the role of courts in holding other branches of government accountable, but also on the Court's approach to cases of gender violence. The issues to be decided would have far-reaching consequences and the potential to alter radically the relationship between the state and those it should protect from violent crime. It goes without saying that any step toward creating greater accountability for the impact of crime on South Africa would not be taken lightly.

Unfortunately, the five white male judges who presided over the case seemed out of touch with the dramatic shift in judicial attitude required by a constitutional democracy. The judgment is striking in its failure to

The five white male judges who presided over the case seemed out of touch with the dramatic shift in judicial attitude required by a constitutional democracy

even consider the effect of the Constitution, or to engage at all with the constitutional imperative to develop the law to accord with the rights and obligations set out in the Constitution. It was as if the Appeal Court wanted to insist that private law—that sphere of law that concerns individuals' status and relationships—was somehow immunised from the legal impact of the enactment of the Constitution. This marked reluctance to engage with the constitutional issues of the rights of women to the state's protection of their physical integrity, safety and security clearly presented by Advocate Breitenbach in his argument, foretold the disappointing judgment.

Unsurprisingly, the appellate court dismissed the appeal, with costs. It found that the state did not owe Carmichele a duty to prevent Francois's release from custody, that the prosecutor was under no obligation to oppose his release, and that the state and Carmichele were not in a 'special relationship'.

Pama reports feeling decidedly depressed at the judgment, believing the case was over. Being very conscious that they had now lost twice, Pama describes feeling as if he had received a 'black eye' from the Cape High Court and a 'broken nose' from the Supreme Court of Appeal: 'I could not help feeling that the Constitutional Court would cut my head off.' However, when Andrew Breitenbach recommended that they appeal to the Constitutional Court, Alix showed the resolve and determination that had marked her whole approach to the case and agreed to press on.

Round three

Carmichele duly approached the Constitutional Court for relief. Following argument on 20 March 2001, the Court handed down its judgment on

16 August 2001. Authored by Justices Ackermann and Goldstone, the judgment at last handed victory to Alix.

One of the country's leading advocates, Wim Trengove SC, joined Carmichele's legal team for this round of the fight. Alix's Constitutional Court case was also bolstered by a submission by the Gender Research Project of the Centre for Applied Legal Studies (CALS) at Wits Law School, argued by Advocate Janet Kentridge. Not only did this boost the Carmichele team's morale, knowing at last that they were not alone in their fight, but the CALS submissions generalised the case beyond Alix Carmichele and connected it to the broader struggle for women's human rights and gender equality in South Africa. As the CALS submission framed the issue: 'Sexual violence and the threat of sexual violence goes to the core of women's subordination in society. It is the single greatest threat to the self-determination of South African women.'

The case was important for another reason: as a step down the road of developing South Africa's law in line with the Constitution. The common law —that body of law historically decided and drawn upon in subsequent cases as binding authority—must be developed in a way that takes account of the Constitution, especially the Bill of Rights. It cannot atrophy and become like an insect caught in amber; rather, it must grow organically as required by the demands of constitutional democracy. Here, the constitutional rights to life, respect for and protection of dignity, freedom and security of the person, personal privacy and freedom of move-

The common law ... cannot atrophy and become like an insect caught in amber

ment were all in play. The delictual common law on what constitutes a duty of care and negligent conduct in such circumstances was now a work in progress. Old principles must be revisited and shaped to conform to constitutional imperatives. As the Constitutional Court judgment set the issue: 'Section 39(2) of the Constitution provides that when developing the common law, every court must promote the spirit, purport and objects of the Bill of Rights. It follows implicitly that where the common law deviates from the spirit, purport and objects of the Bill of Rights the courts have an obligation to develop it by removing that deviation.'[5]

For this reason, the Constitutional Court specifically noted that neither of the two earlier judgments in the case—by the High Court and Appellate Court—had taken account of the relevant provisions of the Bill of Rights or the consequent obligation to develop the common law in light of the Constitution.

On the merits of the case, the Constitutional Court dealt with the claim against the police separately from that against the prosecutors. On both legs, however, the Constitutional Court found that a duty existed to do far more to prevent violence against women.

The Constitutional Court judgment was significant for at least two reasons: it was the first time that the Court asserted the importance of the new constitutional normative framework, and it extended this normative framework, now required to be applied by judges in deciding disputes in the area of private law. It refused to defer to the Supreme Court of Appeal's view that private law, and, in particular, the law of delict (claims for a civil wrong), was unaltered by the Constitution.

Pama, who could not travel to Johannesburg for the handing down of the judgment, reports that when he got the call from his correspondent attorney who had attended court, he raced to the top of the wooden staircase in his Knysna law offices, bellowing 'We won!' He emotionally called Alix and the other members of the legal team to report their victory. The result attracted massive media coverage —probably as some rare but welcome good news in the fight against crime.

Round four

The win in Braamfontein on 16 August 2001—nearly four years after the trial started in Cape Town in September 1997—did not mean the end of this now marathon matter. The case was referred back to the High Court in Cape Town where the trial continued on 7 March 2002, with the same legal teams as had appeared in the Constitutional Court. In effect, the reversal on appeal by the Constitutional Court of Judge Chetty's grant of absolution from the instance meant that that new order replaced it—the application for absolution was denied. This meant that the respondents, the State, was required to begin its defence of the claim in the continuation of the trial. The State called the police officers and prosecutor as witnesses. Prosecutor Louw conceded that her decisions not to oppose Francois's release on his own recognizance on 6 March 1995, and again after his return from Valkenburg, on 15 April 1995, were mistakes. The police officers called to testify confirmed that they were aware of Francois's earlier conviction and had other knowledge of his deviant past, but had bungled passing on this information effectively.

The testimony of the main investigating officer, in particular, demonstrated why Trengove SC is considered such an outstanding trial lawyer. Inspector Klein, in the police service in Knysna since 1985, was closely cross-examined on what little he did to ascertain the details of Francois's previous conviction for indecent assault. He claimed to have spoken to Mrs Coetzee on Sunday 5 March 1995 in Hornlee about Francois, testifying that she had told him that Francois was a good boy, was a father figure in their home, contributed to their household expenses, had passed matric and wanted to study further. She testified that Francois should be released on his own recognizance because she did not have any money for bail. However, she denied ever having any such conversation about her son with Inspector Klein.

To corroborate this conversation, Inspector Klein had relied on an entry in his police pocket book. An entry, squeezed between the other entries on page 16, and running over the fold in the middle onto page 17 (instead of continuing on the next line on page 16), recorded 'Noetzie MAS 26-03-97'. Trengove put it to Inspector Klein that this entry was fabricated and inserted after March 1995 in order to bolster the evidence of his investigation.[6] This was denied; he claimed that this was the way he made notes in his pocket book. However, no other entries appear in this fashion in the entire pocket book. Moreover, this conversation should have occurred on 26 March 1995, but the date recorded in the pocket book is two years later, in 1997. The final nail in the coffin of this testimony's credibility was that Inspector Klein recorded a 'MAS' case number in this entry, testifying that this was the case number for the case against Francois for the assault of Eurena Terblanche. However, other police testimony confirmed that the system of numbering cases with 'MAS' commenced in April 1996. Prior to that, cases of this type would have borne a 'MR' case number. The case number for the Terblanche assault was MR-26-03-95. It was therefore clear that Inspector Klein had tried to bolster his evidence, plugging the hole where a proper investigation of Francois's prior criminal conduct should have led the police.

Judge Chetty's new judgment found that the police and prosecutor's conduct fell short of the standard requiring that they act with care and diligence

Judge Chetty delivered a new judgment, ultimately finding the police and prosecutors jointly and severally liable to Carmichele for the damages she suffered as a result of the attack, and ordered the state to pay her legal costs. Crisply put, Judge Chetty's new judgment found that the police and prosecutor's conduct fell short of the standard requiring that they act with care and diligence. Carmichele finally had established the state's liability for Francois's attack. In the ordinary course, the matter would then have proceeded to consideration of what damages, if any, had been caused and what compensation, if any, should result.

Round five

However, three months after the re-start of the trial, on 3 June 2002, the State applied for leave to appeal this latest defeat. Alix's affidavit opposing this application described how she was 'dumbfounded' by this development. She went on to explain how '[a]t the hearing in the Constitutional Court, one of the Justices said that he did not want to see this case "yo-yoing" through the South African legal system. It would be most unfair to me for this to happen. The whole ordeal has left me feeling tired and now despondent once again. I cannot understand what benefit an appeal will bring to the [state]. This case should be dragged on for years with no resolution or closure and ultimately a waste of taxpayers' money.'

Precedent & Possibility

It is worth pondering why the State chose to pursue the appeal of Chetty's judgment. It makes one wonder whether the State's legal advisors had read the Constitutional Court's judgment which made clear that the Constitution was there precisely in order to come to the aid of claimants like Alix, rather than simply pursue the appeal because that avenue was procedurally available to them.

In any event, Judge Chetty refused leave to appeal, and the State then applied directly to the appeal court in Bloemfontein for leave to appeal. After the granting of such leave, the appeal was heard on 3 November 2002 and, later that month, the Court, which had previously found against Carmichele, confirmed her victory.

Unfortunately, this hearing further underscored the journey still to be undertaken before the judiciary comprehends and is sensitive to the traumatic position of survivors of violent sexual assaults. At one point in *'If we grade this* the hearing, Judge Louis Harms, the most senior member of the *as rape cases go, it* Bench who presided that day, commented that only 'attempted *merits less than* rape' by Francois had been established here, and that Alix's *five out of 10'* specific injuries were 'superficial' (notwithstanding the multiple surgeries required to repair them). He then commented on Francois's actions, to the visible discomfort of his judicial colleagues, that 'if we grade this as rape cases go, it merits less than five out of 10.' Admittedly, his colleague, Judge Ian Farlam, hastened to add moments later 'I don't know how you rate rape. But if you put attempted rape with attempted murder, it becomes very serious indeed.' Adding, 'your danger to society does not depend on whether there was penetration or not.'

This exchange prompted Carmel Rickard to write in her *Sunday Times* column that weekend,

> How could any judge think of 'grading' rape, of actually assigning a value to its severity? What does that say to the woman involved about her ordeal and how it is viewed by society? And given the ferociousness of the attack, why would this case be 'less than five out of 10'? Was it so 'low', simply because the young woman regained consciousness many hours later—surely not; after all, another few seconds of the pressure from his fingers, and she could have been dead. Why should it 'merit' lower than a five on the judicial Richter scale simply because her injuries appeared superficial?
>
> I kept asking myself these questions, but there was another even harder one: if these words had shocked me deeply, how would the woman who had actually lived through the experience be feeling if she had been here? How would she feel about the ability of judges to understand the impact of her trauma? What would happen to her confidence that the legal system could ensure that she and other women are taken seriously when they report and describe a sexual attack?

Judge Harms also earned himself the 'Mampara of the Week' award from *Sunday Times* columnist Hogarth with the comment:

Hogarth is loath to test the patience of court officers such as Judge Louis Harms by honouring them in this space. But Judge Harms had made a very strong case against himself as reported elsewhere. . . . He was applying his mind to an old case where a man had attacked a woman, sat on her, punched her in the face, bit her, then dragged her some way before knocking her head, threatening to kill her and throttling her until she was unconscious. Then he pulled off her clothes and attempted to rape her before leaving her for dead. So, what did the good judge have to say about these grotesque violations? 'if we grade this as rape cases go, it merits less than a five out of 10', said he. As judges go, two out of 10.

Of course, Judge Harms's comment cannot be simply dismissed as insensitive. It also reveals the tragic and infuriating fact that South Africa's courts are so mired in the torrent of cases caused by the very worst criminal conduct, that degrees of reprehensibility present themselves. Only by comparing cases, can courts make some sense of the facts before them in any particular case and deliver appropriate judgments.

An anecdote from this appellate hearing bears repeating, demonstrating some of the challenges of this litigation.[7] At one point during Trengove's argument, Judge Harms commented to him that his cross-examination had troubled the Court, given that it used inappropriate and offensive language, and seemed to infuse Francois's attack on Alix with a sexual element. As the Court adjourned for lunch, the judge provided counsel with the page reference to the cross-examination that had so offended the Court. Distressed at this, and unsure as to what the learned judge could have been referring, Trengove immediately reviewed the record of his cross-examination. There, a question had been put to a witness, dealing with what Francois said to Alix while he held her leg as she lay on

An anecdote from this appellate hearing bears repeating, demonstrating some of the challenges of this litigation

the passage floor. The transcript of the testimony was that Francois 'het oor en oor vir haar gesê dat sy moet hom naai'. This was a most unfortunate typographical error. It should have read that Francois 'het oor en oor vir haar gesê dat sy moet *omdraai*'. After the lunch adjournment, a relieved counsel could advise the Court of this mistake.

In the end, Judge Harms, notwithstanding the public criticism, wrote an important judgment on behalf of the Court, confirming that Carmichele was owed a duty by the state, that such duty was not met here and that the state's appeal should be dismissed, with costs of two counsel. Round 5 to Alix.

But how many more rounds. . .?

Notwithstanding taking her fight to five courts over 13 years, Alix had still not recovered any compensation for her injuries. She returned to court in April 2008, armed with revised and updated expert evidence detailing the basis for her compensation claim. This process of evaluation by her own, and the state's, experts—including a psychologist, psychiatrist, industrial psychologist, ortho-paedic surgeon and physiotherapist—meant that she was forced to relive the traumatic attack and its impact on her life. She told an interviewer in October 2007 that she 'was dissected like a rat to determine how much [the state] has to pay. I had to reveal my deepest, darkest secrets, my most private thoughts and feelings. Now everything I think or feel is in a report and will be in the public domain.'[8] This humiliating and invasive experience of the legal system is not uncommon for survivors seeking justice and compensation. In September 2008, Judge Cleaver awarded R673 772.00 in damages to Alix. This was supposed to cover past medical expenses, past loss of income, her loss of earning capacity, future medical expenses and general damages. However, this parsimonious amount is unlikely to cover the true costs of pursuing justice for 13 years; Alix could end up owing money to her legal team. As a result, she has had little choice but to file for leave to appeal this judgment to a full Bench of the Cape High Court.

In interviews with the authors, Alix recounted her disappointment with the legal system. She described the immense discomfort she felt of having her private physical and emotional space intruded on in the countless hours of examination by expert doctors and the state's lawyers, and of being exposed to humiliating cross-examination during her two days on the witness stand at the damages trial (for example, questioned at length on line items in her bank statements ranging from how much she spent on groceries to insinuations that she hid income). The way the legal system exacts evidence and proof from victims of crime is defective and undignified. It take years, and much cost, to sue for justice, while it also spawns more conflict.

On a national level, violent crime statistics and incidents of sexual assault on women remain horrifically high

Not only did Alix have to recount the horrific experience of the assault (which the state's counsel minimised by referring to as a 'scuffle' throughout the hearing), but also defend her life choices in minute detail. So, her decisions to end personal relationships, relocate cities or accept work each had to be explained and justified. In her sense that the victim becomes re-victimised by the law, Alix is not alone. Nor is she likely to be the last to suffer this way.

On a national level, violent crime statistics, and incidents of sexual assault on women, remain horrifically high. While the *Carmichele* case is undoubtedly a triumph and has radically changed the law, it also reveals the limitations of using law alone to secure redress and prevent the mistakes here. In fact, millions of rands of claims brought by victims of crime are believed to be pending against the state using the *Carmichele* precedent. From this one can deduce that she was one of many failed by law enforcement in South Africa. Indeed, this fact only compounds the sense of disappointment for Alix. All of this fight would be 'worth it' or justified in some way if her case had radically changed the situation for other victims of crime. But it did not. While the legal precedent opens another avenue for accountability, true justice and fair compensation remain illusory. It all seems the proverbial hollow victory, and confirms the incremental and imperfect way in which the legal system seeks to deliver justice. One can also conclude that this avalanche of claims speaks far more about the failure of our institutional crime-fighting than the undeniable success of one lawsuit to provide a legal avenue for compensation to victims of crime.

A review of the criminal justice system by the Business Leadership Group and Business Against Crime in February 2008 highlighted the crippling impact of a lack of adequate resources on law enforcement. Of the 2 125 227 crimes reported in 2006/07, 1 160 117 (or 54.5%) were undetected, meaning that they were not investigated at all. Of the 1 048 497 that were detected, and excluding those complaints that were withdrawn or determined to be unfounded, 797 665 crimes resulted in charges being brought to court. Once there, these cases join an ever-growing backlog. The average caseload per month in the High Court is 285, of which the finalisation rate is 1,4 cases; in the Regional (Magistrates) Courts the average caseload is 6 659, with a finalisation rate of 11; and in the District (Magistrates) Courts, the caseload is 81 587, with a finalisation rate of 31. These courts sit daily for an average of only 3 hours 20 minutes in the High Court, 3 hours 55 minutes in the Regional Court and 4 hours 2 minutes in the District Court.

The average caseload per month in the High Court is 285

The same review showed how investigative resources are under immense strain in South Africa. The 22 519 detectives in the police service have only 6 513 vehicles, 1 879 cellular telephones and 3 503 computers with which to perform their work. There are only 1 691 crime scene experts and 923 forensic experts. Yet, in 2005/06, they were called on to process 342 778 crime scene enquiries (including 106 183 fingerprints found), 974 892 criminal enquiries and 777 107 non-criminal enquiries. Prosecution success rates also call for pause. For example, only 7.3% of reported and detected property crimes result in conviction.

Thus, low morale and motivation are regrettable, but understandable, given the enormity of the demands on law enforcement personnel and resources, especially when coupled with the scale of the caseload requiring attention at every stage of the criminal justice process.

Determined to end on an optimistic note, it is worth remembering that the Constitutional Court judgment certainly did open the way for others to follow Alix's hard-beaten path to justice. Two cases in particular demonstrate how Carmichele's case takes us further along the bridge to Mureinik's culture of justification.

First, was the case of *Van Eeden v Minister of Safety and Security*, decided on 27 September 2002 by the Supreme Court of Appeal. Ghia van Eeden sought damages in delict from the state for the injuries and loss she suffered as a result of her sexual assault, rape and robbery by one André Gregory Mohamed in August 1998. In the words of the judgment, he was 'a known dangerous criminal and serial rapist who had escaped from police custody in Durban on 22 May 1998. Mohamed escaped from police cells, where he was being held for an identification parade, through an unlocked security gate. At the time, he was facing no fewer than 22 charges, including indecent assault, rape and armed robbery committed in the Durban area. Within six days of his escape, he resumed his sexual attacks on young women, this time near Pretoria. The appellant was the third victim of the latter series of attacks.'[9]

The trial judge had dismissed her claim, finding himself bound by the Supreme Court of Appeal's decision in the first *Carmichele* judgment (round two above). However, by the time the Supreme Court of Appeal heard the appeal, the Constitutional Court's decision in *Carmichele*, overturning the former court's judgment, had been delivered. The Supreme Court of Appeal therefore had the opportunity to engage immediately and directly with the newly evolved common law understanding of the state's duty to prevent crime in light of the constitutional normative framework. The Supreme Court of Appeal therefore found that the failure by the state to prevent Mohamed's escape gave rise to delictual liability to the subsequent victim of crime committed by this escapee.

The three policemen were subsequently convicted of rape and kidnapping

The second case to consider was that of *N K v Minister of Safety and Security*,[10] decided by the Constitutional Court on 13 June 2005, and, like *Van Eeden*, benefited from the exceptional lawyering of Wim Trengove SC. This case, similarly, involved a claim to recover damages in delict from the Minister of Safety and Security for the harm suffered by a claimant, identified by her initials as 'NK', as a result of being raped and assaulted in the early hours of 27 March 1999. Ms K's 'assailants were three uniformed and on-duty police sergeants. Ms K who had had an argument with a boyfriend with whom she had been out for the evening was looking for a telephone to call home when she met the police officers at approximately 4 o'clock in the morning. They offered her a lift home which she gratefully accepted. Thereafter they took her to a deserted place, raped and abandoned her. The three policemen were subsequently convicted of rape and kidnapping, and sentenced to life in prison by the Johannesburg High Court.'[11]

Judge O'Regan wrote the judgment for the unanimous court considering the vicarious liability of the Minister for Safety and Security for these police officers' conduct. She concluded, as set out in the Court's summary of the judgment, that 'although it is clear that the policemen's conduct constituted a clear deviation from their duty, there nevertheless existed a sufficiently close relationship between their employment and the wrongful conduct. Three factors lead to the conclusion that the Minister is liable: First, the fact that the policemen bore a statutory and constitutional duty to prevent crime and protect the members of the public—a duty which also rests on their employer (the Minister); secondly, the fact that the applicant accepted an offer of assistance from the policemen in circumstances in which she needed assistance, it was their duty to supply it and it was reasonable of her to accept assistance; and thirdly, the fact that the wrongful conduct of the policemen coincided with their failure to perform their duties to protect the applicant.'[12]

The judgment emphasises that the Constitution mandates members of the police to protect community members and that for this mandate to be performed efficiently reasonable trust must be placed in members of the police service by members of the public.

All of these cases, and the many others that followed, demonstrate how law can be used to expand the meaning and reach of the common law, and to ensure constitutional justice for the many South Africans who remain victims of crime. Unfortunately, this precedent has not altered the fact that the country faces a truly massive crime wave or that the justice system is alienating, frustrating and unsatisfying for many of its litigant-users. Nor has it apparently created sufficient incentive for the state to dramatically enhance its law enforcement and crime prevention resources. But it must surely be a step in the right direction.

Endnotes

1   The authors are indebted to attorney Perino Pama whose copious notes and file on the *Carmichele* case invaluably provided comprehensive materials, including statements and testimony excerpts, enabling this chapter to reconstruct events underlying the litigation. Accordingly, except where otherwise indicated, this chapter uses attorney Pamas materials as its factual basis.

2   'Darkness and Light and Dreams Worth having'. *Business Day* (5 October 2007).

3   Unfortunately, the authors have been unable to locate the exact *Fair Lady* article in which this quotation appears, but obtained it from attorney Pama. Any correction or further information is invited and welcome.

4   Similarly, the authors obtained this quotation from attorney Pama, quoting, in turn, a *Fair Lady* article.

5   Paragraph 33 of the judgment.

6   Authors' interviews with Trengove SC.

7   *Ibid.*

8   *Ibid.*

9   Paragraph 2 of the judgment.

10 2005 (9) BCLR 835 (CC).

11 Constitutional Court Media Summary issued 13 June 2005.

12 *Ibid.*

ten

Conclusion

T he title of this book employs four key words: 'precedent', 'possibility', 'use' and 'abuse' (of the law). Each word requires analysis.

Establishing a precedent

We invoke the term 'precedent' both in the traditional legal sense and in a more specific political context. The essence of the legal doctrine of precedent is the imposition upon judges of a duty to follow legal rulings as set out in previous judicial decisions. Recently, the Constitutional Court has observed that the doctrine of precedent serves 'to enshrine a fundamental principle of justice: that like cases should be determined alike'.[1] It also promotes the principles of legal certainty, rationality and equality, in that a litigant can claim injustice if a previous ruling on identical facts was not applied to her. An example is the case of *Carmichele*. The lower courts, being the High Court and the Supreme Court of Appeal, both followed precedent in refusing to grant Alix Carmichele any relief. It required the Constitutional Court to unshackle the restrictions of a precedent which gave little recognition to the constitutional principle of accountability before the law acknowledged Alix's claim.

In an overtly political context, a case may establish a precedent by judicial endorsement of the prevailing political discourse or it can legally censure opponents of those in political power. Thus, in the *Rivonia* trial, the state succeeded, where it had failed previously in the five-year long Treason Trial, to obtain a judgment that imposed a legal censure on its political opponents who were judged to be violent terrorists. For two decades thereafter, the National Party government employed the judgment in the *Rivonia* trial to justify its further repression of legitimate political opposition. The judgment was used expressly to contrast the 'Western' standards of apartheid with the 'godless communism' of the ANC.

As we noted in Chapter One, the role of the political trial has been described in a leading work by Otto Kirchheimer as serving to authenticate state action against its political opposition. The use of a legal standard, however nebulous or refined, to eliminate actual or potential foes of those in power provides, at the least, a veneer of justification for repressive action. As

Kirchheimer notes, legal authentication of state action 'removes the fear of reprisals or liquidation from multitudes of possible victims, and encourages a friendly and understanding disposition towards the security needs of the power-holders on the part of their subjects . . . In proceedings to which the public has some access, authentication, the regularising of the extraordinary, may under favourable circumstances be transformed into a deeper popular understanding.'[2]

In short, a political trial involves the use of criminal law by the state to legitimate its moves against political opposition. The courts, rather than the security police chief, determine the 'legality' of political conduct. Viewing these developments, the public gains confidence in that a legal justification has been shown to exist for the crackdown, and that society is still run by rules rather than by official caprice.

Within this framework, the *Rivonia* trial was a classic form of the political trial. On the strength of the conviction of key members of the ANC leadership, the state claimed that its opponents were no more than violent criminals. *Rivonia* was followed by many similar trials throughout the next two and a half decades as the Nationalist government continued to seek justification for its continued repression of political opposition. As the intensity of political opposition to apartheid grew during the 1980s, the template of *Rivonia* was invoked in two major political trials—in Pietermaritzburg in 1985 and at Delmas shortly thereafter. In both cases, the state prosecuted senior members of the United Democratic Front on grounds of treason, terrorism, murder and subversion. *Rivonia* served the state as an important precedent for these trials.

> *Precedent connotes the binding legal and political force of law. It captures the history of our legal system: the good, bad and ugly*

Precedent connotes the binding legal and political force of law. It captures the history of our legal system: the good, bad and ugly. Not all legal concepts derived from the Roman-Dutch and English systems of law were bad. Far from it—the conceptual tools of much of our law are clear, flexible and logical. The current challenge for courts is more about the content than the existence of these concepts—as the *Carmichele* case illustrates. But precedent also connotes a history of judicial bigotry, excessive deference to racism and authority and, on occasion, judicial bravery and steadfast adherence to principle.

Possibility—an improved future

The word 'possibility' seeks to capture the constitutional ambition to leave behind a past saturated with racism, sexism, homophobia and egregious political intolerance. It was a past often accompanied by state-sanctioned violence which, despite the obdurate public refusal to admit to such conduct during the long period of apartheid, was revealed in its full horror during the TRC hearings and the *De Kock* and *Basson* trials.

South Africa did not experience a revolution in 1990. The erstwhile warring parties engaged in intricate negotiations, culminating in a Constitution which promised the possibility of political and social transformation. The term 'transformation' connoted the constitutional imperative to assume control of government and its institutions, change the political and legal concepts that had emerged during apartheid and reconfigure them in the image of non-racial and non-sexist democratic principles.

Of course, precedent constrains possibility, as we saw possibility in the chapter devoted to the seemingly interminable litigation initiated by Alix Carmichele with great bravery and hope, only to be confronted by pre-constitutional precedent and the state's determined use of it to frustrate the finalisation of her case.

That cautionary lesson came some years into the constitutional journey. In 1995, the seemingly endless, liberating possibility that the newly created Constitutional Court could and would break with apartheid precedent was evident in the judgments delivered in the *Makwanyane* case which found the death penalty to be unconstitutional. There have been subsequent examples of this power to break with the past but, perhaps, none more striking than the parties who participated in a recent marriage ceremony.

Gay marriage : possibility to reality

In early January 2008, Zackie Achmat married Dalli Weyers. The wedding took place on a glorious summer afternoon in Lakeside, Cape Town. It was presided over by Judge Edwin Cameron who, in his remarks to the couple, spoke of a need for the marriage ceremonies of gay couples to be 'plain'. By this, he did not mean that they should not be special occasions, reflective of the unique nature of the couple. He meant that a gay marriage should be regarded as a singularly important event in the lives of the couple but ordinary in the sense that it reflected an accepted norm in the new South Africa.

A gay marriage should be regarded as a singularly important event in the lives of the couple but ordinary in the sense that it reflected an accepted norm in the new South Africa

It was clear to the large group of invited guests that this claim could easily be embraced by the wide spectrum of South African society who attended, including Afrikaner whites from Ficksburg, the home of Dalli Weyers, as well as prominent members of the ANC, such as Nosizwe Madlala-Routledge. The wedding was replete with political symbolism. Both Edwin Cameron and Zackie Achmat have been critical players in the fight for the dignity and equality for gay and lesbian South Africans. Achmat has not only played a vital role in the fight on behalf of all HIV/AIDS residents in this country, but has also been a prominent gay rights activist. So too has Cameron who exercised a profound influence on the anti-discrimination clause in the

Constitution and was the author of majority judgment in the Supreme Court of Appeal that recognised that our law should be developed immediately to recognise gay and lesbian marriages.

The wedding symbolised the extent of one journey already travelled along the constitutional bridge. Before 1994, South African law contained numerous homophobic provisions. But, at the CODESA negotiations, the political parties agreed to a Constitution which became the first in the world to explicitly outlaw discrimination based on sexual orientation. Viewed against the country's history, it was a surprising but most welcome development.

The reasons for the National Party's acceptance of an anti-discrimination clause, which included sexual orientation as one of the prohibited grounds, have never been made clear. To be sure, the legal experts on all sides who assisted the various political parties were significantly influenced by the carefully argued and erudite memorandum of Edwin Cameron and Kevin Botha. This document, in which they eloquently argued for the inclusion of such a clause, was written on behalf of an NGO, the Equality Foundation, and directed to the negotiators at an early stage in the constitutional negotiations.[3]

There is also an illuminating story of late-night negotiations concerning the inclusion of sexual orientation as a ground of discrimination. Kobie Coetzee, the then Minister of Justice, was a man not well known for his clarity of language in either English or his home language, Afrikaans. Late into the night, he was obscurely objecting to the inclusion of this provision in the anti-discrimination clause. Finally, the ANC negotiators realised that the objection was based on the argument that a clause which outlawed discrimination against sexual orientation would allow for a constitutional attack on the crime of bestiality.[4] One of the ANC negotiators then put it to Mr Coetzee that, while he might be worried about the sexual activities of some of his voters, the ANC had no such problems. A roar of laughter broke the tension and the deadlock. That was the last serious objection raised against the provision.

A series of cases followed the inclusion in the Constitution of an anti-discrimination clause, which were designed to secure recognition of the rights of gays and lesbians. In 1999, a challenge was brought against the criminalisation of private consensual sexual acts between gays and lesbians. In this dispute, known as the sodomy case, the Constitutional Court had no difficulty in finding that the crime of sodomy had to be struck from the body of South African criminal law. Pierre de Vos has written reflectively of the court's break with the past and thus of the possibility recognised in the judgment: *'In a way no court in the world has ever done, the Constitutional Court rejected the very basis of different treatment of gay men and lesbians'* 'It is difficult to overstate the power of the rhetoric in [this] case. In a way no court in the world has ever done, the Constitutional Court rejected the very basis of different treatment of gay men and lesbians by rejecting the notion of normal and abnormal sexuality . . .'[5]

A year later, the Minister of Home Affairs was brought before the Court to defend the discriminatory impact of a provision in the immigration laws which afforded special protection to permanent residents, who were engaged to marry South African citizens, while ignoring the rights of same-sex life partners in the same position. Finding this discrimination to be constitutionally impermissible, Justice Ackermann said of the legislation: 'The message is that gays and lesbians lack the inherent humanity to have their families and family lives in such same-sex relationships respected or protected. It serves in addition to perpetuate and reinforce existing prejudices and stereotypes. The impact constitutes a crass, blunt, cruel and serious invasion of their dignity. The discrimination, based on sexual orientation, is severe because no concern, let alone anything approaching equal concern, is shown for the particular sexual orientation of gays and lesbians.'[6]

Finally the big kahuna arrived before the courts, namely the right of gay and lesbian couples to be married

The next case involved Kathy Satchwell, a judge of the Johannesburg High Court.[7] She successfully took the Minister of Welfare and Population Development to court on behalf of herself and her partner, arguing that the exclusion of a provision for a pension to the surviving same-sex partner in a statute was discriminatory compared to the potential provision of a pension for the surviving opposite sex spouse of a judge. Then, the Constitutional Court held that the provision in childcare legislation that confined the right to adopt children to married heterosexual couples, to the exclusion of same-sex couples, conflicted both with the principle of what was in the best interests of the child and the inherent right to dignity of same-sex couples.[8]

Finally the big *kahuna* arrived before the courts, namely the right of gay and lesbian couples to be married. The case of *Fourie* concerned a constitutional challenge to the common-law definition of marriage and to a provision in the Marriage Act that preserved the institution of marriage exclusively for heterosexual couples. Neither the Supreme Court of Appeal nor the Constitutional Court encountered any judicial difficulty in finding that same-sex marriages required legal recognition. The differences between the judges turned on the role the Court should play in making the necessary amendments to the existing marriage laws. In turn these approaches hold important implications for the manner in which courts initiate social change through their judgements. Judge Edwin Cameron, in the majority judgment of the Supreme Court of Appeal, and Justice Kate O' Regan, in a minority judgment in the Constitutional Court, held that the common law should be developed to read into the law the necessary words that would, with immediate effect, permit same-sex couples to marry. By contrast, Judge Ian Farlam, in a minority judgment in the Supreme Court of Appeal and Justice Albie Sachs, on behalf of the majority of the Constitutional Court, held that the resolution of this extremely sensitive issue should be deferred for one year in order to allow the legislature time to consider the question and craft a legislative solution.

The difference in approach between Cameron and O'Regan, and the majority of the Constitutional Court, emerges clearly from the following passages in their judgments. Judge Cameron writes:

> The task of applying the values of the Bill of Rights to the common law thus requires us to put faith in both the values themselves and in the people whose duly elected representatives created a visionary and inclusive constitutional structure that offered acceptance and justice across diversity to all. The South African public and their elected representatives have for the greater part accepted the sometimes far-reaching decisions taken in regard to sexual orientation and other constitutional rights over the past 10 years. It is not presumptuous to believe that they will accept also the further incremental development of the common law that the Constitution requires in this case.[9]

In contrast, Justice Sachs said:

> This is a matter that touches on deep public and private sensibilities. I believe that Parliament is well-suited to finding the best way of ensuring that same-sex couples are brought in from the legal cold. . . It is my view that it would best serve these equality claims by respecting the separation of powers and giving Parliament an opportunity to deal appropriately with the matter. In this respect, it is necessary to bear in mind the different ways in which the Legislature could legitimately deal with the gap that exists in the law. . . Parliament should be given the opportunity in the first place to decide how best the equality rights at issue could be achieved. Provided that the basic principles of equality as enshrined in the Constitution are not trimmed in the process, the greater the degree of public acceptance for same sex-unions, the more will the achievement of equality be promoted.[10]

Parliament voted by 230 votes to 41 in favour of the Bill allowing same-sex civil marriages and civil unions for unmarried opposite and same-sex couples. The Civil Unions Act came into force on 1 December 2006, making South Africa the fifth country in the world and the first in Africa to legalise same-sex marriages. On the day of their marriage, Zackie Achmat and Dalli Weyers walked physically and symbolically along the path to the canopy set up for the ceremony paved by a law which fully recognised the marriage of those who had been consistently regarded as 'other'. On that happy day, work on the construction of the constitutional bridge was certainly evident.

The use and abuse of law

These two concepts capture the dialectical quality of law: it can be used as a sword and a shield at the very same time. This quality is evident in the chapters dealing with the pass laws, the coloured vote and the *Rivonia* trial, which show that law can be and is used to buttress the power of the ruling elite and prop up a political *status quo*.

In these cases, the courts employed legal principles to confirm legislation which disenfranchised voters of colour and to classify the political conduct of ANC leaders as criminal conduct. But if a regime seeks to run its affairs by means of the law, it must at least be seen to deliver on the promise of the rule of law. The trilogy of pass law cases is a fine example of the link between the use and abuse of law. The way in which a law that is intended to abuse can be transformed and used to protect the weak is made clear in the following observation by David Dyzenhaus:

> The promise of law that was realised in the two decisions of the Appellate Division (*Komani* and *Rikhoto*) was not just that many black South Africans henceforth knew what the law was that regulated their lives. They also knew what legal rights they had, rights which could be said to entail recognition of black South Africans as having agency within a space that was supposed in terms of apartheid doctrine to be exclusive to white South Africans, and thus deeply undermining of that doctrine.[11]

The pass laws represented a brutal mechanism which treated black South Africans as pawns to be moved at the whim of the mining and industrial houses. But the mechanism was set out in a series of detailed laws. Those laws required interpretation by the courts. Once the law was definitely interpreted by the Court in the *Komani* and *Rikhoto* cases, the discretion of the administrator to act arbitrarily in deciding the fate of millions was severely curtailed. Failure to comply with the laws as interpreted by the courts could, in turn, be sanctioned by the judiciary. The law was a sword of government power but, at the same time, a shield for victims to use against that power.

This complex quality of law is also evident in the nature of the political trial where not even legal censure by the State remains uncontested. In the *Rivonia* trial, the accused put forward their own censure of state action. When the State used the brutal mechanism of detention without trial, it found itself exposed in the *Wendy Orr* case by the same legal system it employed to repress democratic political activity. The State disregarded the needs of HIV-infected pregnant women only to find the TAC engage in lawfare with it, thereby forcing it to retreat from its disregard for those in need of antiretroviral drugs.

There is another aspect to the dialectical quality of law. Litigation is used to enforce a claim, for example, against the State. Through the adversarial process, the plaintiff as the claimant becomes an 'accused', as her life, history and conduct is publicly scrutinised. The roles of the litigant as plaintiff and the recalcitrant state as defendant are now reversed. Sword and shield are easily swapped. The lawsuit becomes 'your story versus my story'. Each party seeks to discredit the other in order to persuade the court that its version should be accepted. At the end of the trial, one side 'wins'. There is no reconciliation and resolution in this brutal process.

The case of *Carmichele* highlights the way in which the legal system can simultaneously be an instrument of abuse of victims of assault by turning them into 'accused persons' and a mechanism by which the State could be held to its constitutional obligations to protect its citizens from being victims of crime.

Lawfare

This relationship between the use and abuse of law can be further understood through the concept of 'lawfare'. In a recent work, John and Jean Comaroff observed that, as society increasingly uses law as a means of control, the targets of the state invoke the cry of human rights to persuade courts that law has an intrinsic quality of accountability, certainty and the recognition of the basic freedom of the individual citizen. In this way, citizens fight attempts to control them through the law:

> . . . politics in many societies is played out more in the courts than it is in the streets, more by the use of law and its disguised violence than by unfettered brutal force, absent of any legal constraint. In an age of constitutionalism and a dominant discourse of human rights, conflicts once joined in parliaments, by means of street protests, mass demonstrations, and media campaigns, through labour strikes, boycotts, blockades, and other instruments of assertion, tend more and more—if not only, or in just the same way every where - to find their way to the judiciary. Class struggles seem to have metamorphosed into class actions. . .; people drawn together by social or material predicament, culture, race, sexual preference, residential proximity, faith, and habits of consumption become legal persons as their common plaints turn them into plaintiff's communal identities—against antagonists who, allegedly have acted illegally against them. Citizens, subjects, governments, and corporations litigate against one another, often at the intersection of tort law, human rights law, and the criminal law, in an ever mutating kaleidoscope of coalitions and cleavages.[12]

Why do governments then employ law as a means of political and social control if it can work against social control? The Comaroffs provide a most plausible answer:

> As a species of political displacement, it becomes most readily visible when those who act in the name of the state conjure with legalities to act against some or all of its citizens. Any number of examples present themselves, but the most infamously contemporary is, again, to be found in Zimbabwe. The Mugabe regime has consistently passed laws in parliament intended to silence its critics and then has proceeded to take violent action against them; the media regulations put in place just after the presidential election of 2002 are a case in point. Operation Murambatsvina ('Drive out Trash'), which has razed informal settlements and markets, forced people out of urban areas,

and caused a great deal of hardship, ill-health, and death under the banner of 'slum clearance', has recently taken this practice to unprecedented heights—or depths.[13]

The Zimbabwe example shows how a government becomes increasingly desperate for legitimacy in a global world which insists upon a commitment to legality and human rights, at least on paper. Even tyrants like Mugabe crave some legitimacy!

The 2008 election in Zimbabwe reached an impasse when the government-controlled electoral commission realised that Robert Mugabe had lost the election: the government employed its conventional tactic of extra-parliamentary thuggery to prevent a defeat at the polls from being implemented by the inauguration of Morgan Tsvangirai as president. Significantly, when the opposition approached the courts to force the results of the election to be made public, the law was invoked to rule that there be a recount of votes and criminal law was used to round up and prosecute election officials to show that the vote count in favour of Mugabe was far larger than that counted for the opposition.

Of course, Mugabe took no risks with the law. While preserving the façade of an independent judiciary, he forced the resignation of a bench of superb judges and appointed several mediocre lawyers who benefited materially from his largesse.[14] This turn to courts, rather than the streets, as a preferred site of struggle leads to the simultaneous influence of public discourse on the courts.

The role of law in the transformation of society: the public as the elephant in the court room

Consider the restraints of precedent stretching back for decades, the excitement of possibility and the unstable quality of law. Examine also the dynamic, almost full-throated public debate about the future of South Africa, including the alternatives of constitutional democracy versus the cult of the leader.[15] The question then arises as to the relationship between the role of courts in the further construction of the constitutional bridge and the impact of public opinion and attitudes. Can the courts function as a site of contest over the construction process? And if so, how, if it steps ahead of public opinion?

Max du Plessis summarises the problem succinctly: 'To strengthen respect for human rights under the Constitution, the Court is expected to be fearless in upholding rights against the sway of public opinion. But to ignore public opinion the Constitutional Court runs the risk of being labelled undemocratic and illegitimate.'[16]

This observation raises a further question: To what extent can courts extend the bridge and help create the kind of transformed society promised in the Constitution without risking the essential condition of legitimacy, which would render courts perilously vulnerable to political attack? In other words, if the judgments of the courts are fundamentally opposed to the dominant political and social outlook of society, that institution may not have the public respectability needed to mount a defence against government attack.

The first case in this book, dealing with the coloured vote, provides a part answer to this question. Throughout the period of the coloured vote crisis, the courts in general, and the Appellate Division in particular, were under severe political pressure. The National Party regarded the will of the people, reflected in its majority in Parliament, as the test for the justification of legal change. Of course, the 'will of the people' meant white people only but the point regarding the importance of public opinion should not be missed.

For some considerable period, the courts resisted the constitutional attack that the National Party launched after its election victory in 1948. By the end of 1956, all but Oliver Schreiner had buckled under consistent legislative and executive pressure. Judges Centlivres and Hoexter, who had been on the same side as Schreiner in the earlier *Harris* cases, now found for the government. Faced with a government determined to win at all costs, these judges clearly considered that they had exhausted the limits of their judicial supervision.

The outcome of these cases needs to be understood within the context of the balance of (white) political forces at the time. When the first *Harris* case was launched, extra-parliamentary opposition to the National Party's proposals was intense. The Torch Commando had initially attracted huge support in its opposition to the constitutional changes. On 28 May 1951, 10 000 protesters marched past Parliament and more than 50 000 gathered on Cape Town's Grand Parade to protest the government's legislative proposals.[17] But by the end of 1953, the Torch Commando had begun to fade from the political scene and with it went the last determined mass political campaign against the proposed constitutional changes. When, in late 1956, the *Collins* case was decided, the judges were on their own. No political support percolated through the walls of the Court to strengthen their judicial resolve to resist these amendments.

The 'will of the people' meant white people only

So what does this history tell us about the present: in particular, what is the scope of the courts' role in a constitutional democracy committed to the transformation of the country?

A tug of war

The lesson learnt from the 1950's is clear: the balance between the use and abuse of law is invariably the subject of intense contest. This contest is never framed exclusively by legal argument based on precedent and the factual matrix

Precedent & Possibility

of the particular case. The balance of contesting political forces and the consequent impact on public discourse is critical to the legal outcome of controversial cases. The courts are increasingly drawn into the vortex of politics. The construction of the bridge is never protected fully from the buffeting winds of political contest and, hence, by extension, public opinion.

For example, in the struggle for the recognition of marriage and other rights, gay and lesbian activists sought to use the law to change a precedent which was the product of a homophobic view of the world which classified gay and lesbian South Africans as a part of the 'other'. Seizing on the promise of constitutional possibility, various organisations used the law to eradicate a series of homophobic precedents. In this strategy, they were successful but their experience remains of importance to our core question: How do courts respond to legal challenges that are not without deep public controversy?

Take the various judgments delivered in the *Fourie* case. The different approaches adopted by the judges do not yield easily to one correct conclusion.

How do courts respond to legal challenges that are not without deep public controversy?

One approach is not obviously more compelling in its application of the Constitution than the other. The key difference turns upon the manner in which judges took account of public support in the formulation of their constitutional responses to the relief to be granted.

The majority of the Constitutional Court considered it important to enlist Parliament's cooperation in the development of controversial legal change. By contrast, Judge Cameron and Justice O' Regan considered that the constitutional text was sufficiently clear for the rights of same-sex couples to be asserted by the Court. To return to Justice O'Regan: 'The power and duty to protect constitutional rights is conferred upon the courts and courts should not shrink from that duty ... Time and again, there will be those in our broader communities who do not wish to see constitutional rights protected, but that can never be a reason for courts not to protect those rights.'[18]

These approaches to public opinion contrast with those in two other cases in this book as stated earlier. In *Makwanyane*, the Court rejected the idea that public opinion held any significance in the formulation of its decision. Judge Johann Kriegler reflected the views of all 11 judges when he wrote: 'The issue is not whether I favour the retention or the abolition of the death penalty, nor whether this Court, Parliament or even overwhelming public opinion supports one or the other view. The question is what the Constitution says about it.'[19]

In *Makwanyane*, the Court was aware that the dominant party in government, the ANC, was clearly opposed to the death penalty. By contrast, public opinion, in all probability, was overwhelmingly against this decision. However, the ANC's public approach that it was not in favour of the retention of death penalty could well have diluted the influence of public opinion.

188

Compare this with the *TAC* case, in which the government not only opposed the TAC's application but the Minister of Health, at one stage, announced that the government would not abide by a decision of the Court if it held against it. However, at the time of the TAC litigation, there was overwhelming public support for the extension of the antiretroviral programme.[20]

In the same-sex marriage case, public opinion was arguably against the decision. Government, even if it was sympathetic to the decision, kept its views to the confines of the Cabinet room and initiated very little legislative reform to close the gap between the constitutional promise of equality and the reality of homophobic practices and attitudes.

In the same-sex marriage case, public opinion was arguably against the decision

These cases reveal the danger of simplistic analysis. Courts are affected by a range of different forces of which public opinion and government's predictable reaction are but two. But they also reveal that, faced with persistent political opposition and, at best, little or lukewarm government support, over the long run, courts will retreat from the protection or construction of the bridge.

That conclusion held true for the Court in its defensive role during the 1950s. In our view, it holds equally for its bridge-building role during the first decade of the 21st century. This consideration of the relationship between public opinion and the outcome of decisions has been sharpened in its focus through the shift from political warfare to a contest about policy, the justification thereof and the allocation of public resources, where the forum for all these conflicts is often the courtroom.

Of course, this is not a problem exclusive to South Africa. Some 105 national constitutions have been passed between 1989 and 2000.[21] More than 40 constitutional courts now exist in the world, including in South Africa, Uganda, Ukraine, Chile, Croatia and Brazil.

John and Jean Comaroff observed of this change during the past 20 years that 'whereas the constitutions promulgated in the decades of "decolonization" after World War II gave little autonomy to the law, stressing instead parliamentary sovereignty, executive discretion, and bureaucratic authority, the ones to emerge over the past twenty years have tended, if unevenly, to emphasize the rule of law and the primacy of rights, even when both the spirit and the letter of that law are violated, offended, distended, purloined.'[22] The turn to constitutionalism has brought about a juridification of politics, or to use the Comaroffs' description, a turn from warfare to lawfare. Governments seek to 'launder brute power in a wash of legitimacy, ethics, and propriety.'[23] For example, the use of criminal law allows governments to justify action against political opponents, from the crude and brutal style of Robert Mugabe to more sophisticated mechanisms, such as the trial and continued incarceration by Israel of Palestinian leader Marwan Baghouti.

For South Africa, two challenges now appear to merge: bridge building and political contest.

The era of lawfare in constitutional South Africa: *S v Zuma*: A recent example

> . . . it does not matter who the judge is, we do not believe that the judiciary would be able to be objective
>
> Patrick Craven, spokesperson for COSATU, reacting to news of the indictment of Jacob Zuma cited in the *Mail & Guardian,* 12 January 2008

> South Africa cannot afford a situation whereby the courts and the judiciary become targets for unwarranted attacks whenever people in the ANC, who think they are untouchable, disagree with their decisions. It will indeed be unfortunate if their bitterness against democratic state institutions is going to be used to advance political agendas and settle scores.
>
> The ANC and its allies must also recognise that the independence of the judiciary is not something that can be upheld only when it suits them. When ANC president, Jacob Zuma, was acquitted of rape, the judiciary was not criticised; when he is charged with corruption, blood in the court is threatened.
>
> *Sunday Times* 19 January 2008

> I like the look of this judge. He looked sober to me
>
> Julius Malema *Cape Times* 12 September 2008

Before we turn to this complex problem, we consider a case that in the loudest way has broadcast the implications of lawfare for the transformative ambitions of the courts.

We have already cited the claims that the State's case against the ANC president Mr Jacob Zuma have been viewed by some of his supporters as a political trial. The role of the courts came under intense scrutiny and public criticism, particularly in the period leading up to a vital judgement given in favour of Mr Zuma in September 2008 by Judge Chris Nicholson in Pietermaritzburg. If the possibility of law was elusive in the light of the challenges to bridge the gap between the majestic promise of the constitutional text and the degrading realities experienced daily by millions of historically still presently disadvantaged South Africans, the task became even more onerous as the judicial institutions were engulfed by party political contest.

By the time of going to press, this judgment was cited as one reason for the dramatic recall of President Mbeki by the ANC, precipitating his resignation and the elevation of Kgalema Motlanthe to the nation's highest office. However, at the time of writing, the political drama is far from over. We are therefore understandably cautious to opine on the implications of the prosecution of Mr Zuma, but believe, too, that it is a critical legal case that we cannot omit from this book. With the necessary *caveat* that all that follows may well be overtaken by events occuring after this manuscript was delivered for publication, we offer the following thoughts on the claims of the use, and abuse, of law.

To appreciate its meaning and import it is necessary to sketch some background to the application decided in favour of Mr Zuma in September 2008. On 23 August 2003, the National Director of the Public Prosecutions, Mr Bulelani Ngcuka, conducted a press conference at which he announced that it had been decided to prosecute Mr Schabir Shaik and a number of corporate entities in which Shaik held substantial interests. A decision had also been taken not to prosecute the then Deputy President of South Africa, Mr Jacob Zuma. It emerged from the evidence used for the successful conviction of Mr Shaik that, between October 1995 and September 2002, Mr Shaik personally, as well as by way of some of the companies which he controlled, made numerous and substantial payments of money to or on behalf of Mr Zuma. On 20 June 2005 the new National Director of Public Prosecutions, Mr Vusi Pikoli, announced that the state intended to prosecute Mr Zuma. This took place a few days after the conviction and sentence of Mr Shaik.

That decision led to a flood of litigation, most of which was characterised by lead counsel for Mr Zuma as a 'Stalingrad operation', to ensure that Mr Zuma would not be prosecuted. This strategy required that every possible legal avenue that could be plausibly advanced would be pursued, to prevent Mr Zuma being tried in a criminal court.

Mr Zuma and his supporters have consistently argued that political interference from ministers of state and political supporters of Mr Mbeki were behind attempts to prosecute Mr Zuma. In short, whatever the merits of the criminal charges on which we cannot express a view, the case was set up in the public discourse as a case of vicious factional party politics being fought out in the courts; political warfare had been replaced (or supplemented) by vigorous and expensive lawfare. The institutions of the legal system were just new fronts in this battle.

The institutions of the legal system were just new fronts in this battle

By September 2008, it appeared that two final legal challenges were open to Mr Zuma. Judge Chris Nicholson presided over what could have been the penultimate option: an application that Mr Zuma could not be legally charged until his right to be consulted about, or make representations concerning, the prosecution had been respected. Mr Zuma's lawyers contended that their client's right to be consulted prior to being charged was sourced in a provision of the Constitution. The other option considered and discussed by Mr Zuma's legal team was an application for a permanent stay, or halt, to the prosecution efforts, had they continued on the grounds that Zuma's right to a fair trial had been totally compromised.

The build-up to the hearing of the application regarding representations was characterised by a sustained campaign of rhetoric and criticism by supporters of Mr Zuma against the key institutions of criminal justice in general and the judiciary in particular. Members of the judiciary and especially the Constitutional Court were described as 'counter-revolutionaries', and the judicial institution was accused of being out of touch with the transformative aspirations of the population. Ironically, on the very morning of Judge Nicholson's decision, the Secretary General of the ANC, Gwede Mantashe, wrote an op-ed piece in a number of national newspapers[24] in which he argued that Zuma could never get a fair trial in South Africa.

Less than 24 hours later, Mr Mantashe had changed his tune on the acceptability of the Bench in South Africa. By then Judge Nicholson had upheld the application and set aside the entire raft of charges brought against Mr Zuma. This was, of course, much celebrated by his supporters, who appeared to ignore the fact that the judgment expressly had made no ruling on Mr Zuma's guilt or innocence.

Less than 24 hours later, Mr Mantashe had changed his tune on the acceptability of the Bench in South Africa

However, Judge Nicholson did not limit his judgment to the technical or procedural finding that the Constitution provided Mr Zuma with, at the very least, the expectation of making representations and that such expectation became a right as a result of an offer made by Mr Ngcuka at the notorious press conference.

Instead, Judge Nicholson proceeded onto broader political terrain, with a further finding that there had been a consistent pattern of interference in the prosecution from members of the executive and, hence, that the independence of the prosecutorial authority was compromised. In effect, the Court inferred that responsibility for the baleful manner in which the case had been prosecuted lay not only at the doors of the prosecutors, but also of the presidency and other prominent members of the executive of the country.

This was lawfare in all its jurisprudential technicolour. The Court made a finding about the manner in which the judicial system in general, and the criminal justice system in particular, had been undermined by the executive arm of government. It was this reckless conduct that had threatened the fragility of these key independent institutions. But, because the Court considered the question of political interference in the prosecution within the confines of deciding an application by the prosecution to strike out certain allegations of political interference and conspiracy from the record of evidence placed before the Court, the judgment, while overtly political, was not required to examine the totality of threats made against judicial institutions in the proceedings. These threats, if proved correct, had come from not only the existing executive but also from the sustained attack upon the judicial institutions launched by the supporters of Mr Zuma.

In this sense, the judgment opened the way to the following criticisms:

> [O]nce Nicholson chose to take on the political issues at stake he was morally and politically obligated to do so wholeheartedly. To rise to the occasion and say loudly and clearly—there are two blocs currently threatening the fragility of our independent institutions, particularly the judicial system. These are the secret authoritarian machinations of the current executive under Mbeki *and* the howling populist mob mobilized in the political defence of Zuma.
>
>   History and our struggle ... for a state that is the opposite of the authoritarian, racist apartheid regime, demanded greater things of the judge. If in defending the judicial system he correctly choose to tackle the one, then he was obligated to also find a way to go for the other. To not do so, in the form that he has chosen to do, is to lay himself wide open to the insinuation that he was simply posturing. Certainly the new incoming regime will be extremely grateful for this judgment for it lets them off the hook.[25]

The judgment also raises further important issues. Judge Nicholson disgorged himself of a careful and reasoned judgment, notwithstanding criticisms which were levelled against it. In this he acted as expected: a fiercely independent judge calling the case as he best saw it. But the judgment was delivered in the context of a vicious attack on the judicial institution. Threats were made to take to the streets if the prosection of Mr Zuma continued and that no effort would be spared to ensure that Mr Zuma would never have to stand trial. The Secretary General of the South African Communist Party, Dr Blade Nzimande, placed the following interpretation on the judgment: 'It vindicates us in our long-held view that the charging of Zuma is not a criminal but a political trial.' To those who contended that the judgment, in its explicit terms, did not exonerate Mr Zuma, Dr Nzimande says 'this is nothing other than an attempt ... to try and rescue their intellectual and moral integrity in the light of a judgemnt clearly shows that Zuma ... can never, ever have a fair trial.' [26]

   The judgment, as well as the decision by the NPA to appeal it, were reasons given for the ANC's NEC decision to recall President Mbeki a week later. Their interpretation or misinterpretation, of the judgment unquestionably changed our country's history. The question that then arises is how that history will judge this judgment. Will it be recorded as a muscular assertion of judicial independence and protection of prosecutorial autonomy? Or will it go down in history in a similar fashion to the final judgment in the *Coloured Vote* case trilogy? As we saw earlier, the *Collins* case was a retreat by the majority of the judiciary in circumstances where the judges felt it prudent to leave the battlefield and possibly return to fight on another occasion, however distant.

   The same doubt may linger about this judgment: Did the Court retreat from compelling Mr Zuma to face trial in the face of the incessant political pressure? More important, perhaps, is the question of whether those who shouted the loudest and threatened most menacingly will consider these to be acceptable tactics for compelling the judiciary to find in its favour in the future?

Lawfare: an extended impact

It is not only in the arena of criminal law that legal contestation takes place. Intellectual property law is employed by multinationals to protect and promote their control over international markets, while NGOs like the TAC threaten to use the law to ensure the production of cheaper and more accessible generic drugs. The Alien Torts Act has been called on to hold multinationals accountable for apartheid crimes, while the Ogoni people unsuccessfully attempted the same strategy against Shell in Nigeria. The law has recently been used as a last resort in South Africa where the political process worked in the opposite direction. The ANC government introduced legislation to abolish an elite crime-fighting unit, the Scorpions. Faced with inevitable political defeat, the opposition political parties supported an application by a concerned citizen, Hugh Glenister, to prevent the implementation of this proposed legislation. This was an example of lawfare where political warfare was perceived to have no effect.

These implications should not be confined to the borders of South Africa. Viewed in this context, this book addresses the condition and implications of both a particular form of constitutional lawfare and more general manifestations of legal battles. The South African record may assist in developing a better conceptual grasp of global developments, particularly in the way lawfare may be engaged by non-governmental organisations against state and multinational power.

The ANC government introduced legislation to abolish an elite crime-fighting unit

The pass law cases, Wendy Orr's litigation and the *TAC* case illustrate engagements with the law to prevent arbitrary and cruel intrusions into the lives of ordinary people as well as the initiation of legal fights to prevent egregious acts of violence against citizens. This book documents how lawfare is simultaneously employed by the state and by those seeking to curb the violence of the state. To be sure, the *Rivonia* trial is a most graphic example of a state which conjured with the law to act against citizens who were its most determined and legitimate political opponents. But the idea of the censure, through a criminal trial, becomes effective whenever it confirms or exploits existing conceptions of values, prejudices or both. If society is united against communism, which it equates with violence, lawlessness and an absence of liberty, a trial which engages the legal censure of communism against political opponents of the state can generate a powerful form of condemnation of opposition to those in power.

The same consequence flows when a political opponent can be denounced legally as a common law criminal, guilty of theft or corruption.

So what does this record mean for the turn to constitutionalism? Briefly, this book shows that the increasing use of courts as a forum for political struggles places the spotlight firmly on a judiciary, invariably unelected, to settle fraught political disputes. And then, in addition, the courts are urged to establish a new precedent, often by non-governmental organisations acting on behalf of constituencies which have become disgruntled with government policy. And in this, the courts are then urged to find the possibility of such precedent in the text of the Constitution, a precedent which may hold far reaching implications for government policy, even beyond the case in point.

In this connection, Max du Plessis is correct: 'If the court appeals only to the public and its sense of common morality in abdication of its constitutional duty it will be too easily dismissed as apologist but if it proclaims the superiority of human rights ideals without attempting to engage with the public and its opinion, it will be criticised for being utopian.'[27] The journey is both difficult and institutionally dangerous.

Our courts in the future: Obstacles on the constitutional journey

The cases described in this book reveal that the constitutional journey never proceeds in a single direction. The dominant direction will depend on the outcome of political and legal contest shaped by the prevailing political discourse, the legal traditions of the country, the available legal materials and existing legal precedents, the facts of the particular dispute, the quality of the lawyering and the ideology of the judiciary. Hence the institution has limits to its role, particularly because of these factors.

Take the following illustration based on our reading of the South African text: the South African Constitution promotes the foundational values of dignity, equality and freedom. Manifestly, these need to be reconciled into a normative system which is not at war with itself. In our view, a libertarian conception of freedom would hardly be compatible with a commitment to a society based, in part, on a substantive conception of equality.

Detailed constitutional provisions make this point clearer. The South African Constitution contains an express commitment to substantive equality and to the constraint of private power exercised in a public fashion. The Constitution ensures that significant limitations are placed on all actors to safeguard the environment. Workers enjoy the express rights to form trade unions, to strike and to bargain collectively. This is not the stuff of Margaret Thatcher's England or of Ronald Reagan's America. What, for example, would happen if a South African Margaret Thatcher emerged to take power in South Africa? How would courts deal with the introduction of policies by the democratically elected government which ran counter to the very foundations of the Constitution? If you wish, substitute Robert Mugabe for Thatcher: the game works equally well.

So let's play the game. Assume the new government wishes to abolish the institution of public healthcare. The courts set aside the legislation as it is in conflict with express provisions of the Constitution which guarantee basic healthcare for all. But the government has been elected to office on a 'privatisation' ticket. It is determined to implement its democratically supported mandate. Either it will cause the Constitution to be amended or change the composition of the court.

Assume that, for political reasons, the new government is unable immediately to implement either of these options. It may have to bide its time, but for how long, if the same result flows from the court when one, two, three or five pieces of further key legislation are also declared to be unconstitutional? There is no reason to conclude that the then government's reaction to the *Coloured Vote* cases was an exception. Whatever the outcome of a Zuma prosecution, the populist storm troopers have announced their willingness to sweep aside the restraints of constitutional democracy as the cause/person/cult so dictates.

The courts set aside the legislation as it is in conflict with express provisions of the Constitution

Where, then, does this leave courts in a constitutional democracy, confronted by the competing sides of lawfare and, if necessary, a resort through populist politics, to warfare? How does the judicial institution negotiate its way between a state which employs the law to assert its own violence and a citizenry which uses the law to defend itself against law's violence? What is the connection between law's use and its abuse?

This book is written in a turbulent time. As is evident from Patrick Craven's statement made on behalf of COSATU and the warning issued in the editorial of the *Sunday Times*, the political climate has become far more circumspect about the role of the judiciary than was the case during the first blushes of constitutional freedom in 1994. Within the next year, at least five of the 11 judges of the present Constitutional Court, including the present Chief Justice, will retire, leaving uncertain the future jurisprudential direction of the Court.[28]

At its 2007 conference at Polokwane, the ANC again raised the problem of the lack of transformation of the judiciary. The meaning of its concern is somewhat puzzling. After all, within slightly more than a decade, more than 50 per cent of High Court judges are black and all but one of the heads of court are black. That represents impressive progress, save in the case of gender. By the end of the first decade of this century, the racial composition of the bench will even more closely reflect the country's demography. So does the call for transformation mean something else? A less independent institution? One more in keeping with the mood of the ruling party?

We do not wish to be misunderstood. No official threats have been issued by the government as yet to eradicate an independent judiciary nor does the current negative discourse approximate that exhibited by Eben Dönges and his fellow National Party cabinet members who had clearly considered the abolition of the existing structure of the courts. But when the present brouhaha caused by the indictment of the President of the ANC, Jacob Zuma, is viewed through the prism of the lessons from the coloured vote cases, warning lights begin to flicker. At the very least, we now know that the journey towards a complete recognition of constitutional democracy will be slow, turbulent and painful.

It is often said that walking in the middle of the road is a sure guarantee of being knocked over by traffic on either side. But the challenge for a judicial institution located in the midst of intense lawfare is to negotiate a path between the apologist and the utopian. Public respect for the courts is critical if the construction of a constitutional bridge is to be continued. And if widespread lawfare breaks out, institutional legitimacy is critical to the continuation of the project. Constitutional construction in the midst of intense political opposition and, at best, halting public support, is likely to end as did the bridge on the cover of this book. Yet, as illustrated in *Makwanyane*, the courts may well have an institutional duty to constrain public opinion if it is to be true to the normative framework promised by the constitutional enterprise. When the government supports the courts (*Makwanyane*) or keeps its counsel (the gay and lesbian cases), the journey along the bridge can lead society far along the path to the society promised in the constitutional text, as illustrated in the wedding of Achmat and Weyers.

> *It is often said that walking in the middle of the road is a sure guarantee of being knocked over by traffic on either side*

This book is not a plea for constitutional essentialism, by which we mean that only through an entrenched Constitution and a Bill of Rights supervised by an independent judiciary can political and economic democracy be sustained. But, as Hannah Arendt noted, concrete rights protect a plurality of views because rights underpin citizenship, which, in turn, is a condition for all politics.[29] Take away the rights of some within society and, for this group, there obviously can be no citizenship. If so, there can be no politics because of an absence of a plurality. And if there is no politics, where, then, does that leave democracy?

The recent outbreaks of xenophobia across South Africa are illustrative. If South Africans are the only 'ones' in the country, then Africans from the rest of the continent are 'others' (they are not like us—they deserve no rights, they cannot be treated as citizens but must be expelled, if need be with great force and brutality). How long before this kind of rejection of those who are 'different' and thus 'other' extends throughout the body politic of the country? This conclusion holds implications for constitutional democracy in countries way beyond the borders of South Africa. The rights struggles which take place are a contest against the imposition of the 'one' and a rejection of all 'others'.

But rights alone are insufficient; hence our warning about constitutional essentialism—the idea that democracy is attained solely or mainly through this legal form. A lesson which emerges from the legal struggles during both the apartheid and constitutional eras is that, when left as the sole defender of a constitutional bridge, the courts will be too isolated to continue construction. At best, the bridge will be excessively dangerous to cross and, at worse, it will be destroyed. Without significant public pressure and political activity to defend the activities of the courts in resisting these political initiatives, the constitutional bridge will ultimately collapse under the weight of governmental pressure. Political activity is required to keep alive the possibility envisaged in the Constitution. In turn, the possibility of law can open up further space for political activity. If that possibility is not exploited by civil society, the likelihood of meaningful transformation is slim.

The human rights culture has proved to be more than simply a transient phenomenon
That this conclusion is not confined to South Africa has become increasingly evident, particularly since the events in the United States on 9/11. As David Dyzenhaus has written: 'Especially since 9/11 there has been a marked decline in the West of executive accountability to the legislature, and judges of apex courts who are reacting to what we think of as 9/11 statutes and executive action find it difficult to steer a path between giving too much and too little deference to the executive and the legislature. They often err on the side of too much, as governments make the claim that they enjoy something like a prerogative power when it comes to questions of national security.'[30]

The politics of justification and the creation of conditions for account-ability in the exercise of public power, so basic to the construction of a constitutional bridge, have enjoyed a relatively fruitful first decade in South Africa. Hence the process of construction of the bridge away from apartheid towards a society based upon democratic accountability may well be a kind of construction which represents an antidote to the risk of increased judicial nodding in the direction of executive action which has so depressingly dominated some legal systems since 9/11.

Surprisingly, perhaps, the call of 9/11 has not been a complete global success for the right. The human rights culture has proved to be more than simply a transient phenomenon. Thus a law lord of the stature of Lord Steyn has excoriated the policy of detention without trial and the accompanying justification of torture and called the detention centre at Guantánamo Bay a stain on American justice.[31]

But the invocation of national security interests clearly has been present in South Africa. In the early days after apartheid, legislation was passed in the form of the Promotion of Administrative Justice Act and the Promotion of Access to Information Act. These laws were designed to promote the fundamental constitutional principles of accountability, transparency and public participation in matters of public interest. Not a decade later, the government has, on occasion, treated these Acts as the Protection of Administration Act and the Prevention of Access to Information Act. It has invoked the war cry of national security to prevent the disclosure of key documents in its legal disputes with the ex-Director-General of the Department of National Intelligence, Billy Masethla, and the National Director of Public Prosecutions, Vusi Pikoli. These cases have, in turn, raised important questions about our government's commitment to the principle of accountability.[32] That raises the problem of courts being employed increasingly to settle outbreaks of lawfare.

Where does that leave us? Our Constitution promises a transformation of precedent away from the very culture that has threatened to take hold in significant parts of the world since 9/11. The narratives we have set out in this book are cause for guarded optimism, the international climate and domestic turbulence notwithstanding. To be sure, the continued construction of the bridge will need more than the efforts of courts alone and an ambitious text. The use of law and the possibility of politics must combine. But left isolated and undefended by civil society, the judicial institutions wither.

The process of constitutional construction has changed some attitudes positively

It is, however, not correct to end on a gloomy note. Progress should be celebrated. The process of constitutional construction has changed some attitudes positively, along with the legal framework that governs the lives of citizens. South African society, in significant parts, is in a radically different space to that occupied but a decade and a half ago.

To return to the Achmat-Weyers wedding, two anecdotes illustrate the possibility of the future. Dalli's brother, all the way from Ficksburg, proclaimed that, at the wedding, he did something he never dreamt was possible: 'I kissed a coloured man out of love'. And Nosizwe Madlala-Routledge, herself a tenacious fighter for healthcare for those who live with HIV/AIDS, pointed to her white husband and said that, when they married, their union was illegal in South Africa. Twenty years later, the law had similarly matured sufficiently to recognise the marriage of Dalli and Zackie.

Bridge-building may be slow and difficult. But a decade after its commencement there remains much to celebrate and to defend, both of recent precedent and future possibility.

Endnotes

1   *K v Minister of Safety and Security* 2005 (6) SA 419 (CC), para [16].
2   Otto Kirchheimer *Political Justice: The Use of Legal Procedures for Political Ends* 6-7.

3   See the background to the negotiations as set out by L du Plessis and H Corder *Understanding South Africas Transitional Bill of Rights* (1994).

4   Bestiality is defined as the intentional, unlawful sexual relations between a human being and an animal. Presumably, Mr Coetzee considered that an accused could defend himself or herself by raising the argument that the crime prevented their expression of their sexual orientation!

5   Pierre de Vos 'The Inevitability of Same Sex Marriage' (2007) 23 *SAJHR* 432-449.

6   *National Coalition for Gays and Lesbian Equality v Minister of Home Affairs and Others* 2000 (1) BCLR 39 (CC) para 54.

7   *Satchwell v The President of the Republic of South Africa* 2002 (9) BCLR 986 (CC).

8   *Du Toit and Another v Minister for Welfare and Population Development and Others* 2002 (10) BCLR 1006 (CC).

9   *Fourie and Another v Minister of Home Affairs and Others* 2005 (3) SA 429 (SCA) para 25.

10 *Minister of Home Affairs and Another v Fourie and Another* 2006 (3) BCLR 355 (CC) paras 138-139.

11 David Dyzenhaus *The Concept of Global Administrative Law* (unpublished paper delivered at UCT, March 2008) 25.

12 John and Jean Comaroff (eds) *Law and Disorder in the Postcolony* (2006) 26-27. The claim for the importance of lawfare needs to be qualified. As apartheid history revealed, the turn to lawfare does not occur consistently. Brutal forms of repression are not far off the menu of those in power. See the incisive criticism of Robin Wright's claim in *Dreams and Shadows: The Future of the Middle East* (2007) that a number of Middle Eastern states like Lebanon, Egypt, Kuwait, Morocco and Syria have leaned towards democracy and rule of law. Max Rudenbeck *New York Review of Books* 2008 (8) 18 shows that, in spite of superficial progress towards the rule of law during 2006, all these countries have retreated to their default position of arbitrary and repressive rule. Repression without law is very much alive as a tool of social control. Recent developments in the ranks of the ANC, including threats to kill for Jacob Zuma if his campaign to become President of South Africa is resisted, provide a disturbing local example of the potential flip from lawforce to warfare.

13 Comaroffs *ibid* 30.

14 Jeremy Gauntlett *Business Day* (15 May 2008).

15 Mondli Makanya *Sunday Times* (3 August 2008).

16 Max du Plessis 'Between Apology and Utopia—The Constitutional Court and Public Opinion' (2002) 18 *SAJHR* 1-38.

17 *Cape Times* (29 May 1951).

18 Fourie *ibid* para [171]. This argument is derived from the insightful analysis of Theunis Roux 'Principle and Pragmatism on the Constitutional Court of South Africa' (unpublished paper 2007).

19 *S v Makwanyane* 1995 (3) SA 391 (CC) para 206.

20 Mark Heywood (2003) 19 *SAJHR* 278-306. In the *TAC* case, this conclusion does need some refinement in that the Court refused to grant the structural relief sought. As explained in the chapter on the TAC, this refusal meant that the Court drew back from the supervisory order sought and thereby declined to exercise supervision over

the conduct of the executive in complying with its order. This is an example, therefore, of the Court not wishing to strike too bold a position against the executive, public opinion notwithstanding.

21 Heinz Klug *Constituting Democracy: Law Globalism and South Africa's Political Reconstruction* (2000).

22 Comaroffs *ibid* 23.

23 Comaroffs *ibid* 31.

24 See *Cape Times*, 12 September 2008.

25 Michael Morris, *Cape Times*, 15 September 2008.

26 *Sunday Times* (21 September 2008). A week later (*Sunday Times* 28 September 2008) former treasurer of the SACP, Phillip Dexter, questioned why the Zuma judgment had not been subjected to the same treatment as but a product of a 'bourgeois court' His answer: 'It's simply because Nzimande agrees with the finding.'

27 Du Plessis *ibid* 39.

28 Legal commentators are already voicing concern about the potential turn of the court towards a more pro-executive approach. David Dyzenhaus *ibid*. 'The pasts and future of the rule of law in South Africa', 2007(124) *SALJ*:734.

29 Hannah Arendt *The Human Condition* (1958).

30 David Dyzenhaus 'The Past and Future of the Rule of Law in South Africa' 2007 (124) *SALJ* 734-761.

31 *Guardian* (22 April 2006).

32 This observation has been made recently by judges of the Constitutional Court; see, in particular the minority judgment of Judge Zac Yacoob in *Independent Newspapers (Pty) Ltd v Minister of Intelligence Services,* unreported judgment of the Constitutional Court, 22 May 2008.